Wired For Happiness

Wired For Happiness

Science-based strategies for living a life of connection, fulfillment, and joy

Fatemeh Farahan, LMFT

Think & Be Press

Wired For Happiness: Science-based strategies for living a life of connection, fulfillment, and joy

Fatemeh Farahan

Copyright © 2022 Fatemeh Farahan

ISBN: 979-8-9869410-0-4

All Rights Reserved.

All rights reserved. No part of this publication may be reproduced, distributed, or transmitted in any form or by any means, including photocopying, recording, or other electronic or mechanical methods, without the prior written permission from the author, except in the case of brief quotations embodied in critical reviews and certain other non-commercial uses permitted by copyright law.

Published by Think & Be Press

Fatemeh Farahan
Fatemeh Farahan, Marriage Family Therapist, PC
10350 Santa Monica Blvd., Suite 310
Los Angeles, CA 90025
(310) 962-5935
www.farahantherapy.com

Fatemeh Farahan, LMFT is available to speak at your business or conference event on a variety of topics. Email us at info@farahantherapy.com for booking information.

*To my parents,
Manoochehr and Shahin Farahan,
who turned the uncertainty and fear of being
immigrants to a world of opportunity, new
connections, and nurturing relationships.*

*To my husband and son,
Ramin and Arya, my blessings, and the greatest
loves of my life.*

Contents

STEP 1: PRIME : *Set the Foundation* 1
CHAPTER 1 : Decoding Happiness 3
CHAPTER 2 : Is Your Brain Working For You, Or Against You? 15
CHAPTER 3 : Priming Your Brain for Happiness 27
CHAPTER 4 : Be Here Now: Meditation and Mindfulness 35
CHAPTER 5 : Make Sleep Your Superpower 53
CHAPTER 6 : Get Moving: Exercise 71

STEP 2: SHIFT : *Redirect Your Emotions, Thoughts and Actions* 83
CHAPTER 7 : Habits: The Building Blocks of a Happy Life 85
CHAPTER 8 : Embrace Your Emotions 111
CHAPTER 9 : Rewire Supercharged Negative Thoughts 133
CHAPTER 10 : Living A Life of Value 157

STEP 3: CONNECT : *Reach Beyond Yourself* 171
CHAPTER 11 : Self-Compassion: Becoming a Friend to Yourself 173
CHAPTER 12 : Building Better Relationships 193
CHAPTER 13 : Happiness From the Inside Out: Finding Gratitude & Savoring the Good 213
References 235
About the author 259

STEP 1: PRIME
Set the Foundation

CHAPTER 1
Decoding Happiness

When I was 12 years old, I declared to the world that I'd never be happy again.

Tears streamed down my face as the plane taxied, preparing to take off from Mehrabad International Airport in Tehran, Iran. I was leaving the only home I'd ever known— or, at that time, ever expected to know—to begin a new life in the United States. And a single thought kept looping around in my mind: *my happy days are over.*

I was miserable. Devastated beyond words. After all, I was losing my friends, leaving behind most of my family, and ditching a lifestyle I enjoyed (and perhaps more importantly, understood) for a new and completely unknown way of life. Leaving Iran for some frightening foreign land convinced my adolescent mind that I was condemned to a life of unhappiness. It wasn't even a question of *whether I would* ever be happy again; it was a deadset certainty that I'd never again feel unbridled joy or satisfaction.

The most difficult part of the move was losing all my connections with friends and extended family. Even as a child, I think I knew intuitively the vital role of connections to our happiness, so I really worked on building a strong network of friends, which have proved to be my greatest blessing and support. In Iran, family is everything—and it includes a wide net of relatives! In my culture, we're always surrounded by a web of love and support. That was something I no longer had in the U.S., a culture that prizes individualism over community and family ties.

Of course, over time, I was able to make connections and adapt to my new environment. In an unshocking twist, I was not, in fact, doomed to a life of misery after leaving Iran all those years ago. But that initial fear of losing my own capacity to live a happy life has stayed with me through the years.

As fate would have it, it was the obstacles that I experienced both when immigrating to the US —and my Persian cultural heritage, which places family and community above all else—that set the stage for my own discovery of what it means to live a happy life. It also became the foundation for a lifelong career helping others find happiness for themselves, anchored in an awareness of the vital role of strong connections and social support for our well-being and fulfillment in life.

We all want to be happy—this is a fact. There may be no goal more universal than the desire to be and feel *happier.* It's an immensely human thing to yearn for. Who doesn't wish they could experience an uptick in happy feelings, joyful thoughts, and contented satisfaction? I mean, if happiness isn't the point, what is?

But what does that mean to be happy? Happiness can be a challenging concept to pin down, given its individual and highly subjective nature. What happiness means to *me* may be completely different from how *you* define happiness. And at times (as evidenced by my teenaged conviction that happiness was only to be found in a life in Iran) we lack a clear sense of what brings us happiness, and we make it something that is conditional on external forces.

Many of us also struggle to identify genuine happiness—that joyful contentment that increases our well-being and life satisfaction over the long-term—from the surface-level, hedonistic types of happiness (you know, those fleeting, momentary pleasures that appear quickly and disappear even faster). If we're going to learn how to live a happier life, we need to first get clear on what happiness really is—and what it's not.

What Happiness *Actually* Is...

Once upon a time, my friend Amir thought he had it all. He was living the good life in a fancy penthouse apartment on the beach, overlooking miles of southern California coast and the Pacific

Ocean. He spent four to five nights a week going out on the town, hitting the swankiest clubs and restaurants in Los Angeles, and often woke up the next morning to some new beauty in bed beside him.

Having become a partner at his law firm by age 40, he had pretty much made it—by any conventional standards, at least. He was rich. He was handsome. He had achieved everything he ever imagined, and reached every goal his parents, and the world, had imposed upon him. In short, everything in Amir's life had been coming up roses for as far back as he could remember and had no reason to be anything but wildly fulfilled and content.

But one evening, as we sat on my patio drinking wine, he opened up to me for the first time about how unhappy, and lonely, he'd felt for as long as he could remember.

"Why am I not happier, Fatemeh? And why do I feel so *lonely* all the time?" he asked. "I don't understand it. That part's really weird because I'm almost never alone. But even beyond that, I'm miserable. Why? I've done everything everyone always told me to do. I have all these things that other people want and strive for... So why do I *still* find myself thinking I'm a complete and utter waste, like some phony who's waiting for the rug to be pulled out from under him? I don't get it."

Amir's ambivalence towards his personal and professional success may seem as puzzling to you as it was to him. How could someone who has a life that so many others could only dream of be anything *but* satisfied with themselves and their place in life? Yet here he was, and he was still unhappy.

Amir's predicament is hardly unique and illustrates the problem so many of us encounter we often don't know what happiness really means, nor do we understand how to get there or what changes we need to make (both within ourselves and externally in our lives) to achieve greater fulfillment. We end up chasing the wrong things, which only take us further away from a life of joy and contentment

Let's take a moment to explore what so often trips us up: hedonic happiness, which often masquerades as true happiness in our minds, and leads us down a path that ultimately leads to the *opposite* of what we're really searching for.

Real Happiness > Hedonistic Happiness

Some of the most successful people in the world have everything they could possibly want and have achieved things that most people could only dream of, and yet they're still not happy. A big part of the problem is that in our pursuit of happiness, we end up pursuing the wrong things—things that bring momentary pleasure but not lasting contentment. There's a basic confusion in our minds about what makes us happy, causing us to seek out *hedonic* happiness over genuine happiness.

Hedonic happiness is the type of happiness that brings quick, short-term gratification (think: having sex, getting drunk, buying an expensive pair of shoes, or the adrenaline rush from skydiving). It's based on pleasure and immediate enjoyment. These feel-good experiences are a natural and important aspect of human existence. There's nothing wrong with finding enjoyment in short-term pleasures (as long as they're not hurting you in the long term, like getting drunk regularly or engaging in risky behavior). The problem with hedonic happiness is its inherently fleeting nature, which means that any feelings of happiness tend to leave as fast as they came. The upshot? We end up chasing things that don't truly make us happy, only to find ourselves confused and discouraged about why we're not happier.

Understanding real happiness isn't an easy task! Especially when we live in a culture that presents us with so many misleading messages about what it means to live a happy life. The challenge of distinguishing true sources of happiness from momentary pleasures has been amplified through common social misconstructions surrounding what genuine happiness looks like. We're bombarded from the day we're born with social cues and pressures to conform to a certain standard of success; and those who don't are often ostracized for expressing any sort of deviation from the "norm" of happiness. Let's look at some of the most common misconceptions about what makes us happy.

Common Misconceptions About Happiness

Cultural messaging tends to falsely promote hedonistic happiness as real happiness, presenting a distorted image of a fulfilling life that leads many people astray in their pursuit of happiness. To help you sort out fact from fiction, I've pinpointed some common misconceptions about what happiness is, so that you can begin to identify what true happiness really looks like for you.

"If I Was Richer, I'd be Happy": Money can buy a lot of things...but, as the saying goes, it can't buy happiness. Once your basic survival needs are taken care of, the luxurious upgrades that come with a pay raise don't tend to do a whole lot for your happiness. While the data on this topic is mixed, the research suggests that more money, as a rule, doesn't mean greater happiness, and that there is only a small correlation between income increases over $75,000 and increased well-being. A landmark 1978 study, similarly, showed that lottery winners weren't any happier than people who did not win the lottery. It also matters *what* we spend our money on. One study showed that people experience greater increases in happiness when they spend money on experiences and giving to others, as opposed to material things.

"If I Accomplish My Goals, I'll Be Happy": When we make happiness a point on the horizon, we end up chasing it forever—with that horizon continually receding into the distance. The idea that achieving a specific goal will make us happy is sort of like the end of a fairy tale: you expect reaching that goal will lead to living happily ever after...but what about *after* happily ever after? When reaching the goal fails to bring the anticipated satisfaction, the mind immediately generates a new goal that we must reach to be happy. Unlike a fairy tale, our lives don't wrap up neatly when we accomplish something. When you look for happiness in the accomplishment of your goals, you'll inevitably end up dissatisfied because there will *always* be another goal to achieve. The process is never-ending and can lead to stress and burnout when we put too much pressure on ourselves to be constantly achieving. While it's important to savor and cherish your accomplishments, don't expect them to be the source of long-term, sustainable fulfillment.

"I *Always* Need to Be Happy, No Matter What Happens": Living a happy life doesn't mean feeling happy all the time! We live in a culture of "toxic positivity" that tells us (often in meme form!) that we should feel happy and optimistic under any and all circumstances. This misconception causes many of us to feel bad about ourselves if we *don't* always feel good. It also leads us to deny and suppress our more painful and uncomfortable emotions, which only amplifies them in the long-term (more on this in the emotions chapter!). The truth is that no one can be happy all the time. It's not possible, nor is it advisable to attempt to live in a state of perpetual joy. There is nothing wrong with you if you aren't happy all the time because true happiness doesn't come from momentary pleasure or joy—it comes from sustained meaning, self-care, and healthy relationships.

"I Have To Make My Own Happiness, On My Own": The belief that one must be fully self-reliant to be happy is ingrained in the American ethos. The ideal of the self-made —someone picking themselves up by the bootstraps and creating a happy life through their own blood, sweat and tears— is baked into Western culture, which is highly individualistic. But the simple fact is that we *need* other people in our lives to be happy. The fictional belief that anyone has *ever* achieved a happy, contented state of mind with *zero* help from outside connections is nothing more than that: a fictional belief. As we'll explore in depth later in this book, connection is at the very heart of happiness.

"I Won't Be Happy if I Face Any Adversity": If there is one absolute in life, it's that you *will* inevitably face obstacles, struggles, setbacks, and disappointments along the way. And that's OK! Happiness is not something that's reserved for when things are going your way. Adversity and failure are part of the human experience, whether we like to admit it or not, and we can still maintain a baseline state of happiness even during trying times. If we can stay present and find the lessons in difficult times—rather than seeing them as personal failure—our challenges can lead to growth and increased well-being in the long run.

"*If* This Happens, *Then* I'll Be Happy": Putting conditions on our happiness is one of the most common mistakes I see my patients make. When we make our happiness conditional on getting what we want or things working out a certain way, we're putting happiness outside of ourselves—instead of recognizing that it's something that we cultivate from within. It also keeps you stuck in the future instead of here in the present moment—the only place where happiness can truly be found! You can't put off finding the good in the present moment, even when life is tough, and you can't expect happiness to magically occur when certain criteria are met. Happiness isn't about perfect timing, or perfection at all. It's about learning to love who and what you are and allowing yourself to be grateful for the things you *already* have.

Ask yourself: Which of these misconceptions feels the most familiar to you? Do you recognize any of these ideas as being part of your own thinking about happiness? There's a good chance that you've adopted at least one of the previously listed misconceptions of happiness—a list that is far from exhaustive.

These happiness myths may have led you, like so many others, to feeling unfulfilled, unsatisfied, or unhappy with yourself and your lot in life, regardless of whether or not you've achieved what you set out to in life. You might feel confused about why the things that you thought would bring you joy, and contentment seem to leave you feeling empty. You may feel anxious or depressed about your perceived failures or shortcomings. Or perhaps you feel disappointed in yourself—who you are, your relationships, what you've achieved in life, where you live or how things have turned out for you—and wish you could feel better. Have you felt a disconnect between who you are and who you think you should be? Do you feel that it's your fault that you're not happier? Perhaps you believe that there's something wrong with you—that you're too inherently flawed or defective to be 'normal' and 'happy' like everyone else.

You're not alone. We all face obstacles and roadblocks on our own path to happiness. In fact, in my nearly three decades as a practicing therapist, the common denominator, with every single one of the thousands of patients I've worked with, is a desire to feel happier. *Everyone* wants to be happy and free from pain and suffering. The real secret I share with my patients is that happiness is less a product of how we feel or what happens in our lives. Instead, happiness comes from what we do. It's about making the decision to be happy and to take small, repeated daily actions to build a happier life over time. This is what rewires our brain over time to create more positive thoughts, experiences, and emotions (more on this in a moment!).

Before we dive into the actions that you can take to cultivate sustainable happiness over time, it's important to understand what true happiness really looks like.

Happiness Is In Your Hands

Here's what it really comes down to: Most people (including countless clients of mine) go about creating happiness in the wrong way. They try to build a happy life from the *outside in*, rather than from the *inside out*. So many clients come to me looking for help changing the circumstances of their lives, rather than seeking to change themselves. But as you'll learn in this book, happiness is an inside job. Even when life is difficult, we can be happy if we have the proper mindset, habits, and commitment to self-care. On the other hand, we can have everything we thought we wanted and still be unhappy if these inner elements are lacking.

So how much control do we really have over our own happiness? Can we just *choose* to be happy—is it that simple? What about things like genetics, childhood upbringing, past trauma, and socioeconomic status?

Many factors go into determining our happiness levels, and psychology researchers admit that happiness may be more complex than can be boiled down into a single clear formula. Things like genetics and upbringing do play an important role, but none of us are a victim of our past when it comes to creating happiness in the present. No matter where we've come from or where we are currently, we have a tremendous amount of power to work with our own inner environment to create the foundation for a happy life.

But there is one thing that researchers agree upon: what we do *matters*. Taking conscious, repeated actions over time goes a long way in cultivating sustainable happiness over time. That's what we'll be exploring in this book. While you can't change your genetic makeup or turn back the clock on your childhood, you can choose what you do today, tomorrow and the next day to rewire your brain, work with negative thoughts and emotions, take better care of yourself, and build stronger relationships. That's a whole lot of power that's in your hands.

Many don't know this, or find this fact hard to believe, since so many of us assume that happiness *can* be bought or earned, in some way, shape, or form. But the facts don't lie. In fact, while income has doubled on average in the past half century, our happiness levels have remained stagnant, and by some indications (such as rising levels of stress, loneliness, and mental illness), we've become less happy despite these economic gains.

As you'll learn in the book, the magic key here is the fact that you have the ability to rewire your brain for happiness. Regardless of your financial, familial, or any other circumstance, you have the innate capacity to change your brain to make it work for you, not against you—more on this very soon! As you'll discover, our actions rewire our brain through the magic of neuroplasticity, which we'll discuss shortly. This is where the rubber meets the road—we can take conscious daily action to change our brain and our lives over time.

As we'll explore throughout this book, there are several proven ways to shift the piece of the puzzle you can control—your own choices, actions, and behaviors—towards the positive; of making the brain work for you, by overcoming the brain's negativity bias that works against you. It's so critical to have this awareness because if you place an outsized importance on your circumstances or environment over your own choices, you're more likely to find yourself chasing hedonic happiness in lieu of the real thing.

The Road to Real Happiness

As you'll discover in this book, true happiness tends to be the result of a few key factors: the self-care and compassion you apply to yourself; the connections you have, with yourself, other people, and the world at large; and the habits and actions you take to make your brain work for you, shift negative patterns of thought and emotion, and live a life driven by your own values (rather than someone else's).

It's important to be aware that happiness looks different for every single person. Some may find happiness in a quiet, simple life in nature, while others find fulfillment in adventure and creativity, and others yet find happiness primarily with family and loved ones.

Think about sometimes in the past that you've felt truly, genuinely happy. Maybe it was hiking through a beautiful trail or lounging in a comfy chair on the porch, reading your favorite book. Playing cards on Sundays with your friends. Volunteering your time to help underprivileged children. Having date nights every week with your partner. Cruising down a country road with the windows down and the music blasting. Enjoying a beautiful meal with your family and closest friends.

We all have our own unique pathways to happiness, but the underlying tools that we can use to get to a life filled with consistent, sustainable feelings of happiness—rewiring your brain to work *for* you—is fairly universal. No matter what the exact destination looks like for you, the path to getting there is largely the same. We must do daily work to overcome our brain's evolutionary bias towards the negative and rewire it in the direction of positive thoughts, emotions, and experiences. It's not difficult, but it does require some time and commitment—and I promise you it's worth every ounce of effort you put in.

To put it simply: *If you want to be happy, you need to get your brain on board first.* And that's entirely possible to do! The brain has a magical ability to change itself, known as neuroplasticity, that's been proven through decades of neuroscience research and peer-reviewed studies, and, if properly applied, is a *guaranteed* method for rewiring your neural networks towards the positive over time. In other words, neuroplasticity can literally build new skills that help create, and then strengthen, neural networks for happiness. And a happy brain equals a happy life!

This book presents a simple, science-backed three-step system for wiring your brain for happiness. Through the **Prime-Shift-Connect** system—which I devised over decades of helping thousands of my clients to build happier lives sustainably, through small, repeated daily actions—you'll tap into the power of neuroplasticity to make your brain work for you, not against you, in your pursuit of happiness. Before we dive into the system, let's look at how, when it comes to happiness, our brain can act as both our greatest ally and our greatest enemy.

CHAPTER 2
Is Your Brain Working For You, Or Against You?

The single most important question in your pursuit of happiness is this: is your brain working *for* you, or working *against* you?

It's a simple enough question. But the answer is tricky, because, well, it's a trick question! The answer as to whether our brain works for us or against us is (drumroll) both! Like the classic thought experiment, the human brain is like Schrodinger's cat: It simultaneously works *for* us, when we utilize *neuroplasticity* to increase our capacity for happiness and contentment, and *against* us, through the evolutionary protective mechanism known as the *negativity bias*.

The Negativity Bias: When Your Brain Works *Against* You

Before I address the way, your brain works *for* you, let's first discuss the way your brain works *against* you: the negativity bias. The negativity bias is sort of self-explanatory, in the sense that it is, indeed, an inherent bias, wired into the human brain, towards negative experiences, thoughts, emotions, and stimuli.

This bias towards the negative causes the brain to react very intensely to bad news or unwelcome inputs, relative to how it responds to good news and positive inputs. The brain has evolved to be constantly scanning for threats, and when it finds one, to fixate on it to protect us from it. What that means is that we tend to notice and dwell on the negative *way* more than the positive (sound familiar?).

Consider your miraculous human brain for just a moment. As the point of origin for all our thoughts, emotions, and actions, the human brain is by far the most incredibly intricate piece of organic machinery in the history of the world. The functional capacity of the human brain, and its ability to literally control every aspect of our physical body and cognitive abilities, is so complex as to be nearly incomprehensible.

But understanding how your brain works is crucial to ensuring you perform at your peak happiness potential by training your brain to work *for* you rather than *against* you. After all, the brain is responsible for *everything*: your ability to read and comprehend this sentence; to feel the book in your fingertips and palm; for all the various thoughts and emotions triggered by the content. Everything you think, feel, sense and experience is a product of your brain operating as it's been evolutionarily designed to.

This evolutionary wiring is where the negativity bias (aka your brain working *against* you) comes into play. As I've said, in the simplest, most primitive terms, the brain is coded to detect threats and protect us from them. This hypervigilance towards perilous situations (real or imagined) has been essential to human survival for thousands of years. As New York Times journalist John

Tierney explains in his book, *The Power of Bad: How the Negativity Bias Rules Us and How We Can Rule It,* "To survive, life has to win every day. Death must win just once. A small error or miscalculation can wipe out all the successes. The negativity bias is adaptive, the term biologists use for a trait that improves the odds of survival for an individual or a group."

This survival slant has programmed the brain to process negative stimuli faster than positive stimuli, steering our focus away from those experiences and stimuli that make us happiest. In other words, we're constantly on alert for things to be worried or upset about, and that's where much of our attention is being directed. We pay way more attention to what goes wrong than to what goes right. *This*, ladies, and gentlemen, is precisely how your brain becomes a barrier to your pursuit of happiness. Your brain doesn't care if you're happy—it just wants you to survive at all costs!

The negativity bias explains why negative moments linger longer (and often affect us more deeply) than positive ones; why so many of us live with chronic worry, anxiety, and fear, approaching life with caution and trepidation; why the brain favors negative experiences over positive for long-term memory storage; and how negative events and information play a greater role in shaping our worldview, belief system and mindset than positive ones.

This skew towards the negative is so powerful, in fact, that negative reinforcement is often significantly more effective for learning and social-emotional development than positive reinforcement. And this inherent overemphasis on negative events and moments-- from real and potential dangers to potentially false or benign ones—has created a warped perception, in modern times, of the world we live in versus the one our brain perceives. The problem is that the brain isn't very good at distinguishing a genuine survival threat from an imaginary one (aka, something that makes us *feel* bad but isn't harmful). A critical email from your boss, an Instagram post that elicits a pang of jealousy or a look at news headlines highlighting war, violence and conflict around the globe can all be perceived as an existential threat to our survival, keeping our nervous system on high alert that contributes to chronic stress, anxiety and depression, and negative health outcomes over time.

You can imagine how the negativity bias would have been tremendously helpful in a world where being eaten by predators or chased by a saber-toothed tiger was your biggest concern. But in a world of relative comfort and safety where *actual* survival threats are relatively few and far between? Less helpful. When you're stuck in a state of anxiety because of a never-ending stream of worries about your work, health, finances, relationships, worthiness as a human being, success in life, and social image, well, it's safe to say that the negativity bias is not working in your favor. It's undeniable that the brain's default focus on negativity isn't a perfect match for modern life.

Neuroplasticity: Making Your Brain Work For You
The good news is that you're not condemned to a life of

neurochemistry-driven perpetual negativity. You can change your brain to work for you instead of against you.

Neuroplasticity is, in the most basic terms, the brain's ability to change and adapt over time. It means that the brain is flexible and amenable to change through repeated conscious efforts. While historically it was believed our brains stopped developing after age 25, the past half-century's exponential expansion in our scientific knowledge of the human brain, proved we were not, in fact, stuck with a set of static neural circuitry.

Neuroplasticity means we don't have to be a victim to a brain that works against us. We can literally reshape the structure of our brain, so it works for us, activating and strengthening positive neural networks and downshifting negative ones. The scientific discovery that the human brain does, in fact, continue to change, grow, and adapt over time—from birth all the way until death—completely revolutionized our understanding of the brain's role in happiness.

Neuroplasticity is the key to overcoming your own negativity bias. Through neuroplasticity, you can consciously strengthen neural connections that focus on and reinforce positive stimuli, while also weakening, or in some cases completely removing, those connections that cause us to focus on the negative.

Neuroplasticity is the backbone of everything we're talking about in this book. It is the driving force for making positive change in your life. It's a fancy word that just means that your brain has the capacity to change itself! When you change your actions, you change your brain. And if your brain can change, *your life* can change as a result. Think of neuroplasticity simply as the way your brain adapts to change based on your experiences each and every day.

How does it work? Your brain is home to nearly 86 billion neurons, which are, essentially, the messengers between the brain and central nervous system. These neurons send instructions to every organ, tissue, and cell throughout your body. Those 86 billion neurons are linked by billions of neural pathways that can be strengthened, or weakened, by the frequency and intensity with which we use them.

Think about it: the more times you walk down a particular hiking trail, the more clearly defined and easy to traverse the trail becomes. On the other hand, a trail that's never walked will quickly become overrun by foliage and be difficult to walk. Thanks to neuroplasticity, we have some control over which pathways become stronger through repeated experiences, and which ones become weaker, eventually dying off. I hope you're already thinking about which neural pathways you might want to kill off (i.e., thinking obsessively about your ex, or getting angry at your kids, stressing over deadlines) and which you'd like to strengthen (feeling gratitude for everything you've been given, feeling confidence and belief in yourself).

Neural networks are the key concept here. They're lines of communication within the brain, made up of neurons, that become ingrained through habitual repetition. The more you repeat something, whether it's a thought or a behavior, the stronger the associated neural network becomes within your brain—increasing the frequency and speed with which those neural networks are used.

Basically, neural networks are the literal lines of communication in the brain that help us execute behaviors automatically. Any neural network-- positive or negative-- can become wired for automatic activation with enough repetition. So, if you *invest* the time in building positive neural networks, as explained by psychologist Deann Ware, then you can rewire a brain that works for you as you pursue happiness (more on the importance of Investing time in the PRIME chapter)

We have the power to change these neural pathways. There are limits to our brain's adaptability, of course. Neuroplasticity can't overcome or foster recovery from certain extreme damage from traumatic brain injuries, for instance. But the fact that you can rewire your brain to increase positive pathways of thought and feeling is astonishing. It's the magical ability that we're going to tap into, in this book, to cultivate sustainable happiness.

While you can't change your genetics or your past, a *huge* percentage of your happiness comes down to your interpretation of the world and the way you choose to act and respond to life's events.

The discovery of neuroplasticity has flipped the script on neuropsychology and therapeutic practices. Contrary to prior beliefs, you can, in fact, physically change the way your brain is wired

When I explain neuroplasticity to my patients, friends, or family, I often find myself returning to a particular story about my son. For most of my adult life, I focused on my career: on expanding my professional resume, academic knowledge, and clinical experience to my fullest capacity. I always wanted to have children, but I knew it would be difficult for me to juggle professional demands with raising a child.

So, my husband and I deliberately chose to wait until later in life to have children, and a decade ago, my son was born. We waited a long time to bring him into the world, and I can't even begin to count the ways he's been a blessing to my life. He's an amazing, smart, talented young man, and a wonderful athlete, too—with a particular talent for water polo.

A couple of years ago, he had an all-star game for his water polo league, but the time and location were horribly inconvenient. I was already exhausted that day. I'd had to deal with several patients in crisis, plumbing issues in the house, and had slept only three hours the night before. Frankly, I was irritated that my son's obligation was causing me stress and found my brain working against me: focusing on the negative aspects in lieu of the many, *many* positive ones I was neglecting.

So, I utilized neuroplasticity to make my brain work for me: reminding myself of all the wonderful things about my son; how much better my life was with him in it; and shifting my perspective to feel lucky I *get* to see my son play water polo, rather than viewing it as something I'm *obligated* to do. This simple perspective shift completely reset my thoughts and emotional state for the rest of the day. And because this is something I practice regularly, returning to gratitude—and thereby quickly and thoroughly transforming the way

I feel—has become easier and easier over time. I've strengthened my neural pathways for gratitude (and overrode pathways of frustration and judgment) through small, repeated actions. *That's* what "wired for happiness"—the title of this book—means. *That's* how you tap into neuroplasticity to make your brain work for you.

With practice, focus, and repetition, neuroplasticity has made my brain work *for* me when it comes to fully enjoying and appreciating my family life and made me excited for his activities and endeavors. As a result, I've found immense joy in being present for the big and small moments of his life—even when things are busy at work!

As a practicing Family and Marriage therapist for over 25 years, I've been witness to every variety of individual unhappiness, and the corresponding lack of fulfilled feelings. Divorce. Anxiety and depression. Midlife crises. Low self-esteem. Lack of direction and purpose. Stress and burnout. The list goes on and on. Underneath all the particulars of the situation, my patients find their way into my office for one simple reason: because they're unhappy. But most of them have little idea *why* —or what to do about it.

Many times, I have seen a patient's brain working against them, and as I mentioned at the start, I have experienced an adversarial brain on occasion, as well. Thousands of patients have expressed a complete bewilderment as to how to change their unhappy feelings by making their brain work for them, with no idea where to even start. But anyone can make their brain work for them, and live a happier, more fulfilled life full of peaceful contentment.

I showed them the way. And I can show you, too.

I've spent my entire career compiling an evidence-based program for living a happier life that utilizes the latest and greatest neuroscientific tools and research advances. I've helped countless patients—many of whom may have felt as aimless as you might feel right now—take the proper steps to rewire their brain towards the positive. Through neuroplasticity, you can take advantage of my three-step **Prime-Shift-Connect** method guided by decades of research.

And if you're willing to trust me, you, too, can make your brain work *for* you. You can achieve real, genuine happiness, and overcome your brain's efforts to work *against* you with the negativity bias. Here's a quick look at the series of sequential, simple steps, which we'll explore in further detail in the forthcoming sections:

1. **PRIME Your Brain**: Like the undercoating of a house, priming habits—which include meditation and mindfulness, sleep and exercise—create the foundation for a happy brain and a relaxed nervous system.
2. **SHIFT:** Upgrade your mindset by shifting your thoughts, emotions and daily habits away from the negative and towards a positive, values-driven life through regular, repeated practice.
3. **CONNECT:** Build deeper connections with yourself, others, and the world around you through self-compassion, relationship-building techniques, and gratitude.

Guided by these three clearcut steps, this book will share the keys to unlocking happiness—true, genuine, *personally meaningful* happiness—and show you the path to living your best possible life. I have done the dirty work for you, combing through reams of data over years, and looking to hard, scientific evidence to uncover the best techniques and personal processes to live your happiest life.

It can be extremely challenging to look in the mirror, declare you're unhappy with your life or yourself, and recognize that you need help in feeling better. That uncertainty can easily lead to a vicious cycle of negative thoughts, emotions, and actions, taking you further and further away from a feeling of happy contentment. But just like you can't fix a problem you aren't willing to acknowledge; you can't fix anything before you accept the need for a solution.

I won't lie to you: making your way from unfulfilled and joyless to a happy jack won't happen overnight. But by now, you've lived a life where your brain consistently works against you rather than for you. Clearly, you *want* to live a happier life. So, if you're willing to put in the work, and learn the tools and techniques, you'll trigger neuroplasticity's magic to build a life of connection, contentment, and joy.

And soon enough, you'll find your brain working *for* you rather than *against* you.

The Wondrous Benefits of Being Happy

But before we get started with priming, a little extra motivation: Science has proven that happiness is not only a wonderful thing, but also the foundation of success, health, relaxation, and peak performance. If you've been working on improving any of these areas of your life, you might consider focusing on your happiness first!

I'm aware that it might sound a little silly to speak of the benefits of happiness, when clearly, the experience of happiness is its own greatest reward. But there are so many other juicy, wonderful things that come along with the experience of happiness that it's worth exploring them further.

Here are some proven ways that happiness benefits us more than we even know:

- **Helps Be More Productive and Professionally Successful**: One 18-month study, focused on job performance, had participants rate their happiness levels upon starting. Those individuals who reported being happiest in the beginning ended the study with higher pay, better promotions, and higher evaluation scores than the rest.
- **Better Physical Health:** A five-decade study of nuns, from the early 20th century, reviewed diary entries from the start of the study for each nun. Those nuns who wrote the happiest and most positive entries had a longer life expectancy than those who were less positive, with the positive living, on average, an additional seven years. Numerous studies (too many to cite here!) support the direct link between happiness and physical health.

- **Less Stress and Anxiety:** The happier you are, the quicker you calm your brain's emotional center. One study, which induced initial anxiety in participants, measured the physiological response of participants to one of three videos: positive, negative, or neutral. Those individuals who were shown a positive video had the fastest reduction in stress and anxiety, showing that the happier you are, the quicker you can reduce anxious feelings. In unsurprising news, happier people also recover more quickly from stress.
- **Peak Performance:** Numerous studies have demonstrated the link between happiness and peak performance in a variety of endeavors. A study of four-year old's asked participants to complete a task. Some were told to think about a happy moment before starting the given task, and those individuals who thought of a happy occurrence were quicker and more efficient than their peers.

Happiness is Coming

If you're still ambivalent and anxious about your ability to change, good news: you're already on your way! By picking up this book, you've taken the first conclusive steps to rewiring your brain, so it works for you rather than against you. That alone is *HEROIC*. Deciding to step outside your comfort zone, and try something new, is hugely difficult—even if what you're comfortable with hasn't been working.

You've already shown that you're *willing* and *capable*, and demonstrated your desire to make significant changes to your life. Now, can you accept the information you're about to learn, and know that you are powerful enough to live the life you desire? I think you can.

If you still have doubts, trust me: so, have countless patients of mine. But having doubt isn't the same as being *unable* to do something, and any journey can seem impossible when your sights are focused on the final destination. Know that this is possible, and that you are wired for happiness. The key to neuroplasticity—to making your brain work *for* you—is repetition, consistency, and above all else, patience, because true happiness isn't about quick fixes or easy work. As the ancient Greek dramatic Aeschylus said, "Happiness is a choice that requires effort sometimes."

I think you're ready. Let's get started with the foundation of priming!

CHAPTER 3
Priming Your Brain for Happiness

I remember watching my father paint our first house in America when I was 14 years old, not long after we moved from Iran. I stood gazing up at him on our front lawn as he teetered on a ladder balanced against the house, painting broad, off-white strokes across the front facade. The color was a drab, almost translucent shade of white—certainly not what I expected our new home to look like with a fresh coat of paint!

"That color is weird," I called out to him as he brushed up and down the wood. "You can still see the wood underneath it, too. Dad, I'm not sure it's working."

My father chuckled at my observation and pointed to the can dangling from its metal hook.

"It's primer paint, Fatemeh," he said. "It protects the wood and keeps the paint in place. You put this on first and let it dry. Then you paint it with the real stuff. You need to keep the underlying layers fully primed so that the house is protected. The primer helps strengthen the wood so that it can weather any storm. Without it, the paint will peel, the wood will damage, and the house will start to fall apart from the outside in."

At first, I was perplexed. It seemed strange, after all, to paint *before* you paint. But as I considered his explanation, I was struck by the clear logic of priming. Later in my life, as a student of psychology and then as a therapist, I found myself often thinking back to the process of priming—and wondering if it might be something we could do for ourselves, too. I learned that a coat of primer could create a base layer of protection that kept a house safe from the storms of life. It occurred to me that perhaps we could prime *ourselves*, creating a strong, sealed foundation to protect our own minds from the impacts of ever-shifting external conditions of our lives over many years.

Through my study of the psychology of happiness—and particularly, my research into neuroplasticity—I learned that there *is* a way to prime your mind for happiness, well-being, and success.

Through the process of priming, which I will detail throughout this section, you will learn foundational habits that work to form a kind of protective undercoat for the mind. These pillars of priming support the brain's capacity for flexibility and adaptation, overriding the evolutionary pull of the negativity bias and helping us to stay happy and strong in the face of life's difficulties. Priming is the integral first step in the three-step **Prime-Shift-Connect** method for achieving happiness that I have taught hundreds of my patients, and which is the subject of this book. By taking this critical first step—even if it's just a baby step at first—we are setting ourselves down the path to long-term happiness and fulfillment.

PRIME Your Brain, Weather Life's Challenges

As I discovered, we can prime our brains for happiness and peak performance—and in fact, this is something that successful, resilient people naturally do! It's actually a very simple process: You work on the underlying foundation—like coating a house with a primer layer before painting—to ensure your brain is ready to maintain a stable basis of strength, positivity and integrity for the long term, no matter what life may throw your way. If you prime your brain, you'll fortify yourself with a strong, protective basis of positive neural pathways, so the tough moments in life are more likely to just roll right off of you—rather than getting in and rotting the wood. It's a way to keep your mind strong and trained on the positive so you're far less likely to fall prey to exaggerated negative responses when things don't go your way.

There's one thing that's guaranteed in life: difficult experiences will find us. We will face pain, adversity, and setbacks. The work of priming asks us to accept this basic reality, and to take small, repeated actions each day to maintain a strong mental foundation that can hold us up, no matter what happens. In other words, priming allows us to stay resilient under any circumstances.

I developed a handy little acronym, PRIME, that captures the five basic steps of creating a mental foundation for happiness:

P - Be **Present** in the moment with mindfulness

R - **Rest** your mind and body with consistent, good-quality sleep

I - **Invest** time each day in self-care

M - **Meditate** regularly

E - **Exercise** often

By practicing PRIME-Ing, you'll soon find yourself embracing the challenges of life, rather than avoiding or fearing them as overwhelming obstacles.

The human brain, as we've discussed, is both a boon and a barrier to our pursuit of happiness. While we humans are blessed with a cognitive functionality unseen anywhere else in the known universe, if we don't know how to properly utilize and harness our brain's power, it can be used against us. We can become our own worst enemy.

Priming is the cognitive sealant that helps our brain to work for us, not against us—work that we'll build upon in important ways throughout the rest of this book. Priming utilizes research-backed steps for changing your brain and boosting neuroplasticity, providing verifiable, drastic effects on its physiological functionality. It leads to improved mood, reduced emotional reactivity, better decision-making, and sharper focus. You'll find that priming creates a layer of protective armor that decreases susceptibility to anxiety, depression, negative thought patterns, stress, and burnout.

So, how do you prime? It boils down to incorporating a simple set of routines within the following three areas— *Meditation / Mindfulness*, *Sleep*, and *Exercise* —into your daily life. Each of these three activities have been proven through thousands of peer-reviewed studies and decades of research to utilize the power of neuroplasticity to create new, positive pathways in the brain and to boost psychological well-being. Remember: it's all about small, repeated actions that rewire our brains and change the way we feel over time. That's the real foundation of a happy life.

Each of the three Priming routines we'll discuss are monumentally helpful in shifting your brain's wiring towards the positive—and being less impacted by the negative.

But how, exactly, do these priming pillars support your brain's ability to adapt? How does consistent sleep, exercise and meditation take advantage of your brain's innate flexibility and set you up for future glory? Let's take a closer look.

Priming: Building A Strong Foundation

Imagine your brain and its interconnected circuitry as one giant roadmap, with millions upon millions of neural networks connecting and crisscrossing each other. Just like the real world, our neural map is essentially a group of roads of varying quality: some are smooth and well-paved, others are dirt roads full of potholes, and others are dead-ends, and some are connected thruways yet to be developed.

The purpose of priming—and the goal of this book, really—is to use our natural capacity for neuroplasticity to strengthen the existing "roads" in our brain that foster positive thoughts and feelings while creating new, exciting pathways that lead towards gleeful exploration, fulfillment, and self-realization. Ask yourself: What pathways do you want to strengthen? What do you want to train your brain to naturally experience more of? Maybe it's self-compassion, or generosity, or gratitude. Maybe it's joy or self-worth. Whatever it is, priming can help you utilize neuroplasticity to change your experience for the better. After you've primed your brain, Step 2— *shifting* your brain away from negative neural pathways and towards positive ones—will be infinitely easier, trust me. In fact, we're *already* starting to change the neural pathways through priming, because the three pillars of meditation, sleep and exercise help us to *feel better* building up our base of positive emotions, thoughts, and experiences so that our brain naturally starts to move more in that direction.

Priming makes *everything* to come...
- Dealing with negative thoughts and emotions
- Cultivating self-compassion
- Living your values
- Creating healthy habits and routines
- Connecting more deeply with yourself and others
- Savoring happiness and living in a state of gratitude

... *that* much easier to accomplish. When the brain is primed with a solid undercoat, everything else we do to change or improve it sticks better. We can paint a new coat of paint, add an addition, or do anything else to make the house more beautiful and functional, and we know that we have the base to keep it strong and healthy under any conditions.

Priming essentially turns a muddy, backwoods path into a fully paved, coast-to-coast freeway. In other words, if you repeat a particular action or behavior over and over, you can strengthen that specific neural pathway, and make it easier for the brain to repeatedly utilize it.

Just like paving a dirt road inside your mind.

If you make the effort to consistently Meditate, Exercise, and Sleep, you'll quickly start to notice positive incremental changes, in both the short and the long term. You'll discover experientially how each of the priming components can reshape your brain and monumentally improve your physical health, including (but not limited to) your cardiovascular, immune, and digestive health.

Turning Down the Stress Response

How does it work? Priming acts on your neurophysiology, the physical structure of your brain and nervous system. It consists of somatic techniques that help to calm the physiological stress response of fight-flight-freeze that gets us locked into negative thoughts and emotions, and instead helps to keep the nervous system into a calm and alert state of "rest and digest"—the state of a positive mood, calm mind, and optimal performance. Just think about how you feel after a night of terrible sleep, versus how you feel when you're rested. Meditation, sleep, and exercise all reduce stress by dialing down the brain's threat response, which keeps us stuck in the negativity bias in an attempt to protect us from something that we think might hurt us, whether it's a driver cutting us off in traffic or an angry email from our boss.

In each of the three following chapters, we'll talk more about the mechanisms by which meditation/ mindfulness, sleep, and exercise help to turn down the stress response and get our physiology into a more relaxed, balanced state. With less stress and fewer alarm bells going off internally, we move out of the hyper-vigilance that creates stress, anxiety, and depression, and into a state of relaxed ease, health, and happiness.

Each component of priming provides verifiable, dramatic effects on our brain function, leading to an improved mood, better decision-making, and sharper focus. You'll find your memory strengthening, creating a layer of protective armor that decreases your chances for anxiety and depression.

There's no question that priming is good for you. Still, many people are resistant to meditation, find a good night's sleep to be a pipe dream, or hate to exercise. If you fall into any of these categories, I've compiled some tips and strategies to help you overcome those initial barriers to just getting started. In the rest of this section, we'll take a deeper look at each pillar, starting with meditation and mindfulness.

A Pre-Priming Disclaimer

But before we get started, an important disclaimer: I know this isn't breaking news. You've probably been told a million times that you need to sleep better, exercise regularly and make time to meditate. In fact, your eyes may be starting to glaze over right about now. You've "heard it all before." We "know" this information—or at least we think we do. But the reality is that most people still aren't consistently meditating, exercising, or sleeping enough. If we were, we wouldn't need so many self-help books and workshops teaching us the secrets of health and happiness! Clearly, something is missing.

Unless you can honestly say that you have impeccable habits when it comes to each of these three areas (and if you do, kudos! You can go ahead and skip to the shift section), the reality is that you need to revisit this information. I've done my best to present it in a new and fresh way that can help you to see the importance of these essential happiness pillars and learn new strategies for implementing them easily and effectively. I ask that you keep an open mind and a humble recognition that there's still more to learn and room for improvement. Be open to changing your approach.

There's a saying in Alcoholics Anonymous: "Your best thinking got you here." Your best attempts to be happy got you to where you are—so be open to going back to basics and exploring the essential building blocks of a happy life in a new way. Remember that you have to prime the walls before you add a fresh coat of paint. Instead of skipping over those critical first steps, be willing to take the time to go back to square 1 and do it right. This is what Buddhists call "beginner's mind," and it's an incredibly powerful place to be. In the words of Zen master Suzuki Roshi, "If your mind is empty, it is always ready for anything; it is open to everything. In the beginner's mind there are many possibilities; in the expert's mind there are few."

And remember, knowledge is just information until you put it into action – and when you put it into action, it becomes wisdom. So before you start zoning out or decide to skip this next section, know this: There is tremendous power in going back to the basics. When it comes to your happiness, try – just try – embracing a beginner's mind. Be open and curious about things that you already thought you knew but may not actually be implementing. It will make everything else you do that much more effective. Are you with me? Let's get started.

CHAPTER 4
Be Here Now: Meditation and Mindfulness

My longtime patient, Emily, scoffed in disbelief when I told her that she should try meditation (not an entirely uncommon response, I'll admit). She looked at me and said bluntly that she'd rather just take a Xanax.

When we first met, Emily had described herself as a constantly frazzled mess, racked with shame about her past, riddled with guilt about the current drama and dysfunction in her life, and anxious and pessimistic about a future that didn't look bright to her. She couldn't ever seem to quiet her racing thoughts or calm her inner distress, and she often struggled immensely to get through her day-to-day activities. Her motivation, mood and mental processing were lagging, and she had given up almost any hope of things ever changing.

Emily could never keep her mind in the present because she was so consumed by past failures, and worried that her future would bring more of the same. Consequently, she found herself unable to enjoy the many wonderful blessings in her life, like her loving husband and three beautiful daughters. Instead, she viewed pretty much everything in her life through a lens of failure and disappointment.

Despite her situation, Emily was resistant to my suggestion to try meditation. It seemed too difficult to do, and paradoxically, too simple of a solution to help solve her problems.

Meditation *is* Medication (without the Side Effects)
If I told you that there was a pill that could improve your focus and attention span, reduce your anxiety, improve your memory, and lower your risk of cognitive decline over time, I bet you'd take it in

a heartbeat—especially when you found out that there were no adverse side effects to worry about.

While it doesn't fit into a capsule, meditation is just such a medication. Even if we've drunk the meditation kool-aid, most of us can't even begin to imagine the miraculous benefits that come from the simple act of sitting silently and focusing our awareness on the present moment.

If it sounds too good to be true, well, it sounded that way to Emily, too. She wasn't the first patient to roll her eyes as I explained the power of meditation, nor would she be the last. As meditation has become popularized in recent years, I get fewer eye rolls, but many more responses of "Sure, I'll try it," with no actual follow-up.

Many people, including most of my patients, turn their noses up at the idea of meditating.

They've been inundated with misinformation or become too numb through countless "mindfulness benefits" blogs and social media posts to wake up to the genuine benefits of a regular meditation practice. They understand that meditation is beneficial, but they have a strong underlying resistance that keeps them from taking steps to build a consistent practice and reap the benefits.

The bottom line, though, is that meditation *is* medication...and yes, without the side effects. Meditation—along with daily mindfulness activities (these are two different things)—is more than just a key component in priming your brain for joyous merriment and personal satisfaction: It's a clinically proven , phenomenally effective way to tap into the magic of neuroplasticity to wire your brain for happiness.

Meditation is an ancient process of mental training that can help you rewire negative thoughts and emotions to find greater clarity, focus and calm. Generally, it involves drawing attention to your breath, sounds, or images in the present moment. There are countless varieties and techniques, but you don't need to worry about any of that just yet. To begin, you only need yourself, a comfortable place to sit, and a willingness to keep your mind open.

But let's sweeten the deal a bit, shall we? Before we get into the actual practice, I want to take a moment to explore the tangible brain benefits of meditation. Meditation and mindfulness can be significant agents of neuroplasticity , leading to a fundamental rewiring and long-term changes in the brain. A pair of studies from Harvard and Yale also provided concrete evidence of decreased brain activation in areas involving stress, anxiety, emotional regulation. Happiness is within your grasp when you prime your brain with meditation and mindfulness—and even a few minutes a day will improve your ability to focus on the positive thoughts, emotions and stimuli that makes you feel calmer and happier.

Decades of research has uncovered countless ways that meditation *literally* changes your brain for the better, altering the structure and functions of numerous brain regions. Here are just a few key examples of the physical brain changes caused by meditation:

Meditation can increase the size of your prefrontal cortex, where the vast majority of executive cognitive functions happen, largely determining what we think and how we choose to act. By acting on the prefrontal cortex (and literally changing its physical structure), meditation can improve your focus as well as your internal and external sensory perceptions—making you more attuned to what's going on inside your body (like a subtle headache after eating sugar) as well as your external environment. In other words, you're more aware and attentive to both internal and external inputs, which can help you to make better decisions.

Meditation can shrink the size of the amygdala —aka your brain's fear center and primitive 'alarm bell'—while reducing its active functionality. This reduction in size and activity has the practical effect of calming our instinctual survival fears and ancestral anxieties, while improving your mood, reducing your reactivity to stress, and increasing ability to regulate your emotions. Simply put, you'll feel less stressed, less anxious, and as stable as a table… emotionally speaking, of course.

Meditation thickens the hippocampus, the brain region primarily responsible for learning and memory. This can drastically improve your ability to learn new tasks while also boosting your brain's memory processes, ensuring that you both remember your friend's birthday, that work email you need to send and the extra ingredients you need to pick up for dinner.

Meditation slows the speed of gray matter degeneration **in** the brain associated with age, decreasing cognitive decline. This means that meditation can, quite literally, increase your lifespan *and* quality of life as you age.

What does this all add up to? A stronger, healthier, and more resilient brain—one that is better able to pay attention, stay focused, regulate mood and emotions, learn, and remember information, and handle stress. Sounds great, right? These examples only scratch the surface of the cognitive and neurological effects and benefits of regular practice. In addition to these physical changes in brain structure and functionality, meditation also increases the volume of gamma waves— brain waves associated with focus and attention— improving your ability to stay focused in the moment, on whatever is happening right now.

But it's not just your brain that benefits from meditation—it's also your body. Part of the reason that priming is so important is that happiness isn't just a function of the mind; it's also a byproduct of a healthy, balanced body. Countless studies have also shown meditation's profound impact on the body, with scientific benefits including:

- Lower blood pressure
- Improved heart health
- Decreased levels of the stress hormone cortisol and lower risk of stress-related diseases
- Strengthened immune system function
- Slower rate of cellular aging
- Cancer prevention

The life-changing benefits of meditation—including, perhaps most importantly, the capacity to be more present to the many gifts and joys available to you at every moment of your life—aren't too good to be true or somehow out of reach. Many of the studies cited above show that these benefits can occur in as little as two months of consistent practice. They've been proven, time and time again, over decades of research. Incorporating meditation into your daily routine can vastly increase your physical health, sharpen your brain's cognitive functionality, improve your mood, and slow your brain and body's natural aging process. What's not to like?

If you're still not sold, you may have a case of what I call "meditation hesitation." Let's address the common misperceptions that may consciously or unconsciously be preventing you from getting to the cushion.

Meditation Hesitation

Meditation is not some mystical practice reserved exclusively for shamans or monks. Meditation is simply a way of connecting with yourself, practicing becoming aware of what's happening in the present moment, and learning to *remain* present, in the moment, throughout each and every day. You sit in meditation for a few minutes every day so that you can learn to operate in a more meditative (i.e., calm, and aware) state for the rest of your waking life. We practice meditation to learn mindfulness: the ability to be aware of who and where you are right now—not getting stuck in the past or future—and to focus your attention on your current interactions with the external world. You're fully here in the moment, instead of being half present and having half your attention drifting elsewhere.

While meditation has been growing in popularity in Western culture for years now, it still goes against the always-busy, hustle mentality we've been taught to value in our society. Doing "nothing" but being present in the moment is a completely different way of functioning than what we've been taught! So, don't be surprised if it seems silly at first to sit in a quiet room doing nothing but focusing on your breath or bodily sensations. We've been taught to value busyness over rest and doing over being, and the practice of meditation asks us to rethink this way of operating. That requires a bit of a shift in perspective, and it's only after you start meditating and experiencing the benefits of the practice that this shift can really take hold.

Most people also think that meditation is about getting rid of thoughts, which can feel like an impossible task. But eliminating thoughts isn't the goal, nor is it even possible!

Go ahead: try not to think about anything right now. Bring your mind to a state of total silence.

How did that go?

Instead of seeking to remove thoughts entirely, your aim should be to reduce the number and intensity of intrusions in your thinking mind. While this may seem intimidating initially, with practice, it can be achieved. Before we talk about how to start practicing meditation, let's look at some other common meditation myths that might be getting in your way.

Meditation: Debunking Common Myths

Myth: You need to be a shaman or monk to meditate.

- Fact: Anyone can practice meditation without being on a spiritual path, and without making any major personal changes in their life. Monks in the Himalayas meditate, and so do stockbrokers on Wall Street—it's an equal opportunity practice for becoming more present and aware, no matter what the rest of your life looks like.

Myth: You'll have to sit in silence for hours to achieve any benefits of meditation.

- Fact: You can tailor your meditation practice to your personal needs and preferences and enjoy the benefits without adhering to a rigorous or time-consuming discipline. Research has shown that as little as five minutes of meditation can reduce stress levels and boost well-being!

Myth: You need to rid yourself of *all* thoughts to be a successful meditator.

- Fact: Telling yourself to stop thinking just doesn't work! It goes against the basic function of the brain. Thoughts popping up is to be expected. It's not about removing the thoughts; it's about changing our relationship with them so that they don't throw us off-course as easily or as often.

Myth: You'll have to adopt a New Age lifestyle and study Eastern philosophy.

- Fact: Again, you can practice meditation without changing yourself or your life. You may choose to study the spiritual principles and philosophy behind meditation, but you absolutely don't have to for it to work for you.

Myth: It takes years of consistent practice to see beneficial results of any kind.

- Fact: You may start to notice positive short-term benefits of meditation in as little as a few days or a few weeks. A 2015 study showed that college students who practiced compassion meditation three days a week for one month experienced more positive emotions and social interactions. Research has also shown that eight weeks of meditation is enough to create measurable changes in your brain, particularly in regions associated with memory, empathy, sense of self and stress reactivity.

Why Meditation Matters

Meditation is one of the best ways to support neuroplasticity and redirect your thoughts and emotions in a more positive direction. It helps us to rewire the brain's natural tendency to get sucked into loops of endless negative thinking which set the stage for anxiety, worry, self-judgment, stress, depression, and a whole host of other things that we don't really want in our lives.

Meditation shifts our focus from noisy inner chatter to a calm, alert awareness of what's going on *outside* of us. As psychiatrist Dan

Siegel notes in his book The Mindful Brain, the right side of the brain takes in external stimuli while the left side processes this information through our thoughts and inner experiences.

Despite the complementary nature of these two processes, both sides of the brain are continuously competing for our conscious attention—and the loud, chatterbox activity of the left side tends to dominate. While our ability to process, analyze and use language to make sense of our experiences is important, this rapid-fire inner dialogue can also make it a real challenge to enjoy what's happening in the present. In fact, the left side is a regular Chatty Cathy, pulling our focus away from the present moment nearly half of the time! And as Harvard psychologists

Matthew A. Killingsworth and Daniel T. Gilbert note , " a wandering mind is an unhappy mind."

A wandering mind—the eternal enemy of mindfulness—has been shown in research by social psychologist Daniel Gilbert and others to be the antithesis of happiness. When our thoughts drift away from the present moment in time, whether they're positive or negative, we're doomed to experience diminished feelings of happiness, both now and into the future. Whenever we're in the moment, we're happier.

Developing a daily meditation routine has been proven to turn down the volume on the left brain's noisy, runaway thoughts. Not only does it help you to be more present and to amplify your right brain's aware, observational nature, but it can also help you feel happier by reducing negative thoughts, which likely comprise a significant percentage of your inner dialogue (we'll talk about dealing with negative thoughts in more detail later).

Think about meditation as a workout for your cognitive functions—like burpees for your brain.

When you exercise a muscle over time, it strengthens and improves its ability to operate. Practicing meditation, or working out your brain muscles, is largely the same. You're strengthening your muscles of presence, focus, attention, emotion regulation, decision-making, memory and much more.

Where To Begin?

Look, I get it: we're all incredibly busy, with a hundred things on our to-do list at any given time. The idea of "finding time to sit silently in a room with my eyes closed"—as one patient of mine lamented—can feel overwhelming. We're hesitant to add yet another task to our list of daily obligations, particularly one like meditation, an activity that many assume will be too boring, too challenging, or a complete waste of time.

But as we've seen, the immense benefits of consistent meditation on your mental and physical health are far too crucial to dismiss in the name of perceived difficulty.

If you find yourself struggling to start a meditation practice, or have no idea where to even begin, practicing mindfulness in your everyday life is a good place to start. You can utilize mindfulness within the context of your daily activities until you're ready to start a formal meditation practice.

Remember that mindfulness *is not* the same as meditation. While mindfulness meditation is a very popular type of meditation (and the one I personally recommend), one does not need to formally meditate in order to incorporate mindfulness into their everyday life.

Mindfulness is defined as the cultivation of a relaxed, alert, non-judgmental awareness of the present moment—that's it. Being mindfulness is, essentially, just being present to whatever you're doing. Practicing meditation of all types can increase your capacity for mindfulness. But the key difference is that meditation is a *technique*, while mindfulness is simply a *way of being*.

Mindfulness is something that you can practice with or without meditation. It's simply a way of staying present in the moment and bringing yourself back whenever your attention has wandered.

Think of this way: mindfulness is something you can *be*, while meditation is something you *do*. Both are connected— and any meditation style will increase your ability to be mindful—but it's important to understand and remember the distinction.

Utilize Mindfulness Techniques in Everyday Life

Mindfulness can be practiced literally anytime, anywhere. It doesn't matter what you're doing, whether you're cooking or brushing your teeth or having a conversation. You can be mindful while you perform any task.

You can try practicing mindfulness while brushing your teeth using these simple steps:

Be fully present when opening the toothpaste. How does the brush feel in your hand?

Notice the speed of toothpaste exiting the tube, or how wide the paste appears on the bristles.

Ask and notice: how does the toothpaste taste? What is its consistency? How do the bristles feel against your teeth, your gums, your tongue?

Notice when your mind starts to wander while you're brushing and bring your awareness back to the sensations in your mouth and body while you brush.

It's simple, but incredibly powerful! You brush your teeth twice a day, but how often do you pay attention while you're doing it? The beauty of this process, of being *present* and *mindful*, is how you can turn your focus to any and everything happening in the moment. The key is to tune into your five senses, using the various sounds, sights, smells, and textures vying for your attention to remain anchored in the present. Focusing on staying present by noticing and being curious about what's happening can improve your brain and body's functionality, and over time, make your pursuit of happiness an achievable goal.

Practicing mindfulness during your daily activities is a great option for people who simply cannot quiet or slow down their thoughts. (People diagnosed with ADD or ADHD, for example, have particular trouble with this.) It's also a good option for those who find that a flood of intense emotions tends to fill the void of thoughts when they begin to silence their mind (as several patients of mine have reported experiencing). If you are unable to sit quietly with your thoughts or find the quiet overwhelming—at least initially—using mindfulness is a great way to begin cultivating an awareness of the present moment within the context of your everyday activities. You can make anything you do a "mindful" activity by committing to bringing your full focus to the activity, tuning into your five senses, and coming back to the moment anytime you become aware that your mind has wandered.

Tips and Strategies for Meditation Practice

Now that you have a better understanding of what mindfulness is and how to introduce it into your daily life, let's explore some tools to begin practicing *meditation* itself, if you choose to begin a formal practice (which, again, I highly recommend!).

- **Start Small**

    Setting yourself up for success by starting small is paramount to long-term success. As with any new activity, it's important to take baby steps towards the end goal. You wouldn't run a marathon if you've never jogged before, right? So rather than immediately signing up for a 10-day vipassana retreat (or expecting your inner voice to click on 'Silent Mode' during your first meditation), start by just sitting for five minutes and focusing on the rhythm of your breath as you inhale and exhale. That's your only job for five minutes: just notice your breathing.

    At the start, this might feel boring or pointless. You may be tempted to judge yourself for 'failing' to successfully meditate. But with practice—and by maintaining an attitude of self-compassion throughout the process—anyone can start down their path towards a more awake and present (and therefore happier) life.

    Meditation is, by its nature, a slow process, and developing mindfulness is a long-term practice. Start with this five-minute breath awareness meditation before trying any longer or more advanced practices. And if you're never able to meditate for long periods, that's OK, too!

Remember, research has shown that as little as five minutes of meditation per day can trigger noticeable mental and physical benefits.

- **Get Comfortable**

When you begin meditating, you're likely to find it difficult to quiet your mind. This is especially true if you're sitting in an uncomfortable seat, or you're situated in a distracting or unpleasant environment! The chances that you'll be able to stay calm and focused on being present are greatly reduced. It's hard to quiet your thoughts—and embrace the present moment—when your attention keeps being diverted to your aching back or hips.

As with any new activity, creating a successful and consistent meditation practice is more likely if you set yourself up to win from the start. Be mindful of your environment, your seat, and your comfort level when beginning a meditation session. That way, you're able to focus all your energy on the present and your existence therein. Sit on a chair with back support if that's more comfortable for you than sitting cross-legged on the floor.

- **Be Realistic**

Because of most people's 24/7, Go! -Go! -Go! mode of operating, it can be challenging to slow down enough to get into a comfortable rhythm with meditation. Meditation requires a conscious effort to overcome our natural tendency for non-stop mental activity, which is not an easy thing to achieve!

Don't expect to achieve a state of mental stillness right away. It's OK if your mind is busy during meditation! Just keep catching yourself and coming back to the present. Removing all thoughts from your brain is impossible, as any experienced meditator will tell you. Individuals who have meditated for years still experience thoughts and emotions arising during and after meditation, so if you don't experience any sort of transcendent breakthrough, that's OK. It doesn't mean that it's not working.

Remember, meditation is about long-term goals rather than short-term results. While you may see positive results after only a few weeks of meditation, the key to unlocking the benefits of meditation lies in consistent practice over time. Consider meditation like physical exercise, which can also be challenging to start. Think of meditation as your new workout regimen. You won't see results right away, but with persistent, repetitive practice, you will be able to rewire your brain and reap the many incredible benefits of neuroplasticity.

How to Practice

Hopefully, the concepts of mindfulness and meditation are much clearer by now. The next step? Start meditating! Don't expect perfection, and always keep in mind meditation is a *practice*. Just do the best you can.

Here are a few tips for getting started:

- **Use a Timer**

  The use of a gentle, unobtrusive alarm timer while you meditate, can remove the stress of time, helping you to drop fully into the moment. If nothing else, it will ensure you aren't checking your phone or interrupting your focus with worries about time. Start by setting the timer for five minutes, and only go up from there when you feel comfortable and ready for longer sessions.

- **Start with Sounds**

  It is generally easiest to drop into a meditative state if you start by noticing the sounds around you, and then switch to the breath. Awareness of sounds is a technique that's often used in hypnosis to help patients drop into a state of deep relaxation. If you try to tune *out* the sounds around you, they'll only become louder and more distracting. By noticing sounds in your environment, paradoxically, they recede into the background of your awareness.

- **Focus on Your Breathing**

    Drawing attention to your breath—literally, the flow of air in through your mouth and/or nostrils, filling your lungs, expelling oxygen throughout the bloodstream—is an excellent way to stay focused on the present.

- **Notice Your Thoughts, Don't Avoid Them**

    The goal isn't to stop a thought, it's to simply *observe* a thought as it comes and goes. Ignoring or suppressing thoughts should never be the goal. Try to notice them as they flow into, and eventually out of, your awareness. You can even say to yourself, "I'm thinking," or "I'm distracted," when it occurs. Acknowledge the distraction, then simply return your focus to your breath.

Meditation Script

If you're still unsure how or where to begin, try this sample meditation script to get started:

1. Find a comfortable seated position and close your eyes.
2. Bring your attention to your body, noticing the feel of your seat supporting you. Try to feel all your bodily sensations at once, throughout your whole body.
3. Start by noticing your breath, either the rise and fall of your stomach as air goes in and out, or the feel of the air flowing in and out of your nostrils.

Whichever feels right for you, choose that.

4. Don't change your breath, just allow it to flow naturally. Breathe in and out at a natural pace.
5. If you notice any sounds around you, just get curious about them and let them play with your eardrums. Don't judge or label them; just notice the sounds, then bring your attention back to your breath.

6. If your mind wanders, simply redirect your focus back to your breath's rhythm. Don't judge yourself for wandering, just gently remind yourself that a wandering mind is part of the process. In fact, congratulate yourself for noticing yourself wandering!
7. Let thoughts come and go without engaging with them. Simply notice them, label the experience as "thinking" or "distracted," and then come back to your breath.

That's it! Stay in meditation for as long as you can, regardless of how little or how much you're capable of when first starting.

To make things even simpler, you may want to start with a meditation app that offers guided audio meditations. Most people are familiar with apps like Headspace and Calm, which have many wonderful and easy-to-use guided meditations. As helpful as these can be, I feel that they provide the more watered-down version of meditation known as "McMindfulness." The meditation app that I recommend to my patients—especially if they are really serious about mediation and want an app that is backed by neuroscience—is called Fit Mind. Not only does it have a variety of amazing meditations, it also includes explanations of why and how the meditation will improve your brain and life. Part of the reason I love this app is because it was based on neuroscience and specifically designed to help you retrain your thoughts and build new habits. The app also features tools for setting goals and tracking your progress, which can help motivate you to continue your practice over time.

Awake in Everyday Life

As you know, reader, life moves pretty fast, and remaining present and mindful to the moments of our lives as they're occurring isn't always easy. There are always things that get in the way; things that distract us, drain us, or drag us down. Showing up for our lives fully requires practice and patience. Taking the time to stop and smell the roses is often the last thing we want to do when we have a million other concerns vying for our attention.

But being mindful of ourselves and the world around us—and choosing to remain conscious in any given moment—reminds us we are a living, breathing human being, part of the larger fabric of this miraculous world around us. Mindfulness is the foundation of connection, which we'll discuss in depth in Part 3. When you take the time to truly observe and contemplate this mysterious world we live in, along with the people, animals, and plants that populate it, the natural result is a sense of awe. This existence is wondrous and mind-boggling in its scope and history! You don't want to get to the end of your life and realize that you missed it.

Life is an amazing thing, as I reminded Emily. Being alive is a wonderful experience to relish and cherish! As Albert Einstein once said, "There are two ways to live your life. One is as though nothing is a miracle. The other is as though everything is a miracle." Practice mindfulness in your everyday life, and you will find yourself living as if everything is a miracle.

When Emily *finally* acquiesced to my suggestion to try meditation, she started small—practicing mindfulness for just two minutes every morning by focusing on being present while she made coffee or did the dishes. Initially, she found it challenging to stay in the moment and to silence her "torrent of thoughts." But she persisted, and within a few months, she was excited to tell me that she was experiencing less anxiety, relief from persistent feelings of guilt, a sharper and more focused mind, and to her surprise, a newfound energy and ability to *carpe diem*, or seize the day. All it took was two minutes a day!

> **CONSCIOUS COMMITMENTS**
>
> **Baby Step:**
> - **Mindful Tooth Brushing**: Bring mindfulness to the act of brushing your teeth, two minutes, once a day. Refer to the instructions in this chapter and use this basic daily activity as an opportunity to practice presence and awareness.
>
> **Bigger Step:**
> - **Five Minutes Every Morning:** For one week, try meditating five minutes each morning, either using the script provided here or a meditation app. If you tend to feel rushed in the morning, just sit up in bed and do it right away after your alarm goes off, and then continue with your morning with a calmer and more balanced mind.

While meditation and mindfulness are a crucial pillar of Priming your brain and body for happiness and high performance, it's only *one* component. Let's dive into the next Priming pillar: sleep.

CHAPTER 5
Make Sleep Your Superpower

My good friend Cristina had been driven to her wit's end by insomnia. She lamented to me one day over a venti latte, "I don't understand it. I'm tired all the time, yet I'm always wide awake in bed."

She had struggled for years with an erratic sleep schedule and had adopted the common band-aid solution of daytime over-caffeination to get herself going, drinking upwards of six Starbucks coffees per day. At night, she took sleeping pills (Ambien, prescribed by her family doctor) to wind herself down. It was a vicious cycle that left her feeling constantly wired and tired.

This was partly a result of the demands of her professional and familial obligations. But even on the best of days, she found it impossible to slow the chaotic whirlwind of thoughts churning nightly through her mind like a late summer hurricane. There was always a meeting, a soccer game, an unfinished task, or some obligation to obsess over internally. Yet the more she tried to force those thoughts out and find the mental calm necessary to fall asleep, the more her mind and body resisted.

As the thoughts circled in her mind relentlessly, she'd usually resort to quieting her brain by chemical means: taking a Valium, drinking some wine, or smoking a joint to calm herself down. Always, it was followed by an Ambien right before she hit the pillow.

Every night, without fail, she slept in fits and starts, and arose to a groggy morning. Exhausted and drained of the physical and mental energy required to function—much less able to operate at her personal level of peak performance— Cristina's mood, focus and memory capacities were greatly diminished.

To state the obvious: Sleep is absolutely necessary for your brain to perform optimally. Without proper sleep, the body goes into stress mode, we get stuck in fight-or-flight, and the negativity bias takes over as our primitive brain constantly scans for potential threats. Clearly, that's not a road that leads to happiness or high performance. Like Cristina, most people understand that sleep is crucial to their health. But there are two possible issues that prevent them from getting proper rest: 1) They struggle to sleep well, or 2) they can't seem to find the time to get a full night's sleep.

If time is the issue for you, I'll put it bluntly: *make the time*. Well-rested people do just about everything more effectively (and often, more quickly) than exhausted people. They waste far less time. I can't begin to tell you how counterproductive it is to try to save time by skimping on sleep, because when we're sleep deprived, literally everything else in our life suffers. We don't perform as well, we make mistakes, we're irritable, and our mood and focus suffer. When we lack proper rest, our ability to function at our fullest capacity is always out of grasp.

But if the issue for you—like so many of us—is poor sleep quality, don't worry: the rest of this chapter will provide a wealth of valuable tools and lifestyle shifts to help you sleep deeper, better, and longer.

Sleep is a critical part of priming that is essential for happiness, overall health and well-being, and neuroplasticity. Even if everything else in your life is going well, if you're not getting enough quality sleep, you simply won't be able to enjoy and make the most of your life. So, before you try to fix everything on the outside to become happier, start with your nightly rest as the critical foundation of a well-functioning mind and body.

Sleep: Why It Matters

Sleep is, technically speaking, the time during a 24-hour day cycle when the brain and body rest, shutting down many functions for a period of mental and physical recovery and rejuvenation. When we sleep, we prepare our brain for our time awake, ensuring that we are primed for maximum functionality and performance. But sleep, paradoxically, is also a very active time. Our brain performs many important functions while we sleep, essentially "cleaning house": flushing out toxins that accumulate over the course of the day, releasing metabolic waste, potentially preventing cognitive decline and neurological diseases. And of course, numerous studies have shown that sleep is essential for neuroplasticity!

Sleep is, in the words of Matthew Walker, professor of neuroscience and psychology, our literal "superpower."

Benefits of a Good Night's Sleep

We all know the blissful feeling of waking up from a deep, full night's sleep. The world is our oyster! We're energized, alert, upbeat and ready to tackle the day. This wonderful feeling is a powerful indication of *just how good* sleep is for your brain and body.

So, what, exactly is a "good night's sleep"? While the amount of sleep required for optimal health and performance varies somewhat from person to person, most people need around eight hours of sleep every night to look, feel and perform their best. When you consistently obtain a full eight hours of sleep, your body and brain's ability to function increases *dramatically*, improving your mood, attention, decision-making, reasoning capacity, memory, immune function and much, much more. In his 2017 book, *Why We Sleep,* Dr. Walker demonstrated that we are a whopping *40%* more likely to remember a new fact after a night's sleep, as opposed to remembering the new item later the same day.

If you're able to sleep the proper length, your brain becomes amenable to neuroplasticity, boosting its pliability to neural rewiring—and thereby increasing the likelihood your brain will work for you. While we're sleeping, the brain makes new neural connections. Research has linked chronic insomnia with neural atrophy (meaning, the death or damage of neurons), while sleep actually promotes the creation of new neurons and new neural pathways. Sleep researchers at NYU showed that sleeping encourages the growth of the dendrites that connect neurons and facilitates the transfer of information between neurons, strengthening neural connections and improving memory.

When we're not sleeping enough, our brain is less flexible and adaptable, and we're more susceptible to the negative effects of stress. Sleep deprivation increases your body's stress response—thereby amplifying your brain's negativity bias—and with it your risk for depression, anxiety, burnout, and negative thoughts and emotions. It's a very direct equation, as research has shown. A 2020 Italian study published in the Journal of Sleep Research found that five nights of poor sleep was enough to trigger a negative emotional bias, leading to a heightened tendency to evaluate emotional stimuli as negative rather than neutral or positive. In other words, when we have under slept, we see everything from a more negative lens, making it much more difficult to experience happiness and emotional well-being.

Besides keeping the negativity bias in check, there are so many ways that a good night's sleep keeps us happy and healthy. Some of the proven benefits of obtaining our body's proper amount of sleep, consistently, include:

- **A Healthy Heart:** Hormones crucial to the health and recovery of the heart and its blood vessels are released during sleep .
- **Improved Cognitive Functionality:** Just one night of proper sleep can improve your cognitive abilities the next day, particularly memory and attention.
- **Blood Sugar Regulation:** Sleep supports metabolism and balances glucose levels, preventing insulin resistance and helping you to maintain a healthy weight.
- **Reduced Stress:** Consistent sleep lowers the level of cortisol in the bloodstream, decreasing the physiological stress response.
- **Reduced Inflammation:** Sleep regulates the immune system, reducing the runaway inflammation that can have detrimental

effects on your health over time. Sleep also reduces neuroinflammation and oxidative stress in the brain.

- **Increased Energy and Focus:** Good sleep increases your energy levels the next day, as well as alertness, focus and concentration, all of which can improve your work performance.
- **Improved Memory:** Sleep plays a crucial role in memory consolidation and retention, particularly deep sleep.
- **Repairs Physical Body:** Your body produces certain proteins during sleep, which play a major role in injury recovery and repairing wear and tear throughout your body.
- **Better Weight Regulation:** Sleep regulates levels of hormones in the body that regulate appetite and metabolism.
- **Improved Driving Skills and Safety:** Fatigue was the cause of 91,000 car accidents in 2017, and a wealth of research shows that a well-rested driver is a safer one.
- **Stronger Romantic Relationships:** Sleep reduces irritability and reactivity while strengthening your ability to communicate clearly and calmly; both proven to bring partners closer together.

The overwhelming evidence doesn't lie when we give our body the sleep it needs (again, about eight hours for the average person), we feel physically stronger, mentally sharper, and more emotionally balanced. And when we're at our mental and physical peak, we are *primed* to live our values, experience joy, connect with others and with the world around us, and find a simpler path to not only managing our life but to thriving.

Get In the (Circadian) Rhythm

If you've ever wondered why, you feel tired and drowsiest at nighttime—when it is darkest and quietest—you can thank your body's circadian rhythm. A critical brain function analogous to the heart's pacemaker, our circadian rhythm controls our sleep schedule, dictating when and how we get tired, fall, and stay asleep, and wake each morning.

When we're able to obtain our body's ideal amount and quality of sleep, we naturally cycle through four sleep stages, ranging from active, 'dreaming' sleep, to quiet, 'restful' sleep. These stages range from those first moments of dozing off—like what you experience when you briefly fall asleep while lying on the couch and then snap back into consciousness—to our deepest slumber.

The circadian rhythm is also responsible for the maintenance of bodily functions while we sleep, including lowering your body's temperature, blood pressure and heart rate. Each of these physiological functions is necessary to maintain a sound night's sleep. Yet for all the power the circadian rhythm has over our sleep schedule, it can be easily disrupted and thrown off course—having major impacts on our sleep quality and duration.

The best way to set your circadian rhythm for sleep is to expose yourself to sunlight sometime between sunrise and 9 a.m. for anywhere from two to five minutes. Avoid wearing sunglasses unless you need them for safety reasons and get out in the sun again in the afternoon close to sunset. Exposure to sunlight is literally the best way to set your internal clock for sleep (we'll explore other methods shortly). If you're interested in learning more about the science of circadian rhythms and how this all works, I refer you to Dr. Walker's book, *Why We Sleep*.

The Four Stages of Sleep

Each of the four stages of sleep plays a major role in our brain and bodily recovery, and research has shown that each stage has unique physiological functions—with each playing a critical role in priming our brain. Brain wave analysis, for example, has shown a variety of activity takes place in each of the four stages, and appears to particularly impact the parts of the brain—namely, the hippocampus, associated with memory conversion and storage. That means that our brain is filing away memories for later retrieval while we sleep and performing critical functions that preserve memory retention over time.

The four stages of sleep are predictable, repetitive, and all equally important in our brain and body's ability to recover and refresh for the following day. We will cycle through each of these four stages 4-5 times per night, with each cycle taking roughly 90 minutes to complete.

1. **Non-REM 1 stage** - The shortest and lightest stage of sleep; it acts as a wind-down stage, as your mind and body fall fully asleep.
2. **Non-REM 2 stage** - This stage reduces production of the stress hormone cortisol (a key chemical in waking and alertness) and plays a crucial role in memory consolidation.
3. About 50% of our nightly sleep is at this stage.
4. **Non-REM 3 stage** - This is the deepest sleep stage, as brain and bodily functions significantly slow down, allowing for bodily repair and rebuilding. (It can be challenging to wake someone from this stage.)
5. **REM (Rapid eye movement) stage** - Commonly known as the "dreaming" stage, the eyes dart around under closed lids, while our bodies remain immobile. REM sleep appears to be crucial for memory, learning, and cognitive processes.

Stage 3 (deep sleep) is the time when the brain rewires itself, allowing for neuroplasticity to occur. It's important that we prepare ourselves properly for deep sleep-in order to support new neural growth and connections and keep our brain flexible and healthy. While you're in deep sleep, the brain is also hard at work reinforcing and strengthening the new neural pathways that you formed during your waking hours. If you skip over this stage, you're losing out big time on your brain's ability to get to work for you.

When our sleep schedule is disturbed, and we don't obtain the necessary amount of sleep in a single night or over time, the consequences can be severe. The risks of sleep deprivation—particularly chronic sleep deprivation and insomnia—are significant.

The Dangers of Sleep Deprivation

Countless studies have shown that the potential damage of sleep deprivation to our physical and mental health is staggering. It's important to have a clear-eyed view of these risks so that we can make better decisions about our sleep—and support ourselves in whatever way necessary to get proper rest.

When you sleep less than seven hours per night (and especially when you drop down into the four-to-six-hour range), you aren't just risking feeling crummy the next day. In fact, if you consistently miss the mark of at least seven, or ideally eight, hours of sleep, your long-term risk for numerous health problems increases over time. Studies have shown that only 1-3% of people can truly function with less than eight hours of sleep per night.

Countless patients of mine have declared their body *only* needs six hours of sleep, despite conclusive evidence from a 2003 study by David Dinges and his colleagues at the University of Pennsylvania that after two weeks of a nightly six-hour sleep, our brain operates equivalently to someone who's been awake for 24 hours straight. As Dr. David Dinges, director of Center for Sleep at University of Pennsylvania, puts it, we accumulate a "sleep debt" that reduces our normal cognitive abilities.

Still, more than one in three adults in the U.S. fail to regularly obtain the necessary eight hours of sleep each night. They also consistently underestimated just how impaired they were from sleep deprivation. In fact, sleep deprivation is so detrimental to human health, that it's been used as a torture and interrogation technique for prisoners throughout the world, and the United Nations has banned it as a cruel and inhumane practice.

The negative short- and long-term impact of sleep deprivation on the brain and body can't be overstated. This includes:

- Increased levels of the stress hormone cortisol
- Lowered reproductive hormones in men and women, contributing to fertility issues
- Increased risk of cancer and death

- Depressed immune system function
- Increased insulin resistance and risk of diabetes
- Increase risk of cardiovascular diseases
- Reduced cognitive function across the board (including mood, memory, learning, focus and decision-making)

If that's not enough motivation for you to take sleep seriously, I don't know what is. Clearly, getting a good night's rest (not just once in a while, but each and every night!) is massively important to both our physical health and our brain's functionality—and, in turn, to our ability to thrive in life.

But what happens when we want nothing more than to sleep well, but we can't seem to fall (or stay) asleep? How can those of us who are prone to sleepless nights obtain those elusive eight hours? As we discussed, one of the most important factors for regulating sleep is *sunlight*. But there are many other factors, too. It's important to note that many other variables, like sleep hygiene, bedtime routines, and what we eat, drink, and do every single day impacts the quality of our sleep. Let's take a look.

Creating a Successful Sleep Environment

Cristina's insomnia wasn't only a result of her stress levels and life demands: it was also the byproduct of improper sleep hygiene. Cristina never kept a regular sleep schedule, often falling asleep on the couch and going to bed at vastly different times from night to night. She often drank caffeine in the late afternoon and evening and would frequently watch TV or scroll social media as a way to unwind right before bed. All these habits, as you might imagine, are major no-no's for good sleep!

If you've ever struggled with poor sleep, then you know how important your environment is to getting proper rest. The noise, level of light and temperature in the room can all impact your sleep quality. If you recall, your circadian rhythm is strongly influenced by light and external stimuli, so what type of environment you sleep in—by choice or by other factors—will strongly influence your chances of sleeping soundly.

A huge factor in our ability to successfully sleep lies in our sleep hygiene, which includes your sleeping environment as well as your daily routines and habits. In many ways, developing a sound sleep schedule comes down to positive preparation and setting yourself up to succeed. It's important to consider every factor of your sleep environment: the temperature, the level of light and sound, the comfort of your bed, or any other environmental factor.

To set up a supportive sleep environment, make sure your room isn't too hot or too cold (the ideal temperature for sleep, according to research, is between 60- and 67-degrees Fahrenheit). Staying in this just-right temperature range actually helps to facilitate REM sleep . If your sleep environment (and, consequently, your body) is too hot, you're unlikely to properly cycle through the stages of sleep, and more likely to wake up exhausted.

If your mattress isn't at an optimal comfort level, the Sleep Foundation offers resources on how to find the best mattress based on your typical sleep position and other needs.

Minimize light and sounds, using blackout curtains or an eye mask, and try a white noise machine if street noise or other distracting sounds are an issue. As I've said, light is one of the key factors influencing our circadian rhythms, as our body is designed to follow the patterns of the sun. Artificial light (including lamps, overhead lights, televisions, phones, tablets, or anything else that generates light other than natural sun or moon light) can negatively impact your circadian rhythm. One-third of our circadian rhythm's effectiveness is dictated by light, and the presence of artificial light (particularly at times of day when our bodies are trained to expect darkness, such as the nighttime) can confuse the body, impacting our ability to fall and stay asleep. Artificial light also inhibits the natural production of melatonin , interfering with our body's natural sleep-wake cycle.

Turning off all artificial lights in the bedroom—and not using any devices within an hour of bedtime—ensures that your eyes and brain are less likely to be startled by those harsh external stimuli. By avoiding devices and artificial lights before bedtime, we are more easily able to drift off to dreamland.

It's not just the presence of artificial light emanating from lightbulbs that keeps us awake, though. We are always bombarded with a cavalcade of information and stimuli from our devices, which is enough to disrupt anyone's ability to power down their brain at night! Some patients have asked me if the blue filter function may help alleviate the light issue on their phone. And yes, it could help. But it doesn't do anything to remove the overwhelming number of stimuli that phones, tablets, or computers present, keeping our brains active and stimulated. If you're playing Candy Crush or watching YouTube videos on your phone while you're in bed, how do you think your brain will ever slow down enough to surrender to sleep?

Now, once you've got your sleep environment set up for success, it's time to look at your daily sleep routine—both at night and during the day.

Master Your Sleep Routine

Like any routine, having one for bedtime greatly increases your ability to consistently perform an activity with success, and helps to make the action feel easy and natural over time as you create new neural pathways through repeated behaviors. When our brains are trained to be in tune with our circadian rhythm, and to expect our nightly slumber at a set time, we are less likely to struggle to get to sleep. It's a simple way of training your body to prepare for rest and start winding down at a certain time in the evening.

AT NIGHT
Create a Nourishing Bedtime Routine

Getting yourself relaxed in the evening is critical for the transition from waking to sleep. At least one hour before you get in bed, switch away from stressful or stimulating activities, steer clear of your devices and TV, and engage in some relaxing activities to help signal to your body that it's time to unwind. You might want to drink a small mug of hot chamomile tea or take a warm bath or shower. Light a scented candle that soothes you, or eat a light snack, like almonds or pistachios, which have high levels of melatonin. This is also a great time for a short walk or meditation practice. Whatever feels most soothing and nourishing for you—that's the best thing to do before bed.

Schedule Your Bedtime

Just because you're not a little kid anymore doesn't mean that you don't need a set bedtime. Resist the urge to simply collapse into bed whenever you're tired or finish a Netflix show. The most important aspect of a bedtime routine is setting a consistent time to fall asleep and wake up every day.

Consistency is a key factor in successful sleep. If you need to set an evening alarm to remind yourself about your sleep schedule, go ahead and do it. According to Harvard Medical School , maintaining a regular sleep schedule (even on weekends and vacations) supports the body's internal clock and can make both falling asleep and waking up easier.

Avoid Artificial Relaxants (and Stimulants!)

If you're tired and chronically getting insufficient sleep, it can be incredibly tempting to turn towards artificial relaxants (like alcohol, cannabis, or prescription sleep medications) to induce sleep, but this band-aid fix can make things a lot worse, both in the short and long term.

When sleep is prompted by a foreign substance, your brain and body won't go through the expected, necessary cycles, diminishing the regenerative powers of sleep. The risk of dependency over a period of time—not to mention the physical toll on your body from the chronic use of any drug or pill—also outweighs the potential benefit of "passing out" in the short term. Plus, there is a wealth of research to show how alcohol negatively impacts sleep quality. Even if you fall asleep faster after a few drinks, you're much more likely to miss out on REM sleep and wake up during the night. As little as one drink a day f or women and two for men decreases sleep quality by 24%.

And of course—be sure to avoid artificial stimulants like caffeine, nicotine and energy-boosting herbs, supplements, or drugs before bed (more on this in a moment).

Do A Mind Dump

If you're eager to shut your eyes and fall asleep each night but find that your inner voice and racing thoughts are getting in the way, you may want to incorporate a practice called "Mind Dumping" into your nightly routine. It's exactly what it sounds like: you dump out whatever is running through your mind, by writing it onto paper. This process literally takes the thoughts out of your head and onto the page, so that you can pick them back up again later if necessary. Think of it as taking out the trash of unneeded thoughts so that you can get to sleep with a clean, clear mind.

A racing mind—much like a wandering mind—is an unhappy one at bedtime. As you know from our discussion of meditation, we have very little control over our thoughts. This can be exacerbated when we try to force ourselves to stop thinking and can ramp up the speed of our inner monologue.

Removing those disruptive thoughts before your head touches the pillow by writing them down on paper helps you process what you're thinking and feeling, so that your mind doesn't have to repeat things over and over in an attempt to find some sort of resolution. This procedure has helped countless patients of mine to quiet their noisy nighttime inner dialogue, allowing them to pick up their mental battle the following day, *after* a good night's sleep. There's a certain relief that comes from making a physical note of something, which gives us permission to say to ourselves, "These matters, but I don't need to keep going over and over it. I'll pick it back up again tomorrow."

All you need to do this is a notebook and a pen on your nightstand. While it may be tempting to use your phone, try not to do this: the blue light can disrupt your sleep, and there's a different level of psychological satisfaction and completion in the act of physically writing something down. Just dump everything out onto the paper from your mind. Write it all down without concern for grammar or spelling; just vomit your thoughts into the notebook unedited. Personally, I find categorizing into lists helps (work, family, finances), but don't worry about organization if it's not helpful for you. The basic idea is to remove the thoughts from your brain so you can allow yourself to rest.

When You Wake Up, Get Back to Rest with NSDR

If you tend to wake up in the middle of the night, a little-known practice called NSDR (also known as yoga nidra) can work wonders for getting back to sleep. Deep sleep is where the rewiring for neuroplasticity occurs, so we want to optimize this as much as possible. You can use this practice almost anytime, anywhere. It's a simple technique that is exactly what it sounds like: you are not actually sleeping, but you are slowing down your thought-flow and brain wave frequency, permitting your brain and body to rest deeply. You'll quiet any anxious or racing thoughts, drop into a state of relaxation and find yourself back asleep in no time. I have an audio script which you can try on my site at https://farahantherapy.com.

DURING THE DAY
Get Some Sun

As we've discussed, be sure to expose yourself to *natural* sunlight, particularly early in the day, ideally within 30 minutes of waking. Personally, if the weather cooperates, I try to start each morning with a stroll through the neighborhood before sipping some lemon water in my backyard. As we've discussed, obtaining sunlight in the morning improves your ability to sleep at night, by ensuring that your Circadian Rhythm is primed to induce sleepiness earlier in the evening.

If you recall, your circadian rhythm is most sensitive to light exposure during the window right after we wake up and right before we fall asleep. The earlier in the day that you are exposed to light, the more likely you are to become tired and ready to sleep at a normal time.

Practice Meditation

Meditation is one of the best natural sleep aids around. When we put in the effort to develop a meditation practice, the sleep benefits are mind-blowing (pun intended). Meditation allows us to turn down the volume on racing thoughts—whether it's your to-do list or an argument with a family member running through your head—and the nervous system's alarm bells, providing the inner quite necessary to remain calm and relaxed in the present moment, both during our meditation and at any other time. "Calm and relaxed in the present moment" is exactly the state you want to be in when your head hits the pillow. A Harvard study found that six weeks of practicing mindfulness (two hours a week total) significantly reduced insomnia, fatigue and depression.

Practicing meditation helps us declutter our minds, reduce our stress levels, and curb the intensity of any negative emotions we may experience. It can reduce the number of distractions that disrupt one's ability to peacefully fall asleep, and calm the inner storm raging at night, when we find ourselves alone with only our thoughts.

Exercise

An active body during the day can support a restful mind at night. The physical benefits of consistent daily exercise are practically endless—including better sleep . Just be sure to exercise at least three hours before bedtime (ideally, in the morning) to keep your body temperature low, give yourself a chance to wind down from intense activity, and provide yourself with the best possible chance at nightly slumber. (Stay tuned: there's more to come on exercise in the next chapter.)

Curb the Caffeine

Think twice before drinking that afternoon latte or after-dinner espresso. Caffeine stays in your system for up to 12 hours, keeping you wired and alert. Although it can have some modest, short-term benefits for cognitive function, it's important to stay clear of having it at least eight hours before sleep in order to get good quality shut eye. I've had many patients who say that they can sleep fine having a double espresso after dinner, but there's no question that even if they're able to fall asleep, the artificial stimulation blocks deep sleep cycles and keeps their nervous system hyper-aroused.

Caffeine keeps us alert by blocking adenosine, a neurotransmitter with an essential function in many biochemical processes, particularly the onset of sleep. It has an inhibitory function on the central nervous system, meaning that it halts many processes associated with wakefulness. Caffeine sneakily attaches itself to the same receptors that adenosine would normally latch onto, preventing the natural drowsiness that occurs as adenosine levels increase. That makes it harder to fall and stay asleep.

Flipping the Script on Sleep

You know from both your own experience—and now, from the research—just how much of a difference a good night's sleep makes in how you feel and function on a daily basis. The difference is literally night and day. I hope you now feel armed with everything you need to make good sleep a priority in your life and address any obstacles in your environment and sleep hygiene (or within your own thinking and mental habits) that may be getting in the way.

Like my friend Cristina, you can flip the script on poor sleep hygiene, change your habits, and utilize mind dumping to settle any negative thoughts rattling around at nighttime. Last year, Cristina began priming her brain with meditation and exercise, which helped to reduce her stress levels and get her out of the constant state of hyper-arousal and hyper-vigilance she'd found herself in. She also started following a strict bedtime routine. This included no devices or television in the bedroom, ditching the coffee (except for one cup in the morning), and getting off the drugs that did little more than temporarily knock her out.

After several months, Cristina was sleeping better than ever, and described herself as feeling happier, lighter, and brighter. Her mood, memory, and focus drastically improved. And she attributes a great deal of her success at her new position at work to her newly rested and vibrant state of being.

Anyone can develop a sound, consistent sleep schedule, and help prime themselves for happiness and high performance. Along with meditation and exercise, rest is a crucial component in priming your brain to rewire itself towards more positive experiences and a more fulfilling life. If you try these suggestions and find that you're still struggling with sleep even after changing your sleep environment and hygiene, consider working with a psychotherapist to address any underlying traumas or stressors that may be keeping you in an activated and hyper-vigilant state.

Conscious Commitments

Baby Step:
- **Let the Sunshine In:** Get out in the sun within 30 minutes of waking up, even if it's just standing on your porch for a few minutes or taking a five-minute walk around the block.

Bigger Step:
- **Get on the Clock**: For one week, commit to following a consistent sleep schedule, getting into bed at the same time every night (ideally around 10pm) and waking up at the same exact time every morning (ideally around 6am). Even if you're not tired that early initially, or you find it difficult to wake up early, stay consistent and give your body time to reset your internal clock.
- **Makeover Your Sleep Space**: Make one positive change to your sleep environment—adjusting the light, sound, temperature, or comfort level of your bed to make it more conducive to sleep—to create a restful sanctuary that's set up for success. Start with just one!

Now, let's explore the third priming pillar, exercise, considering both why it's so important and how to make it a regular part of your daily life.

CHAPTER 6
Get Moving: Exercise

If you're a parent, you know that having a baby pretty much turns your life upside down— *especially* your daily habits. When I had my son, my former five-day-a-week workout regime went right out the window as my sleep became completely disrupted and caring for him became my number-one priority.

I'll be honest with you: it took me a couple years to get back on track. Even then, I still didn't have almost any free time, but I had enough motivation to get back in shape. I was ready to at least try to make something work. To get back in the saddle again, I promised myself that I'd just walk 10 minutes each day down the hill from our house and back. That 10 minutes soon turned into 20 minutes. Eventually, I started looking forward to that part of the day, and it became an hour. Within six months, I had a trainer again and I was consistently doing solid workouts several days a week. I never got back up to five days, but that's OK. Things change. Three days a week with my trainer now feels right to me. On the days that I'm not training, I go for walks around my neighborhood.

It wasn't easy to reestablish my exercise habit—but it was worth every bit of effort I put in. Exercise is a basic pillar of priming that both immediately and over time transforms the way we feel and the quality of our lives. It boosts our brain power, releases feel-good endorphins, and keeps our energy moving in positive directions.

Many of my patients struggle to exercise regularly, even though they want to and know that they should. Susan tried countless workouts—spin classes, HIIT, Zumba—without ever finding one that truly clicked or that she could enjoy. Exercising was just another obligation she didn't want to deal with. Without fail, she'd eventually fall off the wagon and find herself down in the dumps, with her failure to keep her commitment reinforcing an inner story of failure and "not good enough." It was a vicious cycle that wasn't getting her anywhere.

Susan's struggle is hardly unique. She's far from the first person to slip up in their efforts to exercise. While some people enjoy exercise and are naturally motivated to do it because it makes them feel good (if that's you, reader, feel free to jump ahead and keep on exercising!), many more view physical fitness as an unfortunate, if necessary, burden.

But just like meditation and sleep, developing and maintaining an exercise routine over the long run is crucial to priming your brain, triggering neuroplasticity to help you maximize your health and happiness. The benefits of consistent exercise on our physical health are many and well-known, but the impact of exercise on your brain is just as important.

If it seems impossible to get (or stay) motivated, there may be some barriers standing in your way, which we'll look at in this chapter. Know that you're not alone, and that there are proven tactics and strategies you can use to build an exercise routine to last a lifetime. You can obtain the physiological and emotional benefits from exercise and use it to prime yourself for a happy life.

Exercise: The Brain's Key to Happiness

Exercise is pretty much a non-negotiable when it comes to happiness. Physical movement is absolutely vital to the way we feel, physically and emotionally. Think about the energy of happiness: it's not a state of stagnation and lethargy; it's a buoyant, active, and uplifted state. Exercise brings our bodies (and minds) into that state. We *all* know that our brain's reward center is activated during exercise. It's not exactly news to inform you that exercise benefits *every* system in your body, including your cardiovascular, immune, digestive, and nervous systems.

But what's less known is how exercise can literally alter the chemical and physical structure of your brain, in both the short and long-term. There are several surprising ways exercise allows you to tap into the power of neuroplasticity to help your brain work *for* you to find happiness and create change in your life:

Exercise induces a 'Runner's High,' a natural antidepressant and mood boost found during any sustained physical activity, not just running. More than that, exercise has been found to release endocannabinoids, the chemical mimicked by marijuana. The amygdala and prefrontal cortex have a high number of endocannabinoid receptors, and when they're released during exercise, they'll bind to their receptors in the brain's stress centers, reducing the activity in those areas. In other words, you'll be more relaxed, less stressed, and more optimistic about yourself and your life—no drugs needed.

Consistent exercise can slow our brain's natural decline of receptors of dopamine, the neurotransmitter associated with pleasure and reward, with age, allowing you to derive more pleasure from life into your later years This is immensely important, since studies have shown adults lose up to 13% of dopamine receptors with each decade.

Exercise produces lactate in the muscles, which is, in fact, often blamed for post-workout muscle soreness. But it also has a real benefit for your well-being. Lactate travels to the brain, where it has an antidepressant effect and helps to make us more resilient to stress.

Exercise protects our brain from stress and stabilizes the nervous system's fight-flight-freeze response, relieving feelings of anxiety and panic in the process. Exercise also calms the brain by releasing the neurotransmitter GABA, which has a soothing effect that restores balance in the nervous system.

Physical activity increases productivity and keeps our energy levels high throughout the day by stimulating the growth of new mitochondria , our cell's energy regulators.

Exercise strengthens our bonds and connections to other people, improving our ability to trust, or feel part of a group. Exercising with a partner can boost feelings of closeness, and synchronized physical movements are proven to trigger the release of endorphins (neurotransmitters known to induce pleasurable feelings) while making us feel closer to the people we exercise with. Given the immense role of connection in determining our happiness levels, we'll come back to the crucial ways that exercise can build and foster strong relationships later in the book, in our discussion of relationships.

Exercise boosts self-esteem and positive feelings towards one's own body.

All these things help us to accomplish our goals and feel good about ourselves. When we exercise regularly, we provide proof for our minds of what we can truly do when we set out to accomplish something and then physically do it. We are rewarded by seeing the fruits of our efforts. Keeping our own word and honoring our commitments also builds confidence and self-trust and a sense of self-responsibility. Plus, accomplishment in one area of life begets accomplishment in other areas. If you can finish an intense weightlifting session, or climb to the top of a mountain, you may feel that you can face anything the world throws your way.

Think about how we often describe mentally or emotionally challenging situations with physical descriptors, like "It was really an uphill climb, but I made it," "It was a heavy weight to carry," or "That project was a real marathon." Exercise can boost your feelings of courage and bravery, giving you the confidence to know that you have everything you need to face life's challenges. Lifting literal weights, climbing an actual mountain, running a real marathon: these are just a few examples of physical, tangible things you can accomplish with exercise. And if your brain knows you can overcome literal physical barriers and obstacles, it will begin to believe you can overcome *any* barrier or obstacle, internal or external.

All of this is just the tip of the iceberg. When you exercise consistently, you give your brain an opportunity to work for you. As a rule of thumb, the body thrives on activity and the mind thrives on stillness—and getting your body moving can help your mind to be quieter and still! It's a win-win. With regular exercise, you'll soon find that everything just works better, mentally and physically.

How to Begin Exercising If You're Unsure or Unmotivated

'Well, no shit, Sherlock,' you might be saying. *Of course*, exercising is good for us, and *of course* we all want to follow a solid workout routine to gain all the benefits. But you may be asking yourself:

How can I actually start an exercise routine?

How can I keep myself exercising once I start?

How can I get myself to exercise if I truly hate all forms of physical fitness?

These are the three most common questions I'm asked when discussing exercise with patients. Without fail, nearly every single patient will express some degree of uncertainty regarding *how* to start exercising: if they're unsure, they lack motivation and discipline, or they simply haven't found a workout option they like.

As many of us have discovered through trial and error, exercise isn't easy. Finding time to maintain an exercise routine while going about your busy life can be challenging. If you don't know how or where to start, it can discourage you from trying at all. But there's hope on the horizon for those eager to incorporate consistent exercise into their daily lives. You *do* have control over your daily habits, and you can start small to build up routines that will make a huge difference in the long run. Remember, a happy life is the result of small actions performed consistently.

In my professional, and personal, experience, there are two crucial areas of focus that can drastically increase your chances of success: building strong exercise habits and finding enjoyment in exercise through joyful movement. It's important that you like what you're doing, and that you have the discipline to stick to it! These two methods—forming strong habits and moving in a way that feels good and enjoyable—have proven most effective for my patients and myself.

Exercise Habit Forming

There's an entire chapter of this book dedicated to habits, and that's for good reason. We'll dive much deeper into the importance of habits in the next chapter, as part of Step 2, Shift, , but the fact is that the most effective way to begin, and continue, exercising is by starting to form strong exercise habits.

Habits are actions we perform automatically on a day-to-day basis. They are actions we don't have to think about (we just do them!), thereby freeing our conscious mental energy for more important things. Consider how you instinctively turn on the tea kettle first thing in the morning or say 'Bless you' after someone sneezes. These are both habits we had to learn and ingrain into our brains at some point, but they are now mindless and reflexive. It's the process of developing a neural pathway that's so strong that you essentially travel down it with a self-driving, self-directing car, without having to put much of any conscious thought or effort into the process.

Installing a new habit, like exercising for 30 minutes every morning, takes time. But there are ways to make it easier. For now, let's focus on two simple methods for building new habits, *habit stacking* and *temptation bundling*, which are particularly effective when it comes to exercise. And remember start *small* —like, ridiculously so! —to increase your chances of long-term success.

Habit Stacking

Habit stacking, as described by S.J. Scott in his book *Habit Stacking: 97 Small Life Changes That Take 5 Minutes or Less,* involves literally stacking a new habit onto an already established one, which can help you build an exercise habit by combining it with a habit you already follow. For example, if you have the habit of microwaving your lunch each day, you can *stack* an exercise you want to become a habit, like abdominal planks, and perform them while the other habit is in progress. This way, you're building on the automatic nature of the existing habit and rewiring your brain to automatically perform core workouts while your lunch cooks. You're piggybacking off the existing habit to create a new one.

You can take literally any habit that you already perform daily and add an exercise to it. For instance, I wanted to tone and strengthen my arms, so I stacked five wall pushups every time I washed my hands. After several months, I'm up to 20 pushups, and believe me: if I can build up an exercise routine, you can, too. Consider running in place while your morning coffee brews or doing jumping jacks while the shower warms up. Again, this is about starting small, so don't worry that you're not doing enough. Just get started.

Temptation Bundling

Temptation bundling, an idea introduced by researcher Katy Milkman, involves the 'bundling' two actions: one that we *want* to do, and one that we *should* do but don't have as much desire to perform. With temptation bundling, you can build an exercise habit while doing something you like to do, making the exercise feel more enjoyable because of its connection to the pleasurable activity. For me, it's listening to my favorite podcast while I walk around the neighborhood.

For instance, if you enjoy playing video games but want to begin walking on a treadmill or riding a stationary bike, you can bundle them by only allowing yourself to play video games while you walk or bike. Maybe you start going for hikes with your best friend, so you can look forward to one-on-one time together. Or maybe, like me, you only listen to your favorite podcast while you're going for a run or walk. Just remember to start with a short run, rather than pushing yourself too far in the beginning.

Jump for Joy...Literally

Building exercise habits can reduce the mental battle we often find ourselves in with exercising, making it an automatic action that we perform without difficulty or a sense of struggle. But another crucial way to make your brain work for you, and set yourself up for success, is by finding physical activities that induce positive, joyous feelings within you—so you're naturally motivated to do them.

While we may think we have limited options for working out, there is, quite literally, no limit to the varieties of physical activity and exercise at our disposal. Hate jogging? Play basketball. Don't like sports? Go for a hike. Not a fan of nature? Find a workout routine to try in your living room.

Prefer not to 'exercise' when you exercise? Dance it out by sweating to your favorite playlist.

The idea of *joyful movement* —a concept that approaches exercise as something to enjoy rather than endure—isn't new, but it has been underutilized in our current culture. Exercise is often associated with grueling, physically straining activities and movements (think: "no pain, no gain"), but it simply doesn't have to be that way. Joy is a powerful force to harness towards positive change!

As psychologist Kelly McGonigal writes in her book *The Joy of Movement*, the key to successful exercise is getting your body moving and your heart pumping. It's about being active in a way that will keep you motivated over time. As long as your body is moving—no matter the activity, even one that doesn't seem like exercise, such as gardening—you can gain the benefits of exercise while doing just about anything.

Don't be shackled to anyone else's workout preferences. The physical activity that lights your fire is out there waiting. Know that getting fit or staying in shape doesn't need to be a chore. Even if you cringe at the notion of physical fitness, there is some activity out there that will bring you joy, whether it's joy in your activity, or the pleasure of seeing and feeling positive changes to your mind and body.

If there's nothing that you physically enjoy, consider focusing on the after effect. For me, the greatest joy is the mental feeling I get *after* I finish my workout. The joyfulness isn't in the 45-minute HIIT routine; it's in the feelings of satisfaction at the end. Appreciating the positive impacts of physical activity can be a useful alternative if joy, itself, isn't found from any exercise.

In addition to using joyful movement to make it easier and more pleasant to exercise daily and consistently, try these other strategies at your disposal to lay the path towards feeling happy, happy, joy, joy.

Tips and Tricks for Maintaining an Exercise Routine

1. Find a Workout Buddy

We are creatures who crave connection, and the pursuit of our personal fitness goals is no different. In fact, individuals who share their goals with a friend are 33% more likely to achieve them than those who don't. Of course, who you choose to share your exercise goals with will also impact your likelihood of success, so make sure you choose someone who will lift you up, not tear you down.

The benefits of working out with others goes beyond accountability. As I mentioned earlier, the endorphins released during a synchronized physical activity, with a group of other people, have been found to fuel your body's biological need for positive human connections. Sociologist Emile Durkheim coined this phenomenon, when one transcends themselves individually, as *collective effervescence.*

Again, be picky when choosing friends or family members to work out with, as the people you surround yourself with can immensely impact your odds of success. The presence of a positive, uplifting workout partner doesn't just increase your chances of exercising consistently; staying connected to others will increase your feelings of well-being and support you in living a long, healthy, happy life (more to come on this when we discuss Connection in Part 3).

2. Sneak in Exercise

Exercise doesn't have to mean sweating it out at the gym, and you don't need to push yourself to the physical threshold to reap the benefits of aerobic exercise. In fact, simply walking 20 minutes a day can provide drastic improvements in heart health, decreasing your risk for major health problems later in life. Walking can literally add years to your life, and stave off many of the common, inevitable effects of aging.

Just like adding vegetables into a meal, you can sneak in exercise-adjacent activities into your daily life. Perhaps you ditch the elevator and take the stairs in your office building or park your car in the back of the lot, encouraging yourself to walk the extra steps inside. You can also make a conscious effort to get up and walk around the house every few minutes while fiddling with your iPad or take time on a break to get up and move from a seated position. If you work from home, maybe your "commute" is a walk around the block before you sit down at your desk.

Even just standing up and pacing while you're talking on the phone can make a difference.

It's easy to get stuck in a sedentary lifestyle, but it's entirely possible, and beneficial, to extricate yourself from the couch and start moving your body. Being physically active in any capacity gets your blood pumping and reminds you that, in that very moment, *you're alive*. That's worth the effort.

3. Avoid All-or-Nothing Thinking

As you're well aware, human beings are not perfect. We all make mistakes, although we still tend to assume that we're capable of perfection. How often have you missed a workout and then internally chastised yourself for hours? Self-improvement can be a slippery slope, and it's easy to allow the distorted thoughts of your inner critic to become gospel truth. Be conscious of your inner dialogue and notice when a self-improvement project becomes the basis for self-judgment.

Be compassionate to yourself with your fitness goals—with any goals, really— particularly in the beginning. Don't abandon all hope the first time you falter in your physical fitness goals.

Jumping to the conclusion that if you fail once, you'll always end up failing, is patently false.

Trust the late, great Aaliyah: *If at first you don't succeed, dust yourself off and try again.* A misstep or stumble here and there isn't the end of the world. Just keep moving forward, working towards progress.

4. Ditch the Scale

It's easy to prioritize your weight as the ultimate indicator of physical health, above and beyond all other factors. But while your weight does matter as a small piece of your overall health profile, it is nothing more than that: a piece of the puzzle. Your weight is simply a number, and if you obsess over that number—and whether you've lost 3, 5, or 10 pounds—you can quickly lose sight of the greater purpose of exercise for maintaining well-being and living a happier life.

Muscle mass is far denser in the body than fat. Even if you simply perform aerobic exercise—as opposed to anaerobic or strength training workouts—you're likely to increase your muscle mass and, therefore, you might not lose as much weight off the bat as you'd hoped. But take it with a grain of salt: if you look better and feel healthier, you can be confident you're on the right track.

Even if you haven't slimmed down, isn't feeling better a worthy enough goal?

Also notice your mood as you progress with exercise. If you're displeased with your weight or appearance after a few weeks, check your mood: Do you feel better mentally? Are your emotions more stable and elevated? There are a number of benchmarks you can use to track your physical progress, and if you find an improved mood or energy levels, take comfort in knowing you're heading in the right direction.

Conscious Commitments

Baby Step:
- **Add a Walk:** Integrate a walk of at least 10 minutes into your daily routine. Any time of day, in any environment, will do! If you're too busy to leave the house or office one day, just walk up and down the hall while you're on the phone or between meetings.

Bigger Step:
- **One week of the seven-minute workout:** This infamous science-backed micro-workout routine is perfectly engineered to provide as many benefits as possible in a short period of time. Head to the appendix to find a link with detailed instructions and commit to squeezing it in each day.
- **Add one hour of joyful movement:** Whether it's a dance class, a hike with a friend, or any other activity, commit to one hour of joyful movement per week. Even if you're already working out regularly, add something to the mix that's fun and joyful. You can break it up or do it all at once—whatever works for you. Just make sure you get in a full 60 minutes.

Exercise: A Pillar of Priming

Practicing meditation, exercise, and proper sleep habits won't in themselves make you instantly happy and content, but they *will* set you up to succeed in your efforts to rewire your brain, and you'll reap all the benefits that come with it. You will feel better and be healthier—that's a guarantee. You'll have the foundation of a healthy body and an even, calm mind.

Now, what if you don't *feel* like getting exercise one day, don't *think* you can successfully sleep seven or more hours per night, or don't *behave* in mindful ways, or practice meditation? If that's the case, you, like so many of us, may find your brain working against you through your emotions, thoughts, or actions. In Step 2, SHIFT, we'll look at ways to improve your emotional regulation and gain greater self-mastery by shifting your thoughts, emotions and habits in a positive direction.

STEP 2: SHIFT

Redirect Your Emotions, Thoughts and Actions

CHAPTER 7
Habits: The Building Blocks of a Happy Life

When Kacie first walked into my office, she had just moved back to Los Angeles from Nashville, where she'd lived for the past six years, after losing her job and being forced to move back into her parents' house. Once a motivated go-getter, she had slowly but surely devolved into a stay-in-bed slacker (her words, not mine).

"God, I'm such a loser."

In our sessions, she would often repeat this familiar refrain that was clearly looping in her mind.

"I can't even motivate myself to get out of bed most mornings," she said. "I'm so far behind everyone else I know, and I've fallen so far off my own path that I don't even know how to begin finding my way back."

Whenever Kacie started to try to figure out a way out of her predicament, she would get overwhelmed and frustrated, and before she knew it, she was eating a weed edible, ordering McDonald's on GrubHub, and starting a *Twilight Zone* binge on Netflix.

"Seriously, Fatemeh, what's the point of starting something new when, without fail, I almost always immediately give up?" she said. "I'm stuck with my shitty self-sabotaging routine, and nothing's ever goanna change it."

Kacie was in desperate need of a big shift in her life—which would start with a shift in her mindset and her habits. Step one? Some priming to get her back on track. She hadn't worked out in over five months, her sleep cycle had become exceedingly erratic, and she was too anxious to stay present in her life. She often found herself awake until dawn, scrolling her social media feeds and engaging in a downward spiral of "compare and despair," contrasting her seemingly hopeless life with that of her more successful and (as she presumed, at least), much happier friends.

Kacie's feelings of rudderlessness were unsurprising given her current circumstances. Her entire life had been uprooted and overturned. As many people do in times of strife, she resorted to avoidance as a coping strategy. All the bad habits she'd ever struggled with came back to rear their ugly heads. She had regressed from her formerly healthy habits, and with a severe lack of self-compassion and clearly defined personal values, she had no idea how to find the energy and will to replace her bad habits with good ones. She had no idea how to start taking the proper steps to develop—and maintain—the thing she needed the most to create change in her life: positive personal routines.

As her therapist, it was clear to me that Kacie's habits were the place where we had to start. From her sleep habits to her eating habits to her Netflix binging and lack of exercise, Kacie's everyday actions were keeping her stuck in cycles of stagnation, self-judgment, and self-loathing. Her bad habits had dug her so deeply into ruts of negative thoughts, feelings, and behavior that she felt like there was no way out. Talk about your brain working against you! To upgrade Kacie's happiness—and get her life back on track—we had to overhaul her habits, one at a time, shifting negative patterns of thought and behavior into positive ones, and focus on life-supporting habits that would bring her closer to what she really wanted in her life. Out with the old, in with the new! The long journey of getting her life back would begin with one tiny action, one day at a time.

That's what this whole section is about: making the small, incremental shifts in our thoughts, emotions, and behaviors that ultimately create the big shifts in our lives. You can see how Part 1 and Part 2 go hand-in-hand and support one another in the implementation of basic positive behaviors that make you feel better, physically and mentally. This whole time, I've been saying that happiness isn't some blissful experience that magically occurs when everything is going well in our lives—instead, it's the result of many small, repeated acts of self-care, connection, and presence. If you want to understand the current level of happiness in your life, then you need to take a good, hard look at your habits—how they are supporting you and how they may be undermining you—so that you can start to shift your life in a positive direction. Let's get started.

The Potent Power of Habits

Each and every person has a set of personal habits, which are acts they perform, almost automatically, on a consistent basis. Habits are an external expression of the neural pathways that are hardwired into our brains. As our brains get stuck deeper and deeper in these grooves of repeated activity, we get more and more "stuck in our ways."

This can be a good thing or a bad thing, depending on the nature of the habit. Habits, in themselves, are an evolutionary mechanism designed to make life easier for us. These actions allow us to operate at our peak personal ability by removing many conscious choices from our mind. By reducing the number of active, conscious decisions we have to make throughout the day, more mental space is freed up to focus on matters of greater importance.

The way we break bad habits—or create good ones—is through the power of neuroplasticity. Remember that neuroplasticity is the way that our nervous system changes in response to experience. When we change our behavior and experiences, the connections between neurons in the brain also change, creating new pathways. And as new pathways are created, different types of thoughts, emotions and behaviors are reinforced. Our goal is to form new neural circuits by which certain habits are more likely to occur, and others are less likely to occur.

Why? Because good habits are the foundation of a good life. The importance of having healthy habits and regular routines cannot be overstated. When you consider the Greek philosopher Aristotle's assessment of excellence—that preeminence is not a singular act, but the habitual repetition of actions—it's easy to see the vital importance of our habits. The goodness of our lives is the goodness of many individual actions. The vast majority of personally and professionally prosperous people, including Tom Brady, the seven-time Super Bowl champion and undisputed football GOAT, have credited much of their success to an almost automatic set of routines and habits that support their goals and propel them forward every day.

Consider the three pillars of priming: mindfulness, sleep and exercise. Imagine a person whose daily habits are to meditate for five minutes every morning, take a power walk after lunch, and engage in relaxing activities for an hour in the evening before heading to bed at 10 p.m. This person is going to have a *very* different level of well-being and experience of life from someone who is primarily sedentary and doesn't exercise regularly, doesn't meditate, and has an erratic sleep schedule—no matter what else might be going on in their lives. Can you see the difference here? The person with good priming habits is highly likely to feel good more often, have lower stress levels, and be more aware and engaged in their day-to-day life. That makes them much more able to take in the good that's already present—and to create better experiences, feelings, and connections from there.

Take a moment to take stock of your priming habits: What are the good habits you have in place? How's your sleep, exercise, and meditation? What are the bad habits you want to change? When do you tend to get off-track with your habits? Is it when you're stressed with work, or when you're traveling? Being honest with yourself is the first step in making the critical *shift* from bad habits to good ones.

A Force of Habit

As I noted before, habits are those actions and behaviors that we perform with an almost automatic reflex, many of which we take for granted or aren't even aware of. Thinking about the things you do first thing in the morning is another good way to start bringing awareness to the many habits that make up your daily life.

Brushing your teeth after you wake up is a habit. Making a cup of coffee is a habit. Going straight to your email instead of heading out the door for a run, are also habits. Completing a habit takes little to no mental effort, which is good, considering habits make up roughly 40% of our daily actions and they require little to no thinking or planning to perform. When it comes to a habit, as the Nike slogan says, you "just do it"—no preparing yourself, waffling, or debating about whether or not you really want to. You can imagine how much time, energy, and mental bandwidth this saves us over time! Our brain loves efficiency, so it will find shortcuts whenever possible to help us get where we want to go. That's what habits are all about: making it easier to achieve our goals by eliminating unnecessary effort and decision-making.

Here's another example of just how automatic habits can be: when somebody sneezes near you, you may be reflexively triggered to say, 'God bless you,' as if on autopilot. The impulse towards polite speech, like saying "please" and "thank you," is an example of a good habit.

You don't need me to tell you that not all habits are created equal. Just as we have good, healthy habits, each of us also performs any number of bad, unconscious habits on any given day. While some bad habits may be relatively benign, others can fester, locking us into patterns of behavior that take us further away from our goals. Over time, this creates increasing distance between our current state of being, on the one hand, and our values and the person we want to be, on the other—often leading to shame, self-judgment and feelings of deficiency or unworthiness.

Bad habits can be challenging to break because, again, they originate in the deep grooves of hardwired neural pathways. But that doesn't mean they can't be rewired. Changing our actions and changing our brains goes hand in hand. The key is *replacing* (not just removing) the bad ones with positive, healthy habits. (We'll talk more about bad habits and how to replace them later in the chapter.)

Whether good or bad, all habits are built through repetition— doing something repeatedly. My patients often ask about the number of days it takes to build a habit. There's really no magic number. The amount of time needed for building a new habit depends on a variety of factors, including the difficulty of the habit and the person's level of discipline and motivation. The popular notion that it takes 21 days to form a new habit is actually just a myth! According to a 2009 study from researchers at University College London, it can take anywhere from 18 to 254 days to cement a new habit. Some habits can be formed easily whereas others can take much longer to be ingrained. Rather than focusing on the timing, I think the more important question is: *how can you rewire your brain so that the good habits have a better chance of sticking—and the bad ones loosen their grip?* How can you hack into your neurochemistry to get your brain to work *for* you as you strive to implement healthier habits?

Rewire Your Brain, Shift Your Habits

Rewiring your brain to shift your habits requires a bit of brain hacking. There's a three-stage method for rewiring your brain to shift your habits that Dr. Andrew Huberman, Stanford neuroscientist, recommends. Understanding our brain chemicals that support the types of habits we want to cultivate is key, as well as connecting broad phases of the day to those chemicals essentially tapping into your circadian rhythms and optimizing your habits.

He suggests breaking up the 24-hr cycle in to these 3 stages to engage new habits, working with your neurochemistry to ensure the best results. His method of utilizing these stages for habit implementation has proved to be incredibly helpful for me personally and for my patients. I have included a few ways to build in new habits, but one of my favorites is this three-stage method from the Huberman Lab podcast on Strong Habits. I love to nerd out to his podcast, Huberman Lab. If you get a chance, listen to him. He has amazing science-based tools for all things mental health.

He explains these stages based on a typical person's timeline of waking up around 7, and going to bed around 10 p.m. (If you are interested in this method of forming habits, I would highly recommend listening to the whole episode.)

Here is a summary of Dr. Huberman's method:

STAGE 1

If you want to build new habits, it's important to understand how your brain works. 0 to 8 hours after waking certain chemicals like dopamine, norepinephrine, and epinephrine are at their highest levels helping with action, reward, learning, and memory allowing your system to be more focus-oriented, making this stage the best time to take on habits that require the most effort. (i.e., exercise) Consider your most challenging activities here giving you the opportunity to perform more difficult tasks and a better chance of succeeding with new habits.

You can also gear your physiology, and further facilitate your brain to work for you by trying five minutes of sunlight in the morning, some caffeine, and exposure to the cold (i.e., a cold shower). By leveraging both your neurochemical activity and priming your whole system with these simple foundational habits you will also be boosting your energy levels and focus.

STAGE 2

This stage which is 9 to 14 hours after waking begins the decrease of chemicals such as dopamine and norepinephrine, and the increase of the neurotransmitter serotonin that will lead you to be in a more relaxed state. Here it's better to take on habits that are already established or take little effort like journaling. Since this is a stage where our bodies would be winding down for the evening, begin to minimize artificial light and engage in activities that are calming, such as, a hot shower, and meditation.

STAGE 3

It seems that the first two stages trigger neuroplasticity while stage three is where all the juicy stuff really happens. At 16 to 24 hours after waking essentially when most of us are asleep is when the brain puts all our experiences together and consolidates them to memory making it possible to build habits.

This is further proof of the importance of priming, good sleep hygiene and quality sleep.

> **CONSCIOUS COMMITMENTS**
>
> - **Baby Step:** Spend five minutes in direct sunlight around sunset to balance your circadian rhythms and set your body up for better sleep.
> - **Bigger Step:** Take 15 minutes daily as an afternoon or evening break to focus on a more relaxing habit like reading, journaling, yoga or meditation.

Get In the Habit Loop

Now you know how to optimize your habits by tapping into your circadian rhythms and utilizing the three stages of habits, let's look at how to set up a habit loop, a simple set of steps involved in creating a habit.

Here's what it looks like:

- **The TRIGGER:** something that prompts an action
- **The HABIT:** the action cued by the trigger
- **The REWARD:** whatever we obtain or get, tangible or otherwise, from the habit, which is why the habit exists in the first place

A habit loop can be as simple as waking up in the morning, which *triggers* you to perform the *habit* of brushing your teeth, so that you obtain the *reward* of fresh, clean breath and a healthy mouth and teeth. The habit loop is also an important concept to remember when attempting to convert a negative or unproductive habit into a healthy, positive one. We'll come back to this later in the chapter, but first, let's look at the benefits of building habits in the first place.

The Life-Changing Magic of Good Habits

Habits are the essential building blocks of a healthy, happy life. There are countless clear benefits to incorporating positive, healthy habits into your daily life. As you know, we only have a limited amount of mental real estate available to us for thinking and acting at any given moment, so making certain actions automatic allows us to spend our precious energy on matters of importance and enjoyment. That means more time and energy for personally meaningful goals and things that make you happy, like connecting with loved ones or enjoying creative hobbies.

We have so much more control over our happiness than we think. Habits help us to build a personal system to shift our behaviors, thoughts and emotions in ways that increase our happiness drastically over time.

The well-established benefits of good habits for your well-being and your life include:

Enhance prioritization: Habits and routines allow you to focus on the most essential tasks and important priorities. The presence of positive habits and routines helps your dorsal striatum-- a part of the brain crucial to habit formation and our 'action-and-reward' perception -- push you towards taking action towards your priorities, rather than procrastinating. Habits reduce the mental energy expended on unimportant or irrelevant topics (like the loops of thinking we expend trying to get ourselves to do things, or punishing ourselves towards procrastinating), allowing our brain to focus on what truly matters.

Increase your attention span: Habits are all about making your behaviors automatic, reducing your risk of becoming sidetracked, or losing your train of thought. The repetition of positive routines and good habits will encode in your basal ganglia (commonly referred to as the brain's 'habit center'), boosting your prefrontal cortex's energy reserves to focus on new or more pressing tasks.

Lessen your worry: Following a set of consistent daily routines can help regulate your nervous system, keeping your amygdala at bay and limiting the time spent in a 'fight--flight-freeze' response. That means less stress and less worry. By creating stable structures and reducing the level of uncertainty in your day-to-day life, your brain will produce a feeling of predictability and calm that lessens your discomfort with the unknown.

Maximize mental bandwidth: Setting routines ensures your brain's limited mental faculties can focus on what's important. For instance, Nobel Prize-winning physicist Richard Feynman ate the same dessert for 50 years– chocolate ice cream– cutting out that daily choice from his brain's agenda. Clearly, he had more important matters to direct his mental energy towards!

Just as healthy habits and positive routines act as a boon for your overall health and happiness, bad habits can act as immovable impediments in your efforts for growth, leading to feelings of stuckness and self-sabotage—as Kacie found as her habits took her further and further away from the life she wanted to be living.

The Heavy Weight of Bad Habits

If you've ever tried to quit smoking, eat less sugar, or become less sedentary in your everyday life, then you know just how difficult it can be to rid yourself of your ingrained bad habits—and just how strong the pull back to them can be. We all have bad habits, since we're all imperfect creatures. We don't always do what we really need or desire, what we "should" do, or what we know is best for us. And we all struggle to override our brain's deeply ingrained shortcuts and affinity for quick, easy rewards. Bad habits are the epitome of your brain working against you! This is where we find ourselves stuck in ditches: those negative neural pathways that are so deeply wired that we can't seem to get ourselves out of them, no matter what we do.

Many things can get in the way of our attempts to break or replace a bad habit, especially if we've tried and failed before. There're what Dr. Huberman calls "limbic friction," which is somewhat of a complicated concept but for our purposes, I would describe it as the amount of effort required to perform a behavior.

Things like tiredness, anxiety, and distraction create limbic friction, making it harder to resist a bad habit and to make the shift to a good one. This is a big part of why we start with priming—to reduce the factors that make it more difficult for the behavior to become automatic, which is what we're really looking for.

We often turn to bad habits as a way of "numbing out" and avoiding feelings of stress or discomfort or suppressing unpleasant and undesirable experiences (like painful thoughts, emotions, and physical sensations), which often precedes unhealthy actions and behaviors, like reaching for a cigarette or glass of wine. The numbness and avoidance of pain is the reward we get for engaging in the bad habit. It might be the moment you grab a beer, open Instagram mindlessly scrolling, or reach for that second piece of cake. The bad habit momentarily relieves the discomfort while doing nothing to address the roots of the problem that keep it recurring.

So why do we keep returning to these bad habits, even when we know how unhealthy, unpleasant, and unhelpful they are? Well, you can start by blaming your brain—simply knowing what you want isn't enough, on its own, to overcome the brain's evolutionary wiring.

The brain, as you know, favors those neural pathways most often used. When your emotional homeostasis—that ideally steady, balanced baseline emotional state—gets thrown off balance, the brain will usually work overtime to return things to a 'normal' state of calm, regardless of whether that default state of mind is good for you or not. Enter your bad habits. They quickly become your go-to tools for reducing stress and overwhelm. They might help in the moment, but typically they only make things worse in the long run.

Part of the problem comes down to the physiological structure of the brain and the way it connects our behaviors and actions with perceived rewards. As I mentioned before, our prefrontal cortex plays a central role in our ability to process, analyze and perceive the world, but its resources are limited, and it doesn't always win out when other parts of the brain (like the amygdala, our fear center) want our attention—particularly if we are stressed.

When we're under stress, our rational and focused prefrontal cortex tends to downshift and lose focus on matters of importance, according to UCLA neuroscientist Alex Korb. This allows other areas, like the amygdala and its primitive survival instincts, to swoop in and shift our focus to whatever stressor is right in front of us. We shift into survival mode, which makes us lose focus on the big picture as our vision narrows to help us deal with the immediate "threat." This can push you towards short-term, temporary comforts, like finishing that entire bag of Doritos in one sitting. Of course, if a state of stress becomes our default mode of operating, our neural circuitry will reinforce those unhealthy actions.

The brain's struggles with prioritization under stress explains why willpower alone isn't enough to break our bad habits. Even when you *know* what you want and why it matters, if you become upset or anxious along the way, you won't be able to just plow ahead with a level head. You'll reach for the sweet treat again, even after promising yourself for the hundredth time that you'll get off sugar. You'll act against your own interests.

Your ability to think rationally, which the prefrontal cortex largely controls, is diminished under the influence of negative feelings and thoughts; and when the irrational wins out, you aren't likely to push yourself forward in a positive direction. In so many ways, the inability to simply remove a bad habit mirrors the difficulty involved with overcoming negative thoughts or emotions (which we'll get into in the next chapters). The more you push back and try to avoid or grit your way through change, the more likely you are to remain stuck in the same place.

There *is* hope, though. Just as you are *not* those negative thoughts or emotions you feel, you are *not* doomed to repeating your bad habits for all eternity. There are steps to take to overcome and change your day-to-day life, and it all starts with taking one step at a time.

Be (Somewhat) Like Bob Wiley and Take Baby Steps

When it comes to habits, or anything else in life, the journey of a thousand miles starts with a single step—and sometimes a very tiny step!

When you see a person who has established healthy habits, keep in mind what you're seeing: the destination, not the journey. If you want to walk a mile—or if you want to get in shape, quit smoking, start a new career, or accomplish anything else of value—you must start with a single step, even if it's a teeny tiny one to begin with, as scientist B.J. Fogg suggests. That's why I've been offering baby steps, and bigger steps for those who are ready, throughout this book.

This notion is perhaps best illustrated in the classic film, *What About Bob?* (Which, if you haven't seen it, I highly recommend you do so). In the film, the key message from psychotherapist Dr. Leo Marvin (played by Richard Dreyfuss) to his obsessive, agoraphobic patient, Bob Wiley (played by the incomparable Bill Murray) is simple: If you want to change anything about your life, you need to take "baby steps" towards your goals. While this supremely silly film takes the idea in an absurd direction, its lesson rings true, because you can only take things one step at a time.

Meet yourself where you're at and start with the smallest action possible, and then build upon that until—before you know it—you've reached a much larger goal. Another reason we start with priming is because the foundational priming habits make it much easier for us to perform other, more difficult habits by increasing our energy, focus and motivation. Priming supports us in breaking bad habits by reducing the stress, anxiety and exhaustion (i.e. "limbic friction") that causes us to reach for substances and behaviors that don't serve us (like grabbing for a cigarette or a sugary snack, or zoning out on the phone).

Here are the three basic steps to forming a new habit:
- **Go Tiny:** Start with the teensiest, tiniest behavior you can imagine.

- **Plan:** Pick a good place within your daily schedule to incorporate the new behavior.
- **Repeat:** Feed the habit formation each day until the behavior becomes enmeshed in to your daily life.

It can be overwhelming to think about the effort and discipline required to cement a good habit or rid yourself of a bad one. But if it's something you *truly value that will bring real benefits to your life,* then it's worth the commitment to move forward little by little. You can't change everything at once. Research has shown that such all-or-nothing approaches tend to undermine and destabilize our efforts, as journalist Charles Duhigg writes in his excellent book on the science of habits, *The Power of Habit*.

14 Powerful Techniques for Kicking Bad Habits & Developing Lasting Positive Habits

You get it: habits matter. Now, let's put the rubber to the road and explore some simple, effective strategies for removing bad habits, replacing them with good ones, and integrating healthy routines into your everyday life.

1. Write It Down

Make your plan to change a bad habit or start a new one and write it down—literally getting it outside of your mind—ahead of time. By cementing this intention, you're committing to yourself in a tangible way, rather than keeping your goals vague and hypothetical in your head. As James Clear notes in his book *Atomic Habits* (which I recommend reading if you'd like to get more strategies for changing your habits), writing your goals and habits down greatly increases the likelihood that you'll follow through on them.

2. Self-Compassion

So often we think we can bully ourselves into change—but in reality, the opposite is true. As with everything else we've discussed thus far, it's important to be kind and patient with yourself as you go forward on your journey. As I've already mentioned, habits can take anywhere from 18 to 254 day to build depending on a number of factors including the difficulty of the habit and your own level of motivation and momentum. When you're struggling with kicking a bad habit or getting a new one off the ground, remember *why* you're taking these actions: you want to feel happier, healthier, and more fulfilled. Fundamentally, it's coming from a place of caring about yourself and wanting happiness. In Buddhism, this desire for happiness (one's own and others) is the foundation of *bodhicitta*, the attitude of compassion. Try to maintain a mindset of self-compassion to help you stay positive and motivated as you go about upgrading your habits—thereby reducing stress and bringing the energy you need to create change.

Self-compassion is far more effective than self-judgment and self-criticism in helping you reach your goals. Research shows that people who are higher in self-compassion respond better to failure and setbacks. They're more likely to get up again after they've fallen, setting new goals for themselves after failure instead of getting stuck in frustration and disappointment.

Self-compassion might even be your best tool for beating bad health habits: According to Dr. Kristin Neff, a psychologist who studies self-compassion, there's also data to suggest that self-compassion helps people engage in healthier behaviors, including exercising, sticking to their weight-loss goals and quitting smoking.

Don't forget that perfection isn't just unattainable; it's the *enemy* of self-compassion (and progress!). Habit formation isn't always a linear process, and you might have to fail a few times before you get to where you want to be. Temporary setbacks are an inevitable part of progress. Keeping this in mind is imperative when you're working towards incremental, positive changes—one baby step at a time.

3. Learn From Your Mistakes

Once again: nobody is perfect. We all fail, and we all make mistakes sometimes—and these mistakes can be valuable learning experiences! They teach us about what is and isn't working, and whether a new approach is called for. Keep your eyes on the prize and be realistic about the fact that you will falter in your efforts from time to time. Don't beat yourself up in those moments. Don't give up on yourself. Simply try to learn from your missteps and try a different approach if necessary.

4. Mindfulness, Mindfulness, Mindfulness

Surprise! Being more present and aware in your day-to-day life, and utilizing mindfulness techniques and skills, can make it a whole lot easier to adopt newer, healthier habits and routines. Bad habits are generally actions that we engage in on autopilot, so it takes a certain degree of awareness to catch ourselves in the moment and choose to act differently. Practicing mindfulness (refer to chapter 4 for specific practices) can help you identify the negative triggers, behaviors, and rewards that you're aiming to replace. It will also keep you grounded in the present—focused on the day-to-day baby steps that add up to real change over time—rather than dwelling on any perceived lack of progress.

5. Don't Just Remove a Bad Habit; Replace it with a Good One

If you want to change a bad habit, don't channel all your energy into removing it; rather, aim to replace it with a good one. Giving ourselves something positive to focus on (i.e., the new habit), rather than keeping a negative focus on how much we want to get rid of the bad habit, can help you feel more energized and motivated. Focus on what's working and what you want—not what you *don't* want.

For instance, if you want to quit smoking cigarettes and simply decide to quit cold turkey, you'll still have the same triggers—and the brain will have the same desired reward—that led you to smoke in the first place. But when you replace the habit—say, going for a walk and eating some carrot sticks instead of going for a smoke break—you can ease the discomfort within your brain because you're simply shifting the parameters of your behavior.

Keep in mind the "Golden Rule" of habit change, which says if you keep a trigger and reward the same, and insert a new routine in between, you simplify the process of change. This "Golden Rule," as outlined by Duhigg in *The Power of Habit*, is a great way to utilize the habit loop:

Trigger → Behavior → Reward

In essence, replacing a bad habit involves swapping the *behavior* part of the habit loop. Too often, when we want to change a behavior, we aren't completely clued in on what the reward of that behavior is. For example, if you want to stop eating junk food, dig into *why* you find yourself driven to eat that type of food in the first place. What reward are you getting? Is it simply for pleasure? Nourishment? To fill an emotional need? Because you're bored with your day or, perhaps, your life in general? Discovering what the reward is when you perform a bad habit can make swapping it out for a good one that much easier. So, if you find the reason for your junk food habit is boredom, then you look for something that eases your boredom.

6. Find Your Cues

Another way to use the habit loop to replace a bad habit is to develop *new* habit triggers—new ways to cue yourself into a good, positive habit. A habit trigger can be cultivated through:

- **Time** - Time-focused triggers can cue the habit at particular times of day.

  Ex. A mid-afternoon healthy snack to eat healthier.

- **Location** - The environment you find yourself in can support the new habit.

  Ex. Go to the library rather than a bar if you want to read more.

- **Preceding Event** - Place the new habit immediately after an existing behavior or habit (more on this shortly).

  Ex. Go for a walk immediately after breakfast.

- **Emotional State** - When you recognize an emotion, use it to trigger the new habit.

Ex. When you feel anxious, take 10 deep breaths.
- **Other People** - Who you are with, and when, can influence whether a habit will be implemented.

Ex. When you go to visit your sister for brunch, bring fruit instead of pie.

7. Click Into Your Cornerstone Habits

Cornerstone, or keystone, habits are consistent, foundational actions you take in your daily life that are healthy and positive, and tend to lead you towards better, healthier decisions everywhere *else* in your life. These types of habits, which include exercising daily, maintaining a healthy sleep schedule, or meditating daily—yes, the PRIME pillars are perfect examples of cornerstone habits—create a domino effect, triggering positive change in every other aspect of your life, as Duhigg writes in *The Power of Habit*. When you exercise regularly, for instance, you're more likely to eat healthier because you're more aware of your body, and you're also likely to be more productive and focused at work.

Making your bed first thing in the morning, so that you start the day from a place of intention, cleanliness, and organization, is another good example of a keystone habit. When you do this, you're more likely to fulfill your other good morning habits, and to keep your house clean and tidy.

Cornerstone habits can help boost your self-image, create a sense of accomplishment and personal efficacy, and drastically improve your chances for long-term success. If you start with those related to the core components of personal well-being, they'll eventually ripple out into every other area of your life.

8. Optimize Your Environment....*and Your Behaviors*

If you want to achieve any goal, you need to set up your surroundings for success. If you want to eat more fruit as part of your snack routine, but you never buy any and you don't have it in your home, how can you possibly expect to achieve that goal? Or if you want to quit sugar but your pantry is stocked with cookies and candy, it's going to be much more difficult to exercise the willpower necessary to reach your goal. The environment we operate within plays a monumental role in our ability to succeed. It's tough to stay off the booze for instance, when the only place you connect with your friends is at the bar.

Your environment matters—and so do the people you surround yourself with. Positive, supportive people who model good habits will inspire you to follow through with yours, whereas people who have little motivation and encourage you to engage in negative behaviors are sure to make it more difficult to change your habits. If you surround yourself with unhealthy triggers or bad influences, you may be sabotaging your own chances of success. Don't make bad habits any easier than they already are. Instead, force yourself to make a substantial effort to perform the bad ones. Make limbic friction work in your favor!

Setting up a successful environment for implementing healthy habits includes:

- **Cleaning it up:** Removing negative temptations or likely obstacles, such as not buying and keeping things like candy, alcohol or cigarettes.
- **Making it easy:** Arranging the environment to simplify your flow towards positive new behaviors.
  Ex. If you want to ride your bike more often than driving, you can leave the bike by your door, so it's always there and ready when you leave.

Setting yourself up for automatic good decisions, is another great way to avoid returning to bad habits.

Chris had decided to adopt a vegan diet for health reasons, but because of his love for cheese, his life largely revolved around cheese and dairy products. When he talked about the wine tastings he regularly attended, his eyes would twinkle as he'd describe the artisanal cheese platters, he'd indulged in. He even had a special drawer in his fridge dedicated to cheeses.

After a few false starts, Chris was able to shift his environment and set himself up for long-term success. He researched vegan cheese products, sampled a variety of nut and coconut-based options, and discovered tasty alternatives to his beloved, lactose-rich cheese plates. He learned to enjoy olives and cornichons as part of a beautiful hors d'oeuvres spread. He also restocked his cheese drawer with only vegan options, and when he attended a social event, he'd bring his own vegan cheeses to be sure that he could enjoy every occasion to the fullest. Not only did he optimize the environment, but he also replaced a bad habit (eating dairy) with a new, enjoyable, and healthy habit (eating vegan cheese).

9. Create a Delay

Take a pause before you engage in that bad habit! Studies have shown that removing immediate access or triggers—and creating at least a 20-second delay before a bad habit can be done—can dramatically reduce your probability of actually acting on those bad habits. If you want to make your own dinner each night rather than ordering out, delete your delivery apps and amplify the time it takes to order takeout. Removing the negative triggers, and making bad habits more challenging to accomplish, can assist the wholesale replacement of your bad habits with good ones.

10. Treat Yourself

Tap into the psychological benefits of rewarding yourself by only allowing yourself to do something you enjoy *after* you've performed a good habit that you're working on. For instance, if, and only if, you work out in the morning will you then allow yourself to watch an episode of *A Handmaid's Tale* on Hulu in the evening. Or if you follow your vegan or low carb diet all day, then you can have a piece of dark chocolate after dinner. Framing it as an "if ... then" statement can help boost your motivation. You can double or even triple your odds of successfully removing bad habits and adding good ones when you tie a reward to a specifically-achieved goal, regardless of the habit or routine you're aiming to develop.

Another way to work with reward is to celebrate yourself when you succeed. Celebrating even the most minuscule accomplishment—such as not smoking a cigarette for one day—can help trick your brain into believing you've gone further than you have. This makes you much more likely to continue! The brain has no real way of discerning a big accomplishment from a small one, so if you tell yourself, you've done something worthwhile, the physiological reaction will be the same. And don't forget: any accomplishment, big or small, is worthwhile!

Through neuroplasticity, you can retrain your brain to find satisfaction in even the tiniest accomplishments, creating stronger neural pathways towards satisfaction with yourself and your life overall. The road to formulating a new habit isn't always easy, so keep yourself motivated through rewards to keep your energy high and ensure success, as James Clear recommends.

This will lead you to much greater rewards in the long term!

11. Stack Your Habits

If you recall from the exercise chapter, habit stacking is exactly what it sounds like it is: stacking a new habit with another, already established healthy habit. Tying the two together increases the odds that you'll perform both actions in the long run. For instance, if you're eager to start exercising in the morning, and you make a pot of coffee first thing when you wake up, you can stack the two together. So, after you make coffee and enjoy a cup? Go for a run afterwards with that nice, caffeinated buzz.

Building new habits off ones that you're already successful with is a surefire way to set yourself up for future success. By building an unbreakable bond between an existing good habit with an as-yet-unestablished one, you'll ensure that the new habit becomes as automatic as the old one. Whenever possible, use habit stacking with existing cornerstone habits, those you perform every day without difficulty.

Once you've mastered habit stacking, and successfully stacked a new habit, you can create what James Clear calls a *habit staircase*, which involves stacking habits on top of another to create a 'staircase' of sorts, where one habit leads to another. Maybe you have your morning coffee, pair it with a green juice, and then go for your morning run. Suddenly that morning cup of joe has led to two new healthy habits! Or perhaps you start with a habit of meditating for 10 minutes after dinner. Once this habit is ingrained, you can add 30 minutes of reading after meditation. Then after reading, maybe you wash dishes, and after dishes, another positive habit can be added, and so on and so forth.

Remember that habits are the building blocks of a happy life. Stack your way to success!

12. Visualization

One of the best science-backed ways to build a new habit is to visualize all the steps required to perform the new habit. This is another strategy from Dr. Huberman.

Simply think about each of the steps, one at a time. Let's say you want to develop the habit of wiping off your makeup before you go to bed to avoid breakouts. (I know it seems oddly specific, but guess who used this method to clean off her makeup? You guessed it, yours truly!). Here's what I visualized myself doing:

1. Walk into the bathroom
2. Turn on the water
3. Pick up the foaming cleanser
4. Splash water on my face
5. Put the cleanser on my face
6. Lightly scrub
7. Rinse my face

You get the point. This was a surprisingly difficult one for me to implement because I was always so tired at the end of the evening. So, I started by lying in bed and visualizing the steps for a few nights before I started implementing the habit and let me tell you—this simple mental exercise really works! By the third night, I was washing my face and it felt much less effortful. Visualization can help you to increase the chances of completing the task successfully the first time, thus making it easier to turn it into a habit.

13. Temptation Bundling

Here's another key recap from the exercise chapter: Remember that we all struggle to do the things we know we *should* do, rather than the things we *want* to do. Eliminating this dichotomy is crucial to the development of healthy habits and routines. Temptation bundling (as described by behavioral researcher Katherine Milkman) combines an action we know we *should* do with something we *want* to do, thereby boosting our chances of short and long term success.

Temptation bundling is backed by Premack's Principle, which states that more probable behaviors will reinforce less likely ones. In other words, if there's an enjoyable habit or routine you consistently perform (like drinking your afternoon tea), you can bundle the enjoyable action with one you may not be as excited about (writing content for your website).

Not sure what actions to bundle? Start by taking a piece of paper and drawing two columns beside one another: the first listing your pleasurable activities; the second listing those tasks you avoid or often procrastinate on. For everything you list as a pleasure (like reading romance novels), link it with an activity you want to begin, like exercising or drinking green juice. Bundle the temptation of reading romance with exercise (or drinking green juice) by only allowing yourself to read them *if* or *while* you exercise (or sip!).

14. Lean on Your Friends, Family, and Support System

As with any goal, relying on your personal network can help boost your chances of success. Whether you're asking your best friend to be an "accountability partner" and check in regularly on your progress, or you're going vegan with your whole family, surrounding yourself with positive, supportive people can support your progress.

Again, who you choose to confide in or lean on for support *matters.* Surrounding yourself with people whose goals are similar can be a huge boon to your progress. Have dinners with friends who are sober if you're cutting back on alcohol. Find some fun outdoor activities on the weekend with your fit friends if you're looking to lose weight.

> ### CONSCIOUS COMMITMENTS
>
> **Baby Step:**
> - **Keep a bowl of fruit in your kitchen:** Healthy snacking can easily become a keystone habit that supports other healthy habits in your life. Buy some extra apples, oranges, bananas or any other fruit of your choice, and keep it on the counter so it's accessible when you're feeling hungry.
>
> **Bigger Step:**
> - **Tap Into the Power of Visualization:** Visualization is an easy and effective way to support good habits. Choose one particular habit you're looking to implement in your life and take a minute or so every day for at least one week straight to visualize yourself performing all the steps of that habit. (Start with an easier habit, as opposed to, say, running five miles every morning.) As an example, you might want to start making your bed every morning, so you take a few minutes before you go to sleep each night to imagine yourself going through all the steps necessary to make that happen come morning.

Habits: The Journey of 1,000 Miles Starts With A Single (Baby) Step

Let's check back on our friend Kacie. When she came to see me, she was desperate to get off the couch, improve her physical health, return to the professional world, and once again quit smoking. While her process was slow and at times felt disheartening, eventually she was able to take some positive steps forward, starting with one small but mighty change to her immediate environment.

By my advice, Kacie removed the television from her room so she wouldn't feel tempted to spend hours of the day zoning out in front of the screen. This one baby step was the catalyst for a gradual series of bigger steps towards positive change. She then deleted all streaming and delivery apps from her phone and decided to conquer her fear of leaving the cocoon of her bedroom and venturing into the outside world. She started small, with a walk outside each morning around her yard as she drank her morning tea. She still loved tea, even in her lowest moments, and when she was enjoying a freshly brewed cup, it alleviated some of her anxiety about entering the outside world.

Kacie then sat with her mother and listed a number of habits that she wanted to implement, starting with the smallest ones possible (leaving the house, going for a walk, and staying out of her bed after waking up). After she stacked her tea habit with a morning walk, she felt her physical health gradually improve, and she eventually extended the walk from her front lawn to circling the neighborhood for 20 minutes. Baby steps gradually led to big changes in her life—including, over time, a new job and moving out of her parent's place into her own apartment.

She wasn't always successful along the way, and she often wanted to beat herself up for not being *better* or where she *should* be. But with time and practice, she was able to accept that everyone, including her, has successes and failures in life. As she grew in self-compassion, she realized that she was worth the effort she was making to improve herself. Knowing that everyone struggles at different times in their lives, she was able to put her inner critic in the backseat and start speaking to herself with the tone of an inner coach.

We all have the capacity for positive change, and even the worst habits can be reworked or replaced using the proper tools and techniques. Trust me: you got this. Review that list of 13 strategies, knowing that you have plenty of tools in your toolkit for whenever you need them. Now let's turn our attention from our everyday behaviors in the external world to our internal world—and to the thoughts and emotions that shape our actions and the way we see ourselves. As we make shifts in our outer lives, we're also going to practice *shifting* our inner lives by releasing negative patterns of thought and emotion to make way for more positive internal experiences.

CHAPTER 8
Embrace Your Emotions

The reason you're reading this book is because you, like all of us, want to be happy. You wish to live a happy life and to enjoy your experiences.

Now that you've gotten this far, I'll let you in on an important and rather counterintuitive secret of happiness: *living a happy life does not mean feeling happy all the time*. It doesn't even mean feeling happy *most* of the time, for that matter. In fact, attempting to always feel good and "think positive" can actually have the opposite effect. We end up making ourselves feel worse because we're adding a layer of shame and judgment on top of whatever uncomfortable emotion we're *feeling*—which we're probably feeling for good reason!

As you'll learn in this chapter, happiness has more to do with fully experiencing and embracing all our emotions—yes, including the difficult and painful ones—than it does with feeling good all the time.

Here's the truth, which I often remind my patients of *the only people who don't have painful emotions are the ones who are in the cemetery!* Life is made up of successes and failures, happy times, and sad times, struggles and triumphs. It's not a flat line—it's up and down, curved, jagged and often circular! The more we can embrace the ups and downs, rather than trying to always stay in the ups, the happier we'll be.

We need to shift our mindset about happiness from thinking that we should always feel good and think happy thoughts, to instead being able to accept and embrace the full spectrum of the human experience—the dark and the light, the pain and the joy, the heartache, and the love. This mindset shift from *positivity* to *wholeness* is one of the most important aspects of building a happier life. And the ironic thing is, when we learn to accept and express *all* our emotions (not just the good ones), we naturally end up feeling happier more often, and the painful emotions tend to have less power to disrupt our well-being.

In feeling the emotions, we judge as "negative," we're also creating more space to feel things like joy, pleasure, gratitude, and excitement. The key is our ability to *embrace* and *regulate* our emotions. We want to be able to notice and acknowledge what we're feeling at any given moment, find an appropriate way to express it, and then return to a healthy emotional baseline.

Getting To Know Your Emotions

Our days and lives are made up of a constant flow of emotions. Think about the word "emotion": an emotion is literally a movement, or motion, of feeling through our being. What determines your emotional state at any given moment? Your emotional state is an intricate and dynamic dance of thoughts, feelings, bodily sensations, and actions. To break it down into a simple equation:

Our Emotional State = Feelings + Thoughts + Behaviors

It's often assumed that feelings come first: We have feelings, which trigger thoughts, which then lead to certain behaviors. But contrary to this assumption, our emotional state isn't a one-way street. Rather, it's a cyclical, bidirectional chain of reactions, each one connected to and influencing the others. All three factors are intimately linked but are distinct from each other. Understanding the difference is necessary to befriend your emotions and rewire your brain to work for you.

To make sure that we're clear on what we're talking about, let's clarify our terms:

- **Emotions** are the primal, instinctive urges that push or pull us to engage in or avoid certain things; emotions manifest as *feelings* and physical sensations in the body.

- **Thoughts** are the way we make sense of things and situations; we always have thoughts running through our head, constantly, in nearly every waking moment.
- **Behaviors** are, as you might guess, the literal things we do, or the ways we act; behaviors also include the things we don't do or act upon.

These three factors are constantly influencing and triggering each other. The first crucial step to emotional regulation is learning to *notice* an emotion or thought as it occurs. Only when you're able to notice an uncomfortable emotion, or what I call a "supercharged negative thought" (more on this in the next chapter), will you be able to take the proper steps, ensuring that you don't behave in a manner which then triggers further unpleasant emotions and thought patterns.

Have you started to think about how this vicious cycle might be playing out for you? Here's an example around habits, which most people will find at least somewhat familiar: In a moment of stress, you slipped back into a bad habit, like reaching for an afternoon treat after you'd sworn off sugar. This behavior triggers a *thought*, "I always mess everything up," or "I can't get anything right," which triggers an *emotion* like shame, disappointment, or feelings of hopelessness or powerlessness. That emotion might trigger a repeat of the bad habit (the behavior) in an attempt to numb out or avoid the uncomfortable emotions.

Because emotions, thoughts, and behaviors are cyclical in nature, our "behavior chain," so to speak, isn't as simple as a feeling leads to a thought which leads to an action.

Instead, it looks a lot more like this:

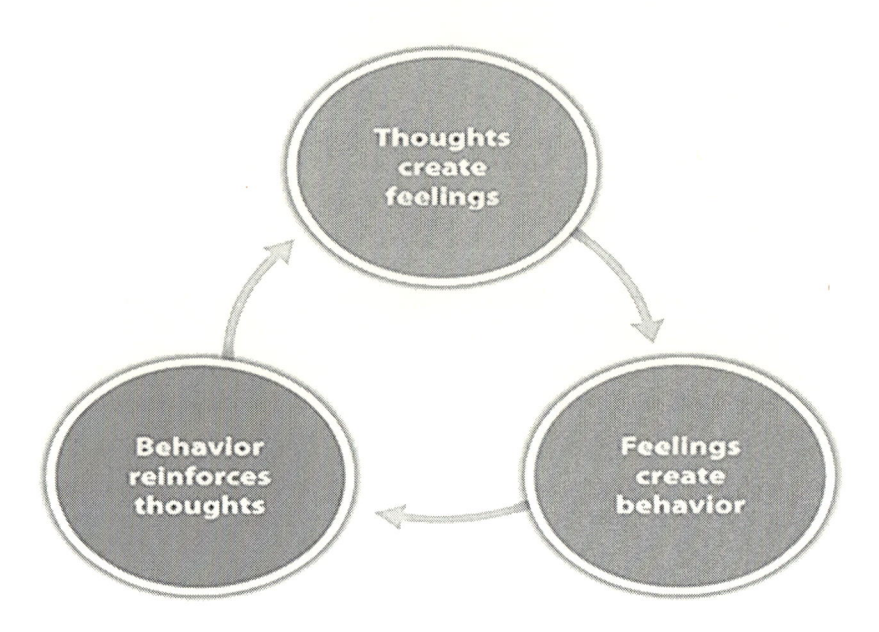

[Diagram: Thoughts create feelings → Feelings create behavior → Behavior reinforces thoughts]

As you can see, any thought can influence an emotion. Any emotion can influence a thought. In turn, both thoughts and emotions largely determine how we choose to behave…and how we behave, then, contributes to another set of thoughts and emotions. In other words, what we think, do, and feel feeds into a perpetual cycle of cause-and-effect, even when the initial cause is unclear.

The Positive Value of Negative Emotions

The whole point of this book is to learn to work with your brain to *be* happier. So, it stands to reason that rewiring your brain to work for you means dealing with your *emotions* and your *thoughts*. Obviously, if you're regularly overwhelmed by difficult emotions or supercharged negative thoughts that consistently send you on a mental tailspin, it's going to have a real impact on your happiness levels.

Emotions and thoughts are not "bad" in themselves. Every emotion is a messenger that contains valuable information for us. We experience each emotion for an important reason! If you can learn to notice and identify uncomfortable emotions—understanding their intended function, acknowledging the message, and acting accordingly—you'll find your brain wired to work for you emotionally. Likewise, if you can activate neuroplasticity to work for you by building new neural pathways based on more truthful thoughts and a less negatively-biased perception of reality, you can recognize and reframe negative thoughts for the distorted falsehoods they are—but we'll get into that a little later.

Given the existence and biological purpose of the brain's negativity bias, we can't completely eliminate negative thoughts or uncomfortable emotions. Nor would we want to! After all, at times, there may be a reason those negative thoughts or uncomfortable emotions manifest. So, the goal isn't to suppress uncomfortable emotions or to replace negative thoughts with positive ones. Rather, we want to replace supercharged negative thoughts with more *realistic* thoughts and accept the uncomfortable emotions as resources and messengers.

When you're unaware of your emotions and don't know *why* you're experiencing them or what they're trying to tell you, you're more likely to judge and suppress your feelings—often triggering supercharged negative thoughts, unwanted behaviors, and a vicious cycle of negativity.

But if you come to recognize your emotions as a resource—something that serves an important and valuable function—rather than an obstacle to be overcome, you can ease the strain of uncomfortable emotions. This is when you'll find that dealing with the inevitable emotional ups and downs of being human no longer needs to be a barrier to living a happy life.

With practice, you can train your brain to recognize your emotions without judgment, allowing you to process what you're feeling with more ease and clarity.

The big mindset shift here is going beyond thinking about your emotions as "good" or "bad," and learning to embrace all of our emotions so that we can get our emotions to work *for* us instead of against us.

Don't Judge an Emotion by Its Cover

An emotion is a primal, instinctive urge and feeling that is meant to keep us safe from harm and support our survival. In other words, our emotions appear to fulfill some sort of purpose or function, whether the emotion is easy and pleasurable, like joy, or immensely uncomfortable, like guilt. There's usually some sort of reasonable purpose for any emotion we feel, meaning, as Shakespeare said: When it comes to emotions, there is no bad or good; only thinking makes it so.

What does that mean, exactly, that emotions aren't bad or good? Well, despite our natural desire to add a judgmental label of *good* or *bad* to every emotion—typically based on whether we experience it as pleasurable or painful—the fact is that when we label an emotion in those black or white terms, we lose sight of what the emotion is telling us. This means we'll often suppress or avoid emotions we label bad, even though this only wires your brain to work further against you. The other response is to overindulge the emotion, get completely caught up in it and let it run the show. We want to avoid either of these extremes, instead finding a middle path of awareness, recognition, and healthy expression.

Our emotions are precious resources. They are an essential piece of the human experience that help us to navigate our daily lives and interactions. They give us valuable information about what's going on inside of us and in the world around us. Judging an emotion as bad and trying to shove it under the rug takes *way more mental energy* than simply recognizing it and releasing it, allowing it to naturally pass through you. Plus, if you can get the message and act accordingly—even if the emotion is uncomfortable—you'll quickly return to more positive and nourishing thoughts and feelings.

Consider the example of anger, an emotion we almost always label as negative. Often, anger arises in response to some kind of injustice or violation. Our anger tells us something *is wrong here*! If we have the awareness to recognize and feel our anger, and to see where it's coming from, it can be a helpful guide to action. Maybe our anger drives us to protest social injustice or to stand up for ourselves when we're being treated poorly. Anger in itself isn't "bad." It only becomes harmful when we either suppress it or let it completely take over and override our rational thinking and good judgment.

Psychologist Paul Ekman created a list of the six primary emotions: anger, surprise, disgust, fear, sadness, and enjoyment. This important list has shaped the way we tend to think about our emotional lives in Western cultures. And with our tendency to categorize emotions as either "good" or "bad"," you can see how those first five emotions Ekman listed would be deemed negative. The upshot? We've been conditioned to assume we'll only experience 'good' emotions one-sixth of the time.

If we assign a judgmental label of "bad" when a certain feeling arises, we're likely to trigger negative thoughts in response... which can trigger *more* "bad" feelings, leading to negative behaviors and actions. Therein lies the problem: instead of just feeling what you're feeling, you're judging what you're feeling. Just remember: the emotion isn't the issue. Your *response* to the emotion is the issue. That's what's making you unhappy and reinforcing the cycles of negativity that you can't seem to get out of.

At the risk of overstating the point, I'll say it again: **emotions aren't good or bad**. Even the most uncomfortable feeling is meant to serve some sort of purpose. If you resist the urge to label an uncomfortable emotion as *bad*, you can reduce the chances of your emotions spinning out of control, spurring further uncomfortable emotions. This can help you to respond reasonably and rationally, without getting caught up in the emotion and derailed by it.

Since emotions are meant to push us towards or away from something, labeling an emotion as 'bad' means that your brain will want to avoid it at all costs. This can lead to you suppressing your necessary emotions by trying to be positive all the time, eventually causing you to explode when the emotion forces its way out of your mind through negative behaviors or thoughts. Have you ever ignored your feelings of anger or frustration about a particular situation—or towards a particular person—until one day you just started yelling or decided that you couldn't take it anymore? That's exactly what I'm talking about here.

Regulating your emotions isn't a matter of categorizing your feelings into this or that group. Instead, it's about learning to simply *notice* an emotion when it occurs, describing it to yourself as comfortable or uncomfortable (without judgment!); and choosing the appropriate action based on a clear-eyed perception of what the emotion is trying to tell you.

Emotional Suppression: You've Gotta Feel It If You Want to Heal It

Caleb didn't want to stay sober, and frankly, he couldn't quite figure out why he had to quit drinking in the first place. He *loved* to get tipsy with his colleagues after work and his friends on the weekend. After a few drinks, he found himself both charming and "in control." What had started as a way to network and boost his clientele list—with business dinners turning into business lunches, "*Mad Men* style"—had become a full-blown addiction. Before a hospital stay forced him to stop, he hadn't gone to bed without a drink in nearly a decade.

"I can't sleep right now, my body is going *crazy* every time I lay down," he told me about a week into his recovery. "My mind goes nuts, and this anxiousness swells inside my chest. My legs and hands keep getting all tingly, and I just want something to soothe my nerves. It's probably just my body withdrawing from the liquor, right?"

Fidgeting and looking away, he added, "I'm just goanna ignore these feelings and soon enough they'll go away."

What Caleb was failing to realize was that his alcohol dependency had long masked a deeper history of emotional suppression. Having a drink has always been a way to numb out; to "take the edge off." He described to me his intense aversion to any uncomfortable emotion or feeling—and for him to even be able to identify that was major progress. Just getting him to admit he *ever* experienced uncomfortable emotions like fear or guilt was like pulling teeth, and it became apparent that having a few drinks was a way to "check out" from whatever he didn't want to feel.

Caleb, like so many of us, had developed his own personal system for avoiding those feelings he thought were *bad*, leading to an endless cycle of numbing and suppression.

But suppressing those emotions didn't alleviate the discomfort they caused. Instead, they were always present in the background, and he had to keep going back to the bottle to get them out of his mind. Finally, after being forced into recovery, Caleb was ready to learn to shift his mindset around his own emotions.

It took some time in therapy for Caleb to be able to recognize his underlying anxiety, guilt, and anger as important resources to be noticed and learned from, rather than something to be avoided at all costs.

Knowledge wasn't enough to change Caleb's relationship with his difficult emotions, but it was an important first step. Once he discovered the purpose of his emotions, learned to notice, and describe them without judgment, and gave himself permission to express them, Caleb was able to begin releasing the pressure valve of all those pent-up feelings inside of him. It all started with a shift of perception that allowed him to see his emotions as *resources*.

Many of us, like Caleb, miscategorized emotions as *obstacles* rather than *resources*. Every single emotion we experience– from the warm, fuzzy ones, to the overwhelmingly painful ones– manifests for some reason. There is some specific purpose attached to each and every emotion we feel or notice, meaning we shouldn't work to ignore or suppress an emotion, even if it feels unbearable.

I Second that Emotion: Learning to Work With Your Emotions

Since emotions exist to fulfill a particular function, it's important we don't actively work to suppress or ignore the emotions that make us uncomfortable. When we do, those suppressive actions become wired deeper into our neural pathways—making it even harder to recognize, process and release that emotion in the future. We train ourselves to ignore what we're feeling, and we end up losing out on the valuable information that our emotions contain.

So how can we begin the important work of learning to recognize and embrace our emotions? It helps to start by looking at them in very objective, non-judgmental terms. Exploring the ways that they manifest in the body and their biological purpose can help.

As noted, before, our *emotions* are primal, instinctive messages sent by the brain to fulfill a specific function or purpose. We often recognize emotions in the form of physical sensations. For instance, "butterflies in your stomach" is a common feeling associated with fear, a sensation of rising temperature is often associated with anger, and a warm glow around your scalp or a sense of openness around the center of your chest is often connected with joy. Sadness can often manifest physically as feeling heavy or deflated.

Recognizing your emotions as sensations in your body can help you remember that they serve a biological function. They're there to protect you from harm and move you towards that which supports your health, well-being, and survival. Think of it as your body's built-in GPS that's always guiding you away from danger and towards your highest good.

The main goal, when working with uncomfortable emotions, is to feel them rather than suppress and avoid them. When we suppress an emotion, it doesn't simply disappear, and it doesn't do anything to actually reduce activation of our brain's emotional center, the amygdala (aka the brain's alarm center). In fact, studies have shown active suppression of uncomfortable emotions can *increase* the activation of the amygdala, meaning we'll actually feel *more* of the emotion that we're trying to ignore.

Once you recognize how an emotion is showing up in your body, the next step is to ask yourself, "Why is this here?" and consider what its function might be.

The Three Functions of Emotions

Emotions are a signal from the brain, designed to motivate us to act one way or another. They are a way of preparing the body to adapt to a certain circumstance. You don't want to ignore them, but instead seek to understand what they're pushing you towards. Every emotion serves one of three main functions:

1. **Adaptive** - As warning signs to prepare to act.
2. **Motivational** - To motivate us to change.
3. **Social** - To help us *connect* with other people.

Adaptive Function: The adaptive function of emotions allows us to choose the proper behaviors or actions for a given circumstance—to *adapt* to our environment and current needs. Every emotion can serve an adaptive function. Here's a list of adaptive functions for a number of common emotions:

Happiness → Feeling of closeness to others
Disgust → Rejection of things that may harm
Anger → Self-defense from being harmed
Fear→ Protection from harm
Surprise → Exploration
Guilt→ Appraisal of your actions
Anxiety→ Avoiding real or imagined danger

Hopelessness→ Maximize your effort and try new approach adaptive You get the picture. There are more functions for every emotion than I list here, but if you can come to understand some of the more basic, universal emotions, you can then expand your awareness and recognition when uncomfortable emotions arise. Starting to label and "catalog" your emotions and to identify their adaptive function will help you to develop a kind of emotional literacy that will make it easier over time to recognize and understand what you're feeling.

Social Function: We often speak through non-verbal forms of communication—much more so than we even know. Given the importance of social connections to our happiness (more on that in Part 3), it makes sense that our emotions would serve a vital social function. For instance, our body language can inform another person of our emotional state, thereby instigating a response that brings us the help or support we may or may not have known we needed.

Emotions help inform us, and the people around us, of what's happening *inside* of us. By expressing our emotions, we can both strengthen existing social connections, and help develop new social connections in the future. Even when we don't verbally say so, our emotions are driving us to connect with other people. Even emotions like guilt and shame are designed to help us avoid harmful actions and to behave in more prosocial ways that secure our most important connections.

Motivational Function: As a driver to act, our emotions often motivate us to behave in a certain manner. And that relationship between motivation and emotions goes both ways. Here are a couple specific ways that emotions function as motivational tools:

Feel It And Let It Go: The 90-Second Rule

Now that you know *why* you're feeling what you're feeling, what does it look like to feel it in a healthy way? What happens when we stop avoiding our emotions, and we just allow them to arise? Most people are afraid that if they feel and express their emotions, they'll be completely overwhelmed by them. But some important research has proven just the opposite.

Motivate to Act: Emotions motivate us to act in certain ways. If we feel nervous before a job interview, it can motivate us to prepare and practice, to ensure we perform as well as possible in the interview.

Motivate To Avoid Danger: Emotions motivate us to pursue survival and avoid things that are dangerous.

Help Make Decisions: Emotions are a motivating factor in every decision we make, both positive and negative.

First outlined by Dr. Jill Bolte Taylor, the "90-second rule" of emotions reveals that the physiological component of an emotion (as in, the actual physical feelings and sensations felt in the body) naturally lasts around 90 seconds. That is, unless we get in the way and drag things out!

In other words, while uncomfortable emotions may *feel* like they'll never end in the moment, the fact is that they *will* end—and much sooner than you may expect. If you can simply ride the wave, like a raft in the ocean, for up to 90 seconds without reacting, you can let *any* uncomfortable emotion pass you by without getting overwhelmed by it or triggering further negative behaviors or thoughts.

If you don't judge the emotion, and you don't suppress or ignore it; but instead, you simply notice and label it without judgment, you'll find that it moves through you in a short period of time. You can let any uncomfortable emotion flow away nearly as quickly as it appeared...or, at the very least, allow it to flow away in *no more* than 90 seconds. You might get another wave of the same emotion, but that second or third wave will also pass in 90 seconds or less.

Consider a moment when you were frightened. Perhaps you couldn't find your phone and feared it had been lost. That initial moment of panic triggers a chemical reaction in the brain, releasing hormones that radiate throughout the body, generating a corresponding physical sensation—like a racing heart or a fluttery feeling in your stomach. Those physical feelings that seem so torturous as they occur *will end* after no more than 90 seconds. The hormones released into the bloodstream when the emotion is triggered in the brain will flush out within 90 seconds of their release, and you'll be free of the physiological reaction that's creating distress.

Armed with this information, you can allow yourself to step back and pause in those moments when you notice an uncomfortable emotion rising. You can observe them as they occur, with a curious and compassionate mind, knowing that it won't be long before it passes through.

The 90-second rule can help you become more comfortable with uncomfortable emotions, since knowing that something will end makes riding out the storm less challenging. Just remember the cyclical nature of emotions, thoughts, and behaviors. Because if you're not careful, you can quickly *restart* a 90-second loop by adding a negative thought or action.

How to Deal with Tricky Emotions

The goal with uncomfortable emotions is to notice them, acknowledge their existence without judgment, and *feel them fully*.

There are many ways to work with challenging emotions. Here, I've put together some of the most effective techniques for emotional regulation that I use with my clients:

1. Apply Self-Validation

2. Use Clear Labels

3. Build a NEST

4. Adopt Emotional Acceptance

5. Ground yourself

Each of these techniques can be helpful in different situations, and they can work together to form a solid toolkit for working with your own emotions. Let's get started.

1. Self-Validation

One of the best ways to regulate and experience your emotions without getting overwhelmed by them is through *self-validation*.

What does it mean to *validate* something?

When one person validates another, they are acknowledging the other person's experience as real, genuine, and, well, *valid*. This is one of the major components of therapy. It's something that I provide to numerous patients on a daily basis: assuring them that their feelings and emotions are valid.

There can be a tremendous sense of relief upon having our own internal struggles and suffering seen and acknowledged. But validation doesn't necessarily need to come from another person. When you self-validate, you're allowing yourself to acknowledge and accept your feelings as a legitimate part of your own personal experience.

If you've ever helped a friend through a breakup or tough time, you know that it's not really about "fixing" the situation or even necessarily trying to make the person feel better. The most powerful thing you can do is to simply be a compassionate witness, letting the person know that you see what they're going through and you're there for them. This is what we want to do for ourselves.

Self-validation is an important part of self-compassion. The more we practice validating our own emotions, the better able we are to recognize our own emotions when they occur and to respond appropriately based on their intended function. All your emotions serve an important purpose, and they deserve to be seen and heard.

Self-validation has been proven to improve emotional regulation, helping us to accept all our own internal experiences.

Here are five simple ways to practice self-validation, which will help rewire your brain to befriend those uncomfortable emotions that we often suppress or avoid:

- **Mindful Presence** - Validate your feelings and emotions when they occur by being mindful of their presence. Being honest about what you're feeling, particularly when it's uncomfortable, and practice simply being present with what you're feeling.
- **Realistic Assessment** - Acknowledge your emotions and seek a realistic appraisal of the situation using objective facts to the best of your ability. This can be a challenge if your emotions and thoughts are often distorted but starting with the facts (what's going on in your body, what happened to trigger the emotion) can help.
- **Educated Guess** - Perhaps you're unsure what emotion you're feeling and aren't even sure *what* to validate. Don't worry about getting it right; just use what you know to arrive at some type of educated guess about what you're feeling.

- **Life Story** - Most of our emotional (and thought) patterns are based in our own personal history. Validate your emotions by remembering your life story and what brought you to this moment and acknowledge that your emotions might be rooted in a painful experience or in your childhood—which is when most of our emotional misconceptions begin.
- **Universality** - Validate what you're feeling by reminding yourself that emotions are universal. Every single human being experiences their own emotional ups and downs, meaning you are just like everyone else: normal for having emotions of all kinds. You might even want to say to yourself kindly, "It's ok. Everyone feels this way sometimes."

2. Label Emotions *Clearly*

You may be thinking that this makes no sense—the whole time I have been telling you to avoid labeling your emotions as good or bad, and now one of the techniques is labeling your emotions! But this type of labeling is different.

The idea here is to identify your feelings and to label your emotions clearly, and in detail. This has been proven to be an effective technique to calm your brain's emotional activity.

When you label your emotions, it not only reduces activation in the amygdala; it also increases activity in the prefrontal cortex, the brain's center of rational thought, decision-making and higher cognition. Giving your emotions a name helps tame your primitive emotional centers and shift your mental activity to those logical processing centers so that you respond with a cool and calm head instead of reacting with fear.

Intense emotions can be terrifying when we don't have any words to describe them. The moment we possess the words to accurately describe the emotion, rather than to judge it, we become less impulsive and reactive when a challenging emotion surfaces. Labeling an emotion takes away its power by reminding us that it's just a feeling. It helps to clarify what's happening in our body, giving us the time and capacity to act on what the emotion is telling us.

When labeling an emotion, be as clear and concise as possible. Try to avoid vague descriptors or letting the labeling spin off into thinking (which can happen very easily!). When you label an emotion, say "I *feel* …" with the emotion felt immediately filled in. You might say:

"I feel guilty."

"I feel embarrassed."

"I feel angry."

"I feel overwhelmed."

The important piece to remember when labeling an emotion is to be direct. Don't beat around the bush here! Simply say "I feel [insert emotion here]," and leave it at that. All you need is a non-judgmental label that describes the emotion when you notice it. No need to start telling stories about why you feel this way or all the times you've felt it before. Bonus points for framing your label as an experience that will end: Try saying, "I feel sad *right now*," reminding yourself that this, too, shall pass.

3. Build a NEST

When you build a NEST for an uncomfortable emotion, you shift from avoidance to acceptance. This process involves noticing your uncomfortable emotions *while* you're actively trying to suppress or avoid them, and then choosing to act properly based on the emotion's function, rather than reacting in a rash or harmful way.

Once you've begun to practice noticing your emotions in-the-moment, you can also begin to recognize those times you simultaneously *avoid* acknowledging or accepting what you're feeling. This is the time to build a **NEST**:

- **N**otice your avoidance - In order to deal with your uncomfortable emotion, you must first notice your own attempts to suppress it.

  Ex. When you feel a fearful twinge in your gut, and you immediately light a cigarette or grab a snack to mask the discomfort.

- **E**xpose yourself to the avoided feelings - Remember that emotions and thoughts, by themselves, *cannot* hurt you. They can be terribly uncomfortable and unpleasant, but they can't cause you physical harm unless you choose to act or react to the feeling.

  Ex. Rather than trying to push away or ignore the physical discomfort from a feeling by compulsively twirling your hair or telling yourself the feelings aren't real, stop and simply feel what you're feeling.

- **S**eek support from family and friends - Surround yourself with the people you love and be mindful to only share vulnerable emotions with those you trust and feel fully supported by.

  Ex. Being open and honest, discuss your emotional difficulty with your spouse, a relative, a dear friend or a mental health professional.

- **T**ake proper action - Take some time to reflect and determine the best course of action as directed by the emotion, or simply let it be felt and pass by.

  Ex. When you find yourself feeling lonely, you choose to go out with a friend, rather than staying home in bed.

Building a NEST can reduce the potential negative impact of your emotions, and help you develop a higher comfort level with embracing *all* your emotions rather than avoiding them.

4. Emotional Acceptance

This last tool is at the very heart of all the previous techniques. Emotional acceptance is just what it sounds like: the ability to willingly accept your emotions and befriend the realities of your life, but it also involves *experiencing* the emotion without resistance. While each of the previously listed tools has some degree of emotional acceptance involved, you can still learn to better regulate your emotions through a basic acceptance of them.

Emotional acceptance means that you stop fighting against reality—a fight that none of us are ever going to win! Just like you can't change the weather outside, you also can't fight the existence of uncomfortable emotions. When you accept your emotions, you can focus your energy and efforts on important matters.

5. Grounding

If an emotional feeling is just too overwhelming to work with in a calm and logical fashion, there are some bodily tricks to help you come back to your center and return to the present moment. These techniques aren't long term solutions, but rather a quick fix to help calm you down before things spiral. There are three types of Grounding techniques you can try, when you can't tap into a realistic mindset:

- **Mental Grounding**: Use your thoughts to ground yourself. Try playing a simple Category game (where you list objects in a particular category, like cities that start with the letter A or types of fish) or drawing an object in your mind, focusing on all the details of construction.

- **Physical Grounding**: Connect back to your body and the world around you. Touch an object near you, like your shirt, noticing the specific details of it, or literally, ground yourself by observing and feeling your feet *on* the ground.

- **Soothing Grounding**: Call to mind thoughts of things or activities that you enjoy putting yourself at ease. List some of your favorite things (like songs or restaurants) or imagine the face of a loved one.

Conscious Commitments

Baby Step:
- For one day, make it your goal to be mindful of your emotions and notice what you're feeling. Label every emotion that you notice and write them down in a notebook (or on your phone or computer if that's easier). Review your list at the end of the day and reflect: What emotions did you feel the most? What patterns do you see? Is there anything that surprises you?

Bigger Step:
- Choose one of the five techniques above (whichever one resonates the most for you) and commit to practicing it for one week with one particular emotion. For instance, maybe you're struggling with anxiety, and you like the idea of grounding. For one week, every time you notice yourself feeling anxious, apply a grounding technique—like pausing and feeling your feet on the ground.

Emotions are Functional, not Fearful!

Living a happy life means embracing the full spectrum of human emotions—the good, the bad and the ugly—and learning to flow with your feelings just like a surfer rides the waves of the ocean.

Shifting your mindset around your emotions is one of the most important things you can do for your own happiness. When we let go of the fear and resistance that we feel towards our emotions, it opens a tremendous amount of energy that we can apply towards more positive and life-enhancing endeavors.

As a final reminder: No matter what you do, you're never going to rid yourself of uncomfortable emotions. So instead of fighting against them and being at war with yourself, the wise response is to form a diplomatic alliance—and learn to work together.

Learning to work with his emotions completely changed Caleb's life. Once he realized that he'd spent most of his life actively suppressing and avoiding his emotions with alcohol, he was finally able to realize that a different approach was needed. He started noticing his emotions as they occurred. He discovered that his uncomfortable emotions shouldn't be feared or rejected, but rather acknowledged and accepted as something that was always trying to help him.

The practice of self-validation became his best friend. For many years, he couldn't believe that everyone felt things like guilt and shame, because he had always seen them as a unique struggle of his own. But by applying self-validation techniques when he noticed a pang of anxiety or sinking feeling of guilt creeping in, he found ways to express and release what was going on inside of him—and soon, those formerly crippling emotional states became manageable.

While shifting your emotions is an indispensable step in rewiring your brain to work for you, working with your emotions alone doesn't always alleviate those ingrained thought distortions that can trigger (and retrigger) uncomfortable feelings. Let's take a deeper look at your negative thought patterns—and learn techniques for shifting them in a positive direction— so you can shift your inner dialogue to feel happier and more emotionally balanced over time.

CHAPTER 9
Rewire Supercharged Negative Thoughts

Emma barely slept the night before her big work presentation. She knew that her presentation could "literally make or break" her entire career, and after months of preparation, the day had arrived. As she mentally rehearsed what she was going to say, doubts began to creep in. What if she had made a mistake in her research? What if she stumbled over her words and "made a complete ass" of herself? What if her mind went blank and she forgot everything she'd practiced?

As Emma drove to work, she was wracked with anxiety at the prospect of having to endure a devastating failure. When the hour of reckoning finally arrived, a cloud of negative thoughts raced through her mind. As she had envisioned many times, she bombed her presentation.

Emma didn't lose her job—much to her surprise—despite being convinced that she'd proved herself a "terrible employee." However, she was passed over for the promotion that she had long hoped for. She decided that day that she would never succeed professionally. Two years later, when she first came to my office, she was still stuck in a tormenting loop of negative thoughts based on the "evidence" of her failed presentation. She couldn't seem to find a way out of her thoughts of failure and a way forward in her career.

Emma's negative thoughts led to negative emotions and unhealthy actions in a vicious, unending cycle. Emma never stopped to question the truth or validity of what her thoughts were telling her. She had plenty of "evidence"—so why wouldn't they be true?

Like so many of us, Emma was at the mercy of a harsh inner dialogue that convinced her that happiness was out of her reach. She'd become locked in a swarm of negative distortion: negative thoughts often feeding painful emotions and self-sabotaging actions, which then, in turn, would conjure further negative thoughts, feelings, and actions.

While we can't completely eliminate negative thoughts, we can use neuroplasticity to shift our brain away from harmful negative thought patterns that create a distorted, false view of ourselves and our reality. We can also learn to pivot from the deeply rooted core beliefs that underlie our thoughts, breaking those habitual mental patterns that get in the way of our happiness.

Negative thoughts, like uncomfortable emotions, shouldn't be dismissed as "bad." They do have a place and a purpose. But when those negative thoughts become distorted by our core beliefs, they can become *supercharged*, which I define as being highly emotionally charged, habitual, and creating a distorted and biased perspective on our life.

At the heart of supercharged negative thoughts are our *core beliefs*: those highly subjective, personal assumptions and opinions that are deeply wired into our brains, largely stemming from childhood experiences. These beliefs form the lenses through which we see the world and interpret our experiences—past, present, and future—sometimes for better, but often for worse.

We all have limiting core beliefs that hold us back from growth, connection, and happiness. These beliefs, whether they're true or false, are deeply ingrained in the brain, forming our strongest and oldest neural networks, and playing an outsized role in directing our emotions and thoughts. Let's look at what exactly core beliefs are, and why they so often end up calling the shots in our pursuit of happiness.

Core Beliefs: Distorting Our Thoughts and Emotional Interpretations

Core beliefs come in all shapes and sizes. They often present themselves in the form of negative self-talk—that inner voice that says, "I am going to fail", "I'm not good enough," or "Just forget it, it's too hard."

Sarah, a recently divorced mother of two who had studied journalism at NYU, had a successful early career with several articles published in The New York Times. But she also had the belief that she wasn't talented enough. As she sought to start writing again after taking several years off to focus on motherhood, she was telling herself that she'd been out of the game for too long and that her success in her 20s must have been a fluke.

"No one is going to hire me," she told me despairingly. "There's no way I can compete with the younger, smarter journalists out there."

Based on her core belief that she wasn't good enough; Sarah had convinced herself that she had no talent and therefore it would be a waste of her time to even try to launch her career again. Her core beliefs drove her thoughts ("I'm not talented," "I'll never get a decent job") and emotions (despair, feelings of shame and unworthiness), which then determined her actions (not applying for jobs), which in turn further reinforced the beliefs, thoughts, and emotions. You can see how this became a vicious cycle.

Have you ever heard the expression "we don't see things as they are, we see them as we are"? That's exactly what we're talking about here.

Core beliefs, first developed during childhood, are how a person comes to perceive themselves and the world around them. Even as an adult, the way you see the world is largely determined by the unique circumstances of your childhood environment. If your home was a chaotic place as a child, you may have formed a belief that the world isn't safe. Or if your needs weren't met, you may have formed a belief that you can't rely on anyone else and that you have to do everything on your own. If your parents weren't giving you the love you needed and craved, you may have internalized this to mean that there's something wrong with you and come to believe that you're not worthy or loveable. These deeply instilled, lifelong belief systems are repeated so often and with such a strong emotional charge that they become etched into your brain, creating some of your strongest neural networks.

Core beliefs are the root cause of many of our most unbearably uncomfortable emotions and supercharged negative thoughts. They cause us to view and perceive the world through our own distorted looking glass, preventing a clear and truthful experience of reality. Instead of seeing the present moment as it is right now, we're seeing the *present* through the eyes of the *past*.

More often than not, core beliefs aren't true, or based in fact; they're nothing more than *opinions* we've adopted as truth. They're how we made sense of our experiences and environment when we were very young. They may have made sense to us at the time, but they rarely make sense in our present context. In fact, while core beliefs are purely *subjective* —completely shaded by your unique life experiences—we engage with them as if they were an *objective* way of seeing and understanding the world.

Have you ever heard the story of the blind men and the elephant? In this classic Indian parable, a group of blind men who have never come across an elephant before try to learn what the elephant is by touching it. One touches the elephant's tail and thinks that an elephant is a rope. Another touches the elephant's side and thinks that it is a wall, and another touches the trunk and imagines that it is a huge snake. The moral of the story is that our subjective experiences and perceptions can be misleading and often don't tell the whole story, even if they feel like objective truth to us.

This story illustrates how we make assumptions and interpret situations based on our own orientation and limited set of data. We don't see the whole picture; we see only one little corner, and then we make false and biased judgments based on our limited view. The problem is that we can't recognize our core beliefs as something distorted because they feel so real to us.

Core beliefs, when triggered, often lead to uncomfortable emotions like shame and guilt, which can lead to supercharged negative thoughts, which then further reinforce the painful emotions. This chain reaction generally leads to negative behaviors—which, in turn, reinforce the negative thoughts and emotions that were initially triggered by the core belief. For instance, if you have a core belief of

"Nobody really cares about me," and a friend doesn't respond to your text, your distorted perception of the situation would tell you that your friend doesn't like you and doesn't want to spend time with you. This might lead to feelings of shame and anger, and a loop of self-judgmental thoughts. What kind of action might you take based on those thoughts and emotions? Maybe you isolate yourself from your friend and decline to spend time with them until they eventually get back to you. But if you saw the situation clearly, you'd be able to recognize that your friend was unavailable for other reasons that had nothing to do with you, and you could have avoided the whole negative cycle.

Here are some of the most common core beliefs:

I'm not good enough.
I'm not supported.
I have to do everything on my own.
Life is difficult.
There's not enough to go around.
Nobody cares about me.
I can't trust myself or others.
Good things happen to other people, not to me.
The world isn't a safe place.
I don't belong anywhere.

What are the core beliefs that have shaped your own thoughts? Are there any beliefs coming up in your mind as you read this?

The list is endless! You can imagine how these kinds of beliefs can cause tremendous harm over the course of our lives. But here's the good news: It *is* entirely possible to pull up the roots of even the oldest and most stubborn core beliefs. Any belief can be challenged, and over time, with awareness and a commitment to change, you can train your brain to rewire itself away from unhelpful, unrealistic beliefs.

Don't Believe Everything You Think

Emma and Sarah were experiencing the power of our thoughts to spiral out of control and convince us of things that are patently untrue. Because of one failed work presentation, Emma had convinced herself that she was a failure and would never achieve any success in her career. Was it true? Absolutely not. Did she believe it? 100%.

Our brains are wired to make connections between different objects of perception, and to see events in terms of cause and effect. This is an important evolutionary function that helps us apply logic to situations, but it doesn't mean that these connections are genuine or legitimate. Sometimes, things go a little haywire. For instance, if you trip and fall when running down the street, you may think that you're clumsy and foolish. But perhaps there was something on the ground that caught your shoe, so the tripping wasn't entirely your fault.

While we may *think* or feel that a connection is real, it may not have any actual causality. It's simply the result of your brain taking a shortcut that leads to a falsehood. Our brain likes to do things as easily and efficiently as possible, which is why we develop habits and strong neural pathways that we return to again and again. Many of our thought patterns become automatic over time so as to free up our mental bandwidth for more important matters. These deeply ingrained neural networks act as shortcuts for the brain, allowing it to perform the countless tasks that it needs to perform in any given moment.

Our brain's capacity to mislead us is an unfortunate side effect of its efficiency and processing capacity. The brain processes more information every second than we could possibly imagine, and to make things more manageable, it relies on neural networks and shortcuts in formulating most of our daily thoughts. In fact, according to Dr. Fred Luskin of Stanford University, a whopping 90% of all thoughts are repeated daily, and, with nearly 60,000 thoughts per day, this means whatever we tend to think most often—

positive or, more likely, negative—is where our mind tends to go back again and again.

Thanks to the negativity bias, the majority of our thoughts will skew towards the negative as a survival mechanism meant to protect us from harm. Now, if the vast majority of our 60,000 thoughts are negative, and 90% of those largely negative thoughts will be repeated daily, how do you think all those repeated negative thoughts are going to make you feel? Odds are, if you're running on autopilot, you're going to have a lot of negative thoughts running through your mind, which you will then likely overanalyze, leading to further negative thoughts. These thoughts can be so convincing that you may decide that *every* negative thought represents the truth of the situation.

But most of the time, this simply isn't the case. If you step back from your thoughts and take a moment for reflection, you'll see that they don't always tell the whole story of a situation. On the contrary: when you examine your thoughts, you may find that they're worth reframing or tossing away entirely.

Negative thoughts can quickly become a self-fulfilling prophecy. If you think this negative thought enough times, it will become hardwired into your brain, and it will become a default thought pattern that you return to again and again. This can lead to recurring patterns and situations in your life that you just can't seem to shake—yet another example of your brain working against you.

Of course, negative thoughts aren't to be dismissed or rejected as being "bad" or "wrong." When properly balanced and contained, they can alert us to potential threats, or warn us away from harmful encounters. They can help us to make wise decisions and avoid getting caught up in harmful situations. Simply put, it's your brain's way of trying to protect you (thanks, brain!).

The thing we must really look out for and be cognizant of is *supercharged negative thoughts*: those automatic, deeply ingrained thoughts, often based on faulty or distorted beliefs and greatly influenced by your unique experiences and environment, that negatively impact our happiness and satisfaction in life.

Supercharged Negative Thoughts: Your Brain Working Against You

We know our thoughts are already heavily biased towards the unpleasant, bad, or negative, which, when repeated enough times, for a long enough time, can become habitual, as happens with any core belief. These negative thought habits, driven by core beliefs, can then morph into negative thought distortions, or what I call *supercharged negative thoughts*. I know this sounds like the name of a Marvel villain, but it's important that we have a clear understanding of just how powerful these types of thought patterns are.

This framework of supercharged negative thoughts (or SNTs) is based on psychologist Aaron

Beck's research into automatic negative thoughts. Beck, who developed Cognitive Behavioral Therapy in the 1970s, described automatic thoughts as thoughts that a person is largely unaware of that strongly influence their emotions and behaviors. I like to call them "supercharged" thoughts because the easiest way to identify them is by way of the intense emotional charge that accompanies them.

SNTs are an unfortunate byproduct of the negativity bias. They are often linked to a core belief, and they almost always lead to elevated levels of stress and anxiety. SNTs are public enemy number-one when it comes to rewiring your brain for happiness, as they can negatively skew your perception of, well, just about everything, leaving you stuck in endless loops of over analyzing.

Not every negative thought is an SNT. It's important to know the difference between plain old negative thoughts and SNTs, which have a handful of distinct and defining characteristics:

They stick to your consciousness and won't let go.
They keep your thoughts stuck in an endless loop.
They convince you that you're able to predict the future.
They are inflexible and impossibly rigid.
They nag you about what you *should* be doing.
They envision the absolute worst-case scenarios.

They make you believe *every* negative thought you have is true.

SNTs are the result of negative thought distortions becoming ingrained in your mental patterns. And beyond making you miserable in the moment, they can also be detrimental to your mental and physical health in the long run. Research has shown that SNTs alter your brain for the worse. They can grow your amygdala—increasing your brain's fear activation—and are known to accelerate the brain's aging process.

As you continue the work of investigating your own mind and shifting your mindset in a more positive direction, it's important to know what type (or types) of SNT is playing on repeat in your own mind (we all have them!). Before you learn how to conquer SNTs and shift your mind towards more clear perceptions and a healthier inner dialogue, let's briefly explore the top 10 most common SNTs so that you can identify which ones you might be struggling with.

A Field Guide to Supercharged Negative Thought Types

A quick note: please don't be scared away by these frightening sounding SNTs! We'll discuss specific strategies to overcome supercharged negative thoughts—and techniques to neutralize each type—so you're able to think in a more clear, calm, and balanced way.

Black and White Thinking - This SNT causes you to think in absolute, binary terms: you *always* fail, you'll *never* find love, *every time* you fall short. With Black and White thinking, you remove any nuance from life and see everything as either all good or all bad. This type of thinking sees everything in stark oppositions: either things are going to work out perfectly, or everything is going to fall apart.

Ex. If I don't finish first in this contest, I may as well finish last. If I'm not first, I'm the worst.

Focusing on the Negative Only - When you get caught in tunnel vision and focus solely on the negative aspects of your life. Any positive information that challenges this SNT is blocked out of your awareness.

Ex. I receive evaluations from my students: 17 of them are positive, but one is negative. I completely ignore the positive evaluations and assume the single negative evaluation is the only accurate one, and it means that I'm a terrible teacher.

Fortune Telling - Nobody can predict the future—but this SNT convinces you that you know what will happen, and it's always the worst possible outcome.

Ex. This holiday season is going to be miserable. I just know it.

Mind Reading - You think you can always tell exactly what someone else is thinking.

And they are *always* thinking something negative about you.

Ex. I called a friend to see if she'd like to go for a walk by the lake, but she says she hurt her knee and needs to stay home and rest. She's lying, of course; I know she just doesn't want to spend time with me or has better plans with friends she likes more than me.

Should-ing - One of the most common SNTs, should-ing causes us to overanalyze what we *should* or *shouldn't* be doing at any given moment, rather than just being present with what you actually *are* doing.

Ex. I constantly tell myself I should be working harder, or I should be as successful as my friends, even though what would really make me happy is to just do good enough and enjoy my family life.

Labeling - This SNT assigns judgmental labels to your feelings or actions. You label your actions or emotions negatively and judge yourself for it.

Ex. If I disappoint someone else, it means that I'm a failure and I'm unlovable.

Taking Things Personally - When another person does or says something to you, you automatically take it as a slight against you. You assume everyone is thinking or acting negatively towards you (as you can imagine, this SNT often goes hand-in-hand with mind-reading).

Ex. I threw a party, but it seems like there are a few people who aren't having a great time. I immediately assume they don't like me and wish they hadn't come.

Blaming - You don't take responsibility for your own actions and circumstances, instead blaming other people or events for your predicament. You tend to see yourself as a victim and refuse to acknowledge your own role in a situation.

Ex. If I hadn't lost my parents at such a young age, my life would be so much better. I'd be married with children, and I'd have a successful career by now.

Minimization - When you tend to discount the importance of an experience or achievement, and instead dismiss it as unimportant or a fluke.

Ex. I trained for months to run my first marathon, but because I wasn't one of the first 20 to cross the finish line, the accomplishment means nothing.

If one or more of these SNT types has taken up residence in your brain, don't despair. Rather than dreading their presence, you can now begin to *notice* yourself having these thoughts and choose to engage with them differently. Once you're aware of a supercharged negative thought, you can take steps to loosen its stranglehold on your mind and free yourself up to experience greater presence and joy.

Now...How to Deal with Supercharged Negative Thoughts

Challenging negative thought patterns isn't an overnight process. While it takes a bit of practice and awareness, you *can* free yourself from SNTs—and trust me, it's worth every bit of effort you put in. The experience of freedom and relief from the tight grip of negative thoughts is one of the greatest gifts you can give yourself. And while it requires some commitment, it doesn't have to be hard.

When it comes to combating negative thoughts, there's no one-size-fits-all approach that works for everyone. In my work with patients, I've identified three of the most effective techniques for shifting your neural networks away from SNTs:

- **Dispute a Supercharged Negative Thought** to Challenge its Validity
- **Reframe a Supercharged Negative Thought** to Shift Your Perspective
- **Use Mindfulness with a Supercharged Negative Thought** to Shift the Pattern

In my nearly three decades working with patients, these three techniques have proven the most consistently beneficial, over time, in helping people to shift their thought patterns to start working for them. Each of these skills engage neuroplasticity to help rewire your brain, releasing SNTs while strengthening more realistic, non-judgmental thought patterns and beneficial neural networks.

You *can* rewire your brain to make SNTs less automatic and to neutralize their impact, both in the short and long term. But there's one absolutely essential thing you must do before you can even consider disputing, reframing, or being mindful of an SNT. You must *notice* the SNT when it happens. Like any problem, if you're not aware of it, then you can't fix it. (You can revisit the mindfulness chapter at any time if you need some extra support here!)

First Things First: Notice What You're Thinking

The critical first step in conquering SNTs is simply *noticing* them. By learning to notice SNTs when they occur, you can start the process of creating distance from them and ultimately replacing them with more constructive thoughts.

Often, we don't step back and become consciously aware of an SNT until we've already been circling in it for a long time. When you catch yourself mid-SNT, you can then begin the work of shifting your brain activity in a different direction.

After you notice an SNT, you can take steps to neutralize and discharge its negative energy, starting with Disputing.

Dispute the SNT with Socratic Questioning, then Take it to Court

We know that our brain can't always be trusted, and our SNTs may be nothing more than a force of habit based on a distorted core belief. To expose a SNT for the lie it really is, one of the best techniques is to *dispute* it with an ancient technique known as Socratic questioning. Once you notice yourself in an SNT loop, ask yourself: *What proof or evidence is there in favor of this negative thought?*

One of the sneakiest tricks of SNTs is the way they convince us that they're real and true. So, it's up to us to make use of our rational thinking capacity to question the factual nature of the thought. Disputing means considering whether the thought is based in reality and coming from a place of truth, or whether the thought pattern is nothing more than a house of cards built on negative assumptions, faulty beliefs, and false evidence.

Using Socratic Questioning to Dispute a SNT

Named after the philosopher Socrates, Socratic questioning is a technique used in psychology to challenge mental falsehoods and uncover the truth of a situation. To apply Socratic questioning to a SNT, ask yourself one or all the following questions:

Are my thoughts on this situation accurate?
Am I basing the thought on facts, or on my feelings?
What factual evidence is there to support my view?
Could I be misinterpreting the evidence?
Am I underestimating my own ability to cope with the situation?
What is the worst-case scenario if the thought is correct?
What good things might happen if I disprove the thought?
What actions can I take to influence the situation?
Am I viewing a complex situation in black-or-white, all-or-nothing terms?
Supposing that the thought *is* true, ask yourself:
o   What's the worst that could happen?
o   What's the best that can happen?

- How likely is either scenario?
- What, honestly, is most likely to happen?
- What can I do to address it?

One thing to keep in mind when you dispute a SNT: don't discount the potential that a negative thought has *some* truth to it. Remember, again, that negative thoughts are a natural mechanism designed to protect us, and not every negative thought needs to be neutralized. If you dispute a negative thought by challenging the evidence for and against its truthfulness, you can come to recognize the difference between garden-variety negative thoughts—those that may have some validity to them—and the more harmful, distorted supercharged ones.

Disputing a SNT...in Court

If you want to dispute a SNT, take it to your own mental courtroom. When utilizing the questions listed above, tap into the power of visualization by imagining yourself as a defense attorney during cross-examination, questioning the validity of the SNT that's currently on the stand.

For instance, perhaps you've noticed yourself struggling with a series of Black-and-White SNTs after missing an important work deadline:

"I failed because I'm a stupid loser. I missed another deadline because I'm lazy and I can't do anything right. I'll probably lose my job."

When you have this thought, take it to court! Dig up evidence that would confirm or disprove the distorted line of thinking. Here's an example of how to use Socratic questioning when disputing a SNT, like the one I just mentioned:

SUPERCHARGED NEGATIVE THOUGHT: "I missed my deadline because I can't do anything right. I'm a failure."

1. Is there any evidence to support the thought that you can't do anything right?

Answer: No, actually. I've done a lot of things right at my job and often perform well. There's no evidence to prove that I *always* fail.

2. Am I basing this thought on facts or feelings?

Answer: I feel bad for failing, and disappointed in myself for not getting things finished on time. Since I have made countless other deadlines and done plenty of good work in the past, I'm not basing this thought on facts; I'm basing it on feelings.

3. What good things can happen if I prove that this thought is inaccurate?

Answer: I can feel good about myself and my positive accomplishments, while being less critical and cruel to myself for my mistakes. I can see that I'm much more than one missed deadline and learn to take proactive steps in the future to avoid leaving things to the last minute.

As you can see, when we're in the grip of a nasty SNT, it takes a bit of discipline and fortitude to fight back and dispute its validity. After all, SNTs are *very* convincing, and they're often extremely forceful in their tactics. But by asking the right questions with Socratic questioning—just like a well-prepared defense attorney—you can poke holes in any negative thought. Over time, disputing SNTs will allow you to rewire your brain to reduce the strength of negative neural networks based on a distorted core belief.

Reframe Your Negative into Neutral Terms

If you find that disputing a SNT isn't enough to reduce the charge or shift your thoughts in a new direction, you may want to take it a step further and *reframe* a SNT. Reframing doesn't mean turning a negative into a positive. Instead, it's about replacing the negative thought with something realistic, non-emotionally charged, and non-judgmental.

When you reframe a SNT, the goal is to shift your point of view—and your neural pathways—towards a clear, neutral, and accurate thought process. Reframing is the third of three simple steps:

1. First, *notice* the SNT.
2. Engage in an honest *reflection and analysis* of the SNT through disputing. Consider what evidence proves or disproves the negative thought.
3. Based on what you discovered in the reflection and analysis, *create* a new thought that is emotionally neutral, truthful, and non-judgmental. Maybe the thought of "Nobody likes me" becomes "I don't have much in common with this particular person, and that's perfectly fine."

Reframing SNTs can be particularly helpful for those who suffer from 'Should-ing'. When you find yourself thinking you *should* be doing this or that ("I should be eating healthier"), try replacing the phrase 'I should" with one of the following:

I look forward to having more energy when I eat healthy.
I love the way I feel and look when I eat healthy.
It's important to me that I am physically healthy.
I'm not the kind of person who dismisses nutrition.
I choose not to eat junk food as a snack.

Let's look at a few other SNT types and how they might be reframed:

Black and White Thinking

"If I don't finish first in this contest, I may as well finish last. If I'm not first, I'm the *worst*."

REFRAME: "I may not have won, but I learned a lot and had a lot of fun on the journey. Winning isn't everything, after all, and everyone loses sometimes."

Focusing on the Negative Only

"One of my 18 students gave me a negative evaluation. I must be an awful teacher."

REFRAME: "17 out of 18 positive evaluations is an awesome percentage overall, and I realize that one bad apple doesn't spoil the whole bunch. I allow myself to feel good about the positive evaluations and investigate the negative feedback from a place of self-compassion and non-judgment.

Mind Reading

"My friend just canceled on me because she says she hurt herself and needs to stay home and rest. She's lying, of course; she just doesn't want to spend time with me or has better plans with friends she likes more than me."

REFRAME: "I give my friend the benefit of the doubt, as I would want her to do for me in the same situation and believe her when she says she is injured. I can't know what she's thinking, after all, but I do know that she cares about me."

Blaming

"If my parents were still alive, and hadn't passed away tragically before I was 30, my life would have turned out better. I'd be married with children, and I'd have a successful career."

REFRAME: "Even if my parents were alive, there's no way to know how my life would have turned out. I've *still* accomplished things I'm proud of, and I can still have a family and successful career."

Becoming Mindful of Your Own Mind

What this all really comes down to is practicing mindfulness with your own thoughts. In fact, in traditional Buddhist thought, investigation of one's own mind is one of the key components of mindfulness. We have to be willing to take a close look at our thoughts, and to question whether what they're telling us is true.

In addition to becoming more mindful of SNTs as they arise, another way to be mindful with SNTs is to focus on a new positive thought, the same way you'd put your focus on the breath or on the act of brushing your teeth. We know that our thoughts never cease, flowing eternally like a Mississippi River through the mind. You can't control or stop thoughts from popping into your mind, but you *can* control which thoughts you *choose* to focus your conscious attention on. So, if you're confronted with a SNT, you can use mindfulness skills to notice and acknowledge the SNT, before redirecting your attention to a more empowering thought of your choosing.

Once you learn to stop engaging or ruminating on SNTs, those neural pathways will wither away over time, and new, more truthful, and unbiased pathways will be created. Eventually, you can reduce or eliminate the negative impact of SNTs, learning to treat them like background noise and not getting caught up in them. You're aware of their presence, but you choose not to engage or become distracted by them.

Beyond basic mindfulness skills (head back to chapter 3 if you need a refresher), two particular practices can be especially effective in rewiring the brain away from SNTs: *Writing it Down*, and *Labeling SNTs*.

Write it Down

Similar to the process of Mental Dumping before bedtime, writing down your SNTs when you notice them can help alleviate their impact—and literally get them out of your head by putting them onto the page. Writing SNTs down on paper can help physically remove them from your mental plate, making it easier to redirect your focus. When you write down SNTs, you're being mindful of their existence, while avoiding directly engaging with them.

Labeling a Thought

Given the almost hypnotic power that unchecked SNTs can have over us, taking the time to simply label a SNT can reduce much of the fear and anxiety they generate, which tends to stem from a fear of the unknown. As soon as you label the SNT clearly, you know exactly what you're dealing with. Rather than letting our imagination run wild with doomsday scenarios, labeling a

SNT helps our brains to expose inflated and exaggerated thoughts for the falsehoods they are.

When you label a thought, you create distance from it, helping your brain to see it through an objective, clear lens. This, in turn, helps neuroplasticity work its magic, slowly shifting your brain's preferred neural pathways from the distorted to the truthful.

Labeling allows you to simply *observe* what you're thinking when confronted with a SNT, rather than *thinking about* or *engaging with* the SNT. It removes the emotional component of the SNT, because there's no emotional connection to a label. You simply say, "This is black-and-white thinking," or "I'm mind-reading right now."

When you label a thought, you're taking the role of an observer; one who happens to be *aware* that they are seeing a situation in all-or-thing terms without engaging further with the SNT.

For instance, you may find yourself ruminating on a professional obligation and worrying about your job. You might label your SNTs as follows:

"*I am noticing* I'm worried about my job."
"*I am obsessing* about my boss's email."
"*I am worrying* about my job."
"*I am dwelling* on my job performance and future."
"*I am having* the 'bad worker' thought."
"*I am remembering* a previous professional disappointment."

Labeling thoughts in this way helps neutralize the emotional impact of SNTs, ensuring that you remain logical and even keeled when a SNT rears its ugly head.

Challenging SNTs with Acceptance and Commitment Therapy Tools

Another way to utilize mindfulness to reduce the impact of SNTs is through Acceptance and Commitment Therapy (ACT). ACT, first developed by Dr. Stephen Hayes, involves a committed willingness to accept thoughts of all types without resistance or suppression. While there are numerous ACT tools available, I've chosen four of the simplest, and most effective, ones to share here. These tools can help distance your focus from a SNT when it occurs, loosening its grip on your mind.

Thank Your Mind

Consider the incredible machinery that allows your brain to do so many incredible things and offer your appreciation. When you notice a SNT, take the time to, quite literally, thank your mind for the thought. Seriously. Say to yourself, "Thank you, brain, for that thought," and allow yourself to reflect on the amazing neurochemical intricacies that lead to a thought existing at all and then let go of the SNT.

A Schoolyard Bully

SNTs often resemble a childhood tormentor: they may appear mean and threatening, but usually they're all bark and no bite. Envision your SNT as a bully during recess and stand up for yourself. When you refuse to let SNTs bully you, they will tend to back down and leave you alone—just like a real bully.

Silly Voices

What if your SNT was being spoken aloud in a ridiculous voice? Imagining this can ease your anxiety and invite a sense of humor and levity. Imagine your SNT being spoken in the voice of Donald Duck or Borat, and you'll realize that it's not so serious after all.

Watch Your Mouth (and Your Mind)

Our words—both the ones we say in our heads and the ones we speak out loud—literally shape our reality. Here's how to use language more consciously to keep your brain working in your favor.

- **The Words You Use** - The actual words you use to describe something can change the way you think, feel, or act about it. For instance, rather than say to yourself, "I was fired" after losing a job, describe it in non-judgmental terms: "I am no longer working at that company." This kind of language helps lift the emotional charge that keeps you trapped in cycles of negative thinking.
- **Don't Use Extreme Wording** - Just as we want to avoid Black and White Thinking, avoid using words like "always," "very," or "never." These words imply certainty when things

are usually much more uncertain than we think. Rather than "I'm always late," try saying "I'm late sometimes" or "I'm working on not being late."
- **Add a 'yet' to It** - When you add the word "yet" to the end of a thought about something you haven't achieved, it implies that there's still time, reinforcing an optimistic and open rather than distorted perspective. Adding "yet" allows you to see yourself in control of your future, rather than beholden to the past. It's OK if you haven't launched your new career… yet. You still have plenty of time.
- **Use Metaphorical Language** - Use metaphorical wording to help frame SNTs in a more positive, less intimidating light—for instance, looking at a relationship that's just ended as a journey rather than a defeat. "I grew a lot as a person during that relationship, and I can take everything I learned into my next relationship."
- **Narrate Your Life as *You* Want** - We are our own narrator of our personal stories. Try reframing your thoughts to see yourself as the hero of your own story, and everything you experienced, or will experience, as part of the story arc.

> ## Conscious Commitments
>
> **Baby Step:**
> - Identify one SNT type that you tend to experience more frequently. Grab a notebook and write down the type, 2-3 examples of how it plays out in your mind, and what emotions and actions it tends to generate.
>
> **Bigger Step:**
> - Choose one SNT type that you want to work with (say, Shoulding), and choose one of the Acceptance and Commitment Therapy techniques (say, Leaves in a Stream) to use with that SNT. Commit to using the technique for one week, every time you notice the SNT. At the end of the week, reflect on your progress and notice if you feel any difference in your relationship with the SNT.

Negative Thoughts are Not You

So, what ever happened to Emma? Emma didn't believe she could be free from the negative thoughts that plagued her. Frankly, her SNTs were wired so deeply in her brain, tied to painful childhood-driven core beliefs, that she couldn't even consider that there might be hope. But, as I reminded her, it wouldn't cost her anything to try, and when I taught her the disputing technique, a lightbulb immediately turned on in her mind.

Having grown up the daughter of an attorney, the idea of asking investigative questions intrigued her. She had fond memories of seeing her father leave for the courtroom with his suit and briefcase, and then telling her at the end of the day what had happened in the trial. She found that it was surprisingly easy and natural for her to ask disputing questions about her SNTs. It was no different from what she'd learned from her father: never relenting when a witness, or a SNT, was confronted with counter evidence.

Over time, Emma was able to notice and dispute most of her SNTs, utilizing neuroplasticity's power to rewire her brain away from entrenched negative patterns. With continual, focused efforts, she found herself getting sucked down the SNT rabbit hole less and less, while noticing a greater sense of lightness, ease and well-being across the board. Through consistent practice, she found that she was no longer beholden to the supercharged negative thoughts that had previously tortured her.

Like many of my patients, Emma was initially skeptical about the techniques I've described here. You may feel similarly distrustful of these approaches and assume that they won't work or that they'll feel too unnatural. Frankly, I couldn't even begin to count the number of patients who immediately denounced these practices as well.

I'd love to tell you there's an easy trick to getting comfortable with these techniques, but the cold hard truth is that these methods and the whole process of rewiring your brain with neuroplasticity simply takes *time*. It's not a quick fix, but over time, it yields real results. You need to execute these practices consistently over long periods to create lasting change.

It's normal for these techniques to feel awkward or silly at the beginning, as I always tell my patients. But be willing to push yourself to try a few methods until you find one that works. (I guarantee you that at least one or two of them will work for you.) I've provided the most effective and helpful tools to rewire your brain away from SNTs; feel free to experiment with different tools for different SNTs based on your needs.

Don't let yourself get derailed by any initial discomfort. If you stay determined over time, you can begin to weaken SNT neural networks, rewiring your brain to work for you rather than against you.

As the saying goes, "Your best thinking got you here." So, be willing to think differently. Try using these techniques and over time you'll experience major shifts in your mindset—and in your life.

CHAPTER 10
Living A Life of Value

"Yep, I've got my PhD in Art History. So what? Now what am I supposed to do?"

I was admittedly surprised by the apathetic, glum tone in the voice of my good friend, Janine, particularly at that moment. I had just called to congratulate her on an incredible accomplishment—completing her doctoral dissertation at Columbia University— but her mind wasn't focused on her once-in-a-lifetime achievement. She wasn't proud and relieved to have reached the end of a decade-plus long pursuit, nor did she seem to find any satisfaction with the fact that she was now a Doctor of Arts.

She knew obtaining her advanced degree was something to hang her hat upon, and had always believed (or, at least, been led to believe) that when she received her PhD, she would have "arrived." She assumed that completing her coursework would result in a level of fulfillment and joy unmatched in her lifetime. But after turning in her thesis, defending her work against a committee of academic faculty, and receiving her Ivy League diploma, she wasn't happy; somehow, she just felt empty and scared.

How was it possible, she wondered, to feel so unfulfilled after fulfilling her biggest life goal? Why wasn't she bursting with pride over her hard-won victory, and why didn't she feel any different now that she had an extra pair of letters behind her name? It was as if everything she'd ever dreamed of—since she first visited the Museum of Fine Arts in Boston at age nine—was a mirage, and she'd been sold a bill of goods by her family, her community, and herself. She had "made it," and yet, she didn't feel any different or better than she had before.

Although Janine was my friend (not patient), I couldn't help but step into my therapist role upon hearing her apathetic and disappointed tone.

"Janine," I said over the phone, "Why was getting your PhD so important to you?"

She listed a litany of rationales: her parents expected it of her; no one would respect a career in arts without a PhD; all her friends had plans to obtain graduate degrees; and she idolized Sigourney Weaver's character, Dana—who restored medieval paintings at the Metropolitan Museum of Art in Manhattan—in her favorite childhood movie, *Ghostbusters II*.

"What is *wrong* with me," she quietly whispered, seemingly begging the world for an answer.

I gently reassured Janine that *nothing* was wrong with her. As she elaborated on her inner torment, the source of her despair became clear. It was the fact that her entire life had been focused on a singular goal—one largely devoid of any deeper personal value or meaning. That was the crux of my dear friend's problem, leading her, like so many others, down a path to disappointment and disillusion wrapped up in a pretty-looking package of goals and dreams. But when we take a closer look, we made the critical discovery that not all dreams are created equal. To live a happy (and meaningful) life, we need to shift our actions, goals, and priorities in the direction of our deepest values.

A Value(able) Life: Finding Happiness *After* Happily Ever After

Personal values are the underlying beliefs and principles we hold which have special meaning we assign to distinguish them from casual or superficial beliefs that act as a navigational guide throughout life. A value can remove the artificiality that often plagues your personal pursuits, because it ensures your actions and goals are sufficiently meaningful to *you*.

Do you know what makes you truly happy? Or what gives your life the greatest sense of meaning and purpose? Honestly, if you were to sit down and ponder what brings forth the strongest feelings of satisfaction and contentment, would you be able to clearly articulate what drives your joy, and why? If you don't, you're certainly not alone (just ask my friend). That creeping uncertainty and constant questioning of how to maximize your time on Earth isn't unique to you.

If you find it difficult to define exactly what it is that brings you true fulfillment—and why—that's perfectly normal. It's not an easy thing to know! If you struggle mightily to understand your life choices beyond the common justification of "that's just what you're supposed to do," then it's almost certain that you're following your *goals* in life, rather than your *values*.

Our goals can either be driven by our values or not. Often, they're driven more by external expectations and a desire to please others than they are by the things we truly value. To be clear, there's nothing wrong with goals, and the process of setting and achieving goals can bring us a sense of meaning and fulfillment. But the important thing is that our goals are driven by our values and in alignment with our values—and, more broadly, that those values are the main thing that are shaping our choices in life. That's what we'll be exploring in this chapter: how to design a life that's in alignment with your deepest values, one that brings true happiness and fulfillment.

So much of our modern culture is dictated simply by surface-level expectations: What success have you already achieved? What milestones have you reached by the age of 25, 30 or 40? What are you working towards in the future? Without even realizing, so many of us live our lives solely to check off a series of boxes: go to college, get a good job, get married, have kids, and so on and so forth. While those are all worthwhile endeavors for anyone to pursue, problems can persist if there's no system of values undergirding the goal.

But to go a little deeper: there *is* a system of values that underlies our ideas of "what we should be doing with our lives"—the problem is when those values are not our own. So often, we adopt the values that have been handed down to us by our parents, and by society, as our own. We're told to get a high-paying, stable job based on our parent's values of security and success, for instance. Or we seek out wealth and a big house because our culture tells us that that's what it looks like to live a good life. So, you can see how our goals—what we strive for and seek out in life—become determined by values that may or may not be our own.

Psychologists talk about this as *intrinsic versus extrinsic motivation*. When we are *intrinsically* motivated to do something, it means that we are performing that activity because it is meaningful and personally significant to us. There's a draw to that particular goal or task that comes from deep within us, and we get real satisfaction from performing that activity. We also enjoy the process itself, not just the destination or reward. When we're *extrinsically* motivated, on the other hand, it means that we're doing something because of outside factors, like wanting to please or impress others, seeking a reward, or trying to avoid punishment. With extrinsic motivation, we're typically focused on the end goal and find less enjoyment in the process.

If you're working towards externally-motivated goals—which you can identify by the difficulty of explaining *why* they matter to you—you will come to find that the fulfillment of these goals does not bring satisfaction or happiness. It's like focusing on the destination rather than the journey itself. Once you get there, your thoughts go straight to: "What now?" Whether it's performing on Broadway, taking a trip to Paris, or becoming a social media influencer, if your goal lacks a deeper meaning, then you're likely to feel empty and confused once you've reached your destination—just like Janine.

To be clear, goals are wonderful to have… so long as they're built upon the fundamental foundation of your values. This is where the real shift needs to happen. But how do you know you're living a value-driven life instead of a goal-driven one? How, exactly, can you identify your personal values and differentiate them from other people's?

Creating a Compass of Values...for *YOU*

Identifying your *personal* values and aligning your decisions, goals and actions with them might initially feel overwhelming. But it's critically important work. Without your own personal *Compass of Values*, you can easily find yourself stumbling through life, seeking fulfillment in the wrong places, and not knowing why major achievements, milestones and possessions fail to bring the happiness you're seeking in them. For this chapter, you'll notice that I've left out the Conscious Commitments section with recommendations for baby steps and bigger steps. In this case, the practice is to clarify your values and shift your life into alignment with them by using the five-step process listed here.

The identification process doesn't have to be daunting—it can be a fun and useful exploration if you know how to approach it. Here are five simple steps, which we'll break down in detail, that can assist you in creating your own compass of values:

STEP 1: Define "Values"

Knowledge is power, even if it's only half of the battle. But just as you can't sail anywhere if you don't know how to read a map, you won't be able to accurately recognize your own personal values—and restructure your life to fit within those values—if you don't know what a value is.

We've acknowledged that goals and values are different, so let's break it down further. Unlike goals, which are specific and often time-sensitive, such as 'become a millionaire in five years,' values are limitless in their timeframe and capacity to help us grow, thrive, and find fulfillment. Values help define the reason for a goal—the "why" behind it—and provide a nuanced understanding of what's driving you to pursue it.

For example, if your goal is to become a millionaire in five years, consider why this goal is so important to you. Are you searching for financial stability, for yourself and your family? Are you seeking the relative freedom and ease that economic comfort provides? Do you wish to have money to feel important? To boost your social status? Or do you wish to obtain wealth to be able to be generous with the people you love and to assist those in need? Will you spend your money ostentatiously, buying designer clothes and fancy cars? How exactly are you planning to obtain the money to achieve your goal—and at what cost (pun intended)?

While goals tend to have a very narrow objective (they either can or cannot be achieved) values are more like guideposts that always guide you along in your life. They don't expire when you complete a goal's mission. Pursuing a million-dollar net worth simply to be rich won't bring you happiness. But pursuing wealth in a conscious way because you value stability and security for your family, and you'd love to be able to help those in need, is a very different story. When you achieve the million-dollar net worth and can feel secure and be generous, your happiness will increase.

STEP 2: Personal Reflection

Now that you understand what values are and how they impact our choices and goals, it's important to take some time to reflect on yourself, your life, and what matters most to you. Through this process, you'll be reflecting on what has brought you the most happiness and fulfillment in your life, what you consider your most meaningful life experiences, and what it is that really gets you out of bed in the morning.

Your values are just that: *yours*. What you value most won't necessarily match up perfectly with anyone else's and valuing one area of life over another is perfectly acceptable. Every single person is an individual, with their own internal wiring, history, and genetic background dictating their unique tapestry of values.

Before we really break things down, it's helpful to start with the biggest values that have shaped your life choices. Here is a list of some of the most common values throughout the world:

Family	Religion	Achievement
Community	Friendship	Entrepreneurship
Knowledge	Justice	Love
Health	Popularity	Peace
Wealth	Wisdom	Success

Take a moment to circle those that are of greatest importance to you and remember: don't define your personal values based on what you think you *should* do, or what you think other people expect. You're the only person who will live your life, and you know yourself better than anyone. Be true to yourself when exploring your values.

To begin defining your personal values, it can help to ask yourself some questions. You might start with things like: what's important to *me*? What do *I care* about? What would *I like* to work towards? These three small queries should get the ball rolling but zeroing in on the personal values that are most meaningful to you can still feel overwhelming.

Here are a few prompts and questions to help single out your values and set you off on the right path.

Imagine you won the lottery, and *every single obligation* you previously had was taken care of. What would you do with your plethora of sudden free time and resources?

If you were attending your 80th birthday party, surrounded by friends and family, what would you want to be said at a toast in your honor? How would you want your life to be remembered and commemorated at that time?

What gets you "in the zone"—like when Joe Gardner plays the piano in *Soul*? This could be a creative pursuit, a pleasurable activity, or anything else that causes you to become so absorbed that you lose track of time. To put it another way, what, for you, epitomizes the phrase, "time flies when you're having fun"?

If the world was to end in 24 hours, who would you want to spend your final day on Earth with? Or if you knew you only had one more week to live, how would you spend the time? Imagine a time when you felt genuinely happy, content with your place and efforts in the world. Picture it in your mind. What was happening? What were you doing? Consider the feelings and thoughts that the memory evokes.

When pondering these questions, write or type up your answers, and review them afterwards, asking yourself what values might be connected to the words or answers you provided.

Based on your own reflections and your answers to these questions, come up with five or six core values that are most important to you and represent what you care most about.

STEP 3: Moving Beyond Basic Values

Now that you've honed in on your basic value system, you'll want to dig down deeper to access the layers beneath the surface of your broad, basic values. The common values listed previously generally correlate with various domains of life (work, family, community, religion, and spirituality, etc.) Based on your selections, you can infer which sectors of your life may hold the greatest importance to you and play the biggest role in your happiness.

Let's take this information and further explore your choices and priorities. If absolutely nothing was holding you back, how would you want yourself to operate within these areas of your life?

If you were the most ideal version of yourself—the full embodiment of who you truly want to be—what would you do, and how would you act? If you're not quite who you desire to be, what are some strategies to becoming this ideal version of yourself? What environments make you feel most like yourself, and where would you prefer to spend more time than you currently do?

Let's say you selected 'Family' as a core value. What sort of sibling, son, daughter, parent, uncle, etc. would you want to be as your ideal self? What sort of interactions and relationships would you like to have? How would you behave differently towards your family members than you do currently? Would you be more present, loving, and attentive? Would you spend more time with your partner or your kids?

Take some time to reflect on your own list of 5-6 values and write a *value statement* describing each value. A value statement of 1-2 sentences can help break down the larger value into smaller, more concise components based on why the value is important to you and how you want it to show up in your life. For example, if you selected *Wealth* as a value, you might jot down something like, "I want to be financially stable," or "I want to have more time to spend with family and less time spent at work."

Based on these values statements, and anything that you feel might be missing from the list you've created so far, start to expand your list and identify some more specific values. Here are some examples of what you might find, beyond the broadest values that form the foundation of your life:

Fun
Creativity
Generosity
Stability
Growth
Integrity
Spirituality
Selflessness
Ease
Independence
Fitness
Leadership

Come up with another list of 5 or 6 deeper values that represent what's most important to you in your life.

STEP 4: Personal Practice Inventory

Now that you've identified your surface-level, basic values, alongside your deeper values, through a process of introspection, you'll want to consider and compare those identified personal values with your current lifestyle, habits, choices, and priorities. Be honest with yourself: Is your current lifestyle helping you in your pursuit of your values, or hindering you from living out the values that matter most to you?

Take some time to reflect on the way you live your life, and the things you spend your time doing. This includes your personal hobbies, personal and professional obligations, relationships, time commitments, where you direct your money and other resources, and any other activities you spend a significant portion of your life on—such as work, exercise, family time, etc.

As you evaluate your current life practices, a picture will begin to emerge of just how aligned your current life is with your stated values. To support this awareness, jot down the specific events and activities—within each value domain—that take place in a given week. Then, estimate what percentage of your overall time is spent on them.

Activity	Domain	Percent of Weekly Time (Column should Add to 100%)

STEP 5: Analysis, Assessment, and Action

The final step in identifying your personal values is a comparison of how you currently spend your time with how you would ideally spend your time if your life was completely in alignment with your values. Take another moment and fill out the chart below by placing the value statements you wrote out before in the corresponding life domain, and then ranking their importance.

When you assign rankings to the value statements, again, be honest about what's most important to you—not what you think other people or society expects from you—and place them in the order of greatest importance to you.

Value Statement	Domain	Rank (1= most important, 5= least important)

Now, compare the chart you just completed with the one from Step 4. Do you spend most of your time performing activities that directly relate to your most important values, or are your current routines and commitments pulling you away from what you've identified as mattering most? Are there any values you consider deeply important to you and yet, perhaps surprisingly, don't devote any time to whatsoever?

As you evaluate and assess your current life versus your ideal, values-driven life, take some time to consider how you can begin to restructure or reorganize your free time to better reflect your values.

Are there ways that you can prioritize and shift your schedule around your values? Developing routines and habits that support your value statements can bring greater fulfillment to your life and help you discover new ways to enjoy life each and every day. What's most powerful about working with your values is how it empowers you to become the active creator of your own life, taking action each day to build the life you *truly* desire—the one that will really make you happy (now and later), rather than just giving you the false promise of a future reward.

Values: Let Yourself Live Every Minute of It

Living a life focused on your values—and making your values the basis of the goals you choose to pursue— provides a deep and profound sense of purpose and clarity of who you are, where you've come from, and where you're going in life. If you take heed of your personal values and take action towards goals that align with what's most important to you, you'll sail your life from port to port, beaming with delight. You'll find that your values act as a compass that guides you through life, not only helping you get to where you want to go, but also giving you the strength and fortitude to weather any storms that you may encounter along the journey.

When I guided Janine through the process of creating her own values compass, she was able to recognize the ways in which her personal goals did actually align with her personal values, particularly her values of Achievement, Knowledge, and Success. This brought a major shift in perspective that changed the way she thought and felt about getting her doctorate. She soon realized that earning her PhD was indeed an accomplishment worth celebrating, and she allowed herself to enjoy her achievements in the present, rather than being panicked about the future.

At the same time, Janine also saw that her decision to pursue a PhD had been driven in part by her parent's expectations (rather than her own values)—and that this had been a driving force in many aspects of her professional and personal life. She recognized that all the pressure she had put on herself to be "good enough" for her parents had sapped much of the joy out of the process of getting her doctorate and left her feeling empty when she received her diploma. She made a commitment to herself, now that she had her PhD, to choose a job and build her new life based on what would make *her* happy, not anyone else.

Additionally, her willingness to investigate her personal values system reaped unexpected insights and rewards—including a surprising realization about her love of Dana Barrett from *Ghostbusters II*. The character was a strong, independent, smart woman who didn't follow society's expectations, didn't apologize for herself, and wouldn't let anything hold her down—not even an onslaught of paranormal threats. This helped Janine to recognize her values of Independence, Strength, Empowerment and Equality, which ultimately led her to take an active role in the political arena, where she became a staunch ally and activist for female equality and women's rights movements.

When you channel your energy into taking actions guided by your values—not superficial goals or the values of other people—you can find a new level of joy and meaning in both the journey and the destination.

Here we turn our focus to *connection*, one of the greatest wonders of life—and one of the most important factors determining our happiness and fulfillment. That's what we're going to explore in Part 3: the way we connect with ourselves, others, and the world as a whole. Once we've primed our brains for happiness and shifted our thoughts, emotions, and actions from old pathways into new and empowering ones, we're ready to connect. The big secret you'll discover? Connection is what life is really all about.

STEP 3: CONNECT
Reach Beyond Yourself

CHAPTER 11

Self-Compassion
Becoming a Friend to Yourself

One of the many gifts of being a therapist is the privileged access that it gives to the inner lives of human beings. In this profession, you quickly learn that the struggles that feel so unique and individual to us are shared by countless other people. Our deepest and most hidden challenges and insecurities are, in fact, universal features of the human experience.

But most of us hold the belief that our struggles are unique to us, and that we are somehow more damaged or worse off than other people. This can give rise to a harsh and critical inner dialogue—and a serious lack of kindness and compassion towards ourselves. I have found that this tendency towards self-criticism over self-compassion is one of the most significant ways that people work against themselves in their pursuit of happiness.

My patient Stephen was convinced that he wasn't deserving of anyone's kindness—let alone his own. Like the rest of us, he's driven by his brain's evolutionarily based negativity bias which led him to a negative outlook on himself and his life.

Stephen's story went something like this: Life was hard, but we can overcome whatever difficulties we face through hard work and determination. We were all capable, he insisted, of picking ourselves up by the bootstraps and overcoming the obstacles in our way. Those who struggled (like him) had failed in some way and had only themselves to blame. They were unworthy of anyone's misguided kindness.

When he expressed this to me, I immediately jumped on two specific words: *blame* and *worthy*.

Why was he placing blame and judgment on himself for struggling to overcome life's obstacles? What if he removed the concept of worthiness entirely, choosing instead to be kind and understanding of his personal challenges?

In one of our sessions, Stephen admitted that he was beating himself up for the fact that his son was sexually abused while he was at a sleep away camp. He felt he should have protected him and that he had failed in his most basic duty as a father.

"It's not your fault, Stephen," I told him. "You're just as worthy of your own kindness and compassion as anyone else is. We're all human, and we *all* experience pain and struggle sometimes."

"Jesus, it can't be that simple, can it? There's got to be more to it than 'I'm human and I deserve compassion *just because'*."

To help the process, I asked Stephen to think about people he knew in his life, and some that he didn't, and to consider their difficulties. As he brought these people to mind, he was able to quickly determine that each and every person he'd ever encountered had their own challenges and struggles—some similar to his, some not.

It slowly dawned on Stephen that he could be compassionate and accepting with himself—and let go of the blame and judgment—while still striving to be a supportive father. After several therapy sessions, he could finally acknowledge that no one was perfect. He seemed to believe me when I made my point: *Every human will inevitably deal with pain in their life, everybody crashes and burns on occasion, and that is more than OK.*

This seemingly simple switch from critical to compassionate is easier said than done. Like everything else we've been discussing in this book, it's a daily practice. But the utilization of *self-compassion* in your everyday life can pay enormous dividends. It's no exaggeration to say that self-compassion is the very foundation of connection: with yourself, with other people, and with your community and the greater whole of life.

Self-Compassion: The Secret Sauce to Resilience

Compassion is a spirit of kindness, understanding and loving concern for human suffering.

When we act with compassion, towards ourselves or others, we are loving, caring, and

forgiving, refraining from assigning blame, criticism, or judgment, no matter the circumstances. It's founded upon the recognition that we're all imperfect creatures, who—by virtue of being living, breathing humans—all experience pain and struggle, and are therefore worthy of kindness.

Self-compassion is the directing of compassion inward rather than outward, adopting an accepting mindset in regard to your own imperfections. It involves a willingness to acknowledge the inescapable reality that every human has flaws, and every person will fail or falter—often because of their own choices and actions. As a human being yourself, you, too, are prone to the same pitfalls as anyone else.

Self-compassion isn't about making excuses for yourself or letting yourself off the hook when you make a mistake or behave poorly. Rather, it is an active state of mind that is unconditionally loving and supportive, even when acknowledging that you could have done better and seeking to improve in the future. Self-compassion isn't something you have to do, like self-care; it's simply a *state of mind* that is the opposite of self-criticism.

No one is perfect! We all fail sometimes. Most likely, we will make a colossal mistake from time to time, too. But that's OK! If you're willing to forgive yourself, you can learn from your mistakes—instead of endlessly judging and beating yourself up for them—and move forward wiser and stronger for what you've been through.

Forgiveness is at the heart of self-compassion, so we'll be giving it a lot of focus in this chapter. It is, in fact, the most crucial component in your ability to be compassionate with yourself. If we can't forgive ourselves, then how can we expect to meet ourselves with acceptance and love? The bottom line is that we all make mistakes. It's not an "if," it's a "when." Mistakes, poor choices and blunders are *going* to happen, and it's inevitable that we'll stumble as we progress along the path of our lives. This is integral to how growth happens! We learn from experience, and we change our approach based on the insights and feedback we get from our experience. If you're able to forgive and gain more awareness, you'll be ready to successfully adopt a mindset of self-compassion.

Dr. Kristen Neff, the leading psychologist studying self-compassion, noted in her research that self-compassion is made up of three basic elements:

1. *Choosing* kindness over judgment during times of pain, remembering that you're a human being who deserves to be treated kindly, no matter the why, how, or what of your present circumstances.
2. *Recognizing* that all people share a common humanity, and contrary to belief, you are not different or separate from the larger human experience.
3. *Accepting* that negative thoughts and feelings are universal aspects of human nature, and not resisting this reality.

Sounds easy enough, right? Yet so many of us struggle to truly understand and implement self-compassion. Being *nice to yourself*, particularly when your pain is self-inflicted, can be surprisingly difficult. Let's take a closer look at what self-compassion is and why it's so vital to living your happiest life.

Understanding Self-Compassion

Tell me: have you ever done something so monumentally dumb that it haunted you for weeks, months, or even years to come? Maybe it was an embarrassing faux pas at a dinner party or an awkward slip of tongue in a conversation with your boss. Or perhaps you made a conscious decision to engage in something you knew was wrong—or would lead to an undesirable outcome—and then found yourself dealing with the consequences.

Maybe you knew you shouldn't spend your last paycheck on a ticket to Coachella, but you did it anyway, and now you're stuck eating ramen noodles and scrambled eggs for two weeks until your next payday.

Or maybe you worked tirelessly for a lifelong dream, like competing in the Olympics as a sprinter. For years, put everything you had towards that goal. You spent days, nights, weekends, holidays, vacations, parties, and every other waking moment working towards that one endpoint of international athletic glory. Yet when the time came to earn your spot on the national team, you tripped out of the blocks and face planted on the synthetic rubber beneath you, as the other competitors—along with your entire life's work—faded from view.

How should you treat yourself in this kind of situation? (And be honest: We all have our own version!) Let's imagine that the stakes are much lower. Recently, for instance, I signed up for a Pilates class after some prodding from a friend. But the day of the first session, I spaced out while binge-watching my brother on *Shahs of Sunset*, and I completely blew off the class. Now, should I have considered myself a hopeless, out-of-shape failure who has zero percent chance of ever following through on her commitments? Should I consider my forgetfulness as an indication that I'm a horrible human being unworthy of happiness or compassion?

Of course, like many of us, my initial reaction *was* a swift, harsh dose of self-criticism. I mentally tore myself to shreds for being so forgetful and lazy. But in reality, I simply made a mistake. It wasn't an indication of anything larger than 'I messed up that one time,' meaning I was worthy of self-compassion in that moment and in others. Self-compassion allows you to forgive, rather than berate, yourself for your unsuccessful or regretful actions. (By the way, this should sound familiar to you! Whenever you notice the black-and-white SNT arising, that's your signal to apply a healthy dose of self-compassion!)

When the damage has already been done, and you're dealing with whatever consequences resulted from your inevitable blunder or failing, criticizing, and judging yourself isn't going to make things any better. Ask yourself: How does it really help you, now or in the future, to allow your inner critic to pile onto your existing pain? When you see yourself as being unworthy of compassion, the unfortunate byproduct is that you stunt your own ability to grow, and you numb your capacity for happiness.

Self-compassion involves an acceptance that failing is part of human nature—because *every single human* is flawed and prone to failure. In times of personal pain or disappointment, you're still willing to forgive yourself and treat yourself with kind regards and warm thoughtfulness.

To get a clearer picture of self-compassion, and learn how best to utilize it with yourself, it's helpful to first know what it *isn't*. Self-compassion isn't conditional, meaning you don't need to *earn* the right to have compassion for yourself.

Self-compassion is also **NOT**....

Self-esteem - While the terms *self-compassion* and *self-esteem* are sometimes used interchangeably, self-compassion is something very different. Self-esteem is how you value yourself based on personal and external judgments. Often, self-esteem is based on comparisons and 'measurable' merits—that is, if you don't match up to whatever arbitrary yardstick you apply to yourself (which we often don't), then your self-esteem can plummet. Self-esteem tends to be overemphasized in our society, but it doesn't always make us happier, and it can fluctuate significantly based on our achievements, status in the eyes of others, and life circumstances. Dr. Neff puts it this way: "Self-esteem is present when we succeed. Self-compassion is a way of relating to ourselves kindly when we fail."

Self-pity - Pity is an attitude of looking down at someone because of their pain, while compassion involves a desire to help or alleviate the pain. It also tends to view pain and struggle in an isolated context, rather than acknowledging it as a universal feature of the human experience. When you engage in self-pity, you tighten the focus on yourself as an individual, overlooking the universality of human suffering.

Being complacent or lazy - When people push back on the idea of self-compassion, which countless patients of mine have done, their reasoning is usually that being compassionate with themselves would somehow be "letting themselves off the hook" or cutting themselves too much slack. They fear that it will dull their motivation and sap their drive to succeed and improve. But contrary to popular belief, self-compassion actually *increases* your motivation for success in the long run (more on this later!).

Unchecked self-indulgence - "Being nice to yourself" is not synonymous with "do whatever you want, whenever you want." Self-compassion simply means being forgiving and kind to yourself for the sake of your long-term happiness and health. If you give yourself permission to succumb to your every urge and desire, you're not practicing self-compassion, you're practicing self-indulgence.

The bottom line is that life is filled with struggles, disappointments, and grievances, and in some way, we are always falling short of where we want to be. That's because we're always a work in progress! Treat yourself like you'd treat a good friend: with kindness, love and understanding.

If you need a little extra motivation to incorporate self-compassion into your life, let's look at the immense benefits of simply embracing an attitude of compassion towards yourself.

It Pays to be Kind: Benefits of Self-Compassion

The scientific evidence of the power of self-compassion is overwhelming—and the data doesn't lie. A large body of research has revealed that self-compassion leads to improvements in:
- Emotional well-being
- Physical health
- Connections with other people, be it friends, family, or acquaintances
- Creativity and motivation

People who practice self-compassion and forgiveness, as opposed to criticism and judgment, have also been found to:

- **Procrastinate less, particularly in times when focus is required.**

    Ex. Instead of getting sucked into reading celebrity gossip and scrolling TikTok, you'll finish your work project before the deadline (if you forgive yourself for missing a deadline in the past).

- **Have improved motivation and self-control skills.**

    Ex. You'll finish painting the garage before the weekend ends, and you were kind to yourself about choosing to lounge around the house the week before (and did not paint, as you initially planned).

- **Demonstrate a greater resilience in the face of difficult events.**

    Ex. Rather than blaming yourself for a tough job market, you continue applying for jobs. You remain calm and forgiving of yourself for the challenges you've encountered in your career.

- **Have better physical health and emotional well-being.**

    Ex. If you skip a week of workouts, you don't decide you're worthless and should never try again. Instead, you accept that you made a misstep and keep moving forward, forgiving yourself and picking back up again where you left off.

- **Increased happiness in romantic relationships and greater acceptance, intimacy, and affection for your partner.**
    People who are higher in self-compassion are less dependent on their partner for self-worth, and less focused on their own personal inadequacies, leading to healthier relationship dynamics and a greater capacity to offer emotional and physical support to their partner.

    Ex. When you practice self-compassion, you're less likely to engage in the SNT of "Mind Reading," worrying that your spouse might be mad at you when they're upset (or wondering why you aren't better, or presuming you caused their pain). You can offer a steadier hand of support to your partner in their times of distress, because you recognize that their pain, like yours, is universal, not somehow "Their fault."

In addition, adopting self-compassion can lead to a stark reduction in both depressive and anxious feelings, while boosting good feelings: namely, your self-esteem and capacity for pleasure.

Self-compassion is practically a miracle cure for negative emotions. It's been shown to support our emotional regulatory systems, decreasing the body's Sympathetic Nervous System (fight or flight response) activation, and thereby downshifting the physiological stress response. In studies, individuals who performed both direct and indirect applications of self-compassion reported a reduction in physiological functions of the Fight-Flight-Freeze system (such as a lowered heart rate) and an increased activation of the body's parasympathetic, or "rest and digest," nervous system.

The bonafide benefits of self-compassion are enormous, and it doesn't take much once you understand it. Applying self-compassion is nothing more than flipping around the Golden Rule:

treating *yourself* the way you'd treat another person (we'll get into specifics of applying the Golden Rule internally in a moment). This is necessary since we're wired to be compassionate towards *others*, but less often to ourselves.

Not Perfect, But Always Real: The Challenge of Perfectionism

The biggest enemy to self-compassion is perfectionism. Our belief that we should be perfect, or that we need to meet some impossibly high standard in order to be worthy, makes it difficult to meet ourselves with acceptance and kindness. It trains our focus on what we perceive to be wrong or lacking about ourselves, instead of on what we're doing right and our innate worth as human beings. If you want to become more compassionate with yourself, it's essential that you take a look at any tendencies towards perfection that you might have—and make a commitment to uprooting any perfectionistic beliefs that tells you that you're not good enough as you are right now.

While aiming for personal 'perfection' may seem like a positive standard to strive for, the reality is that perfectionism sets an impossible standard for success: if you're not perfect, you're a failure—there's no in between.

Obviously, you are *not* perfect, and nobody else in the world is, either. Your efforts to achieve perfection are destined to end in failure (bummer, I know). Given this basic reality, perfectionistic beliefs and behaviors that hold you to impossible standards are the antithesis of self-compassion and a prime example of your brain working against you.

The belief that you must be perfect in order to be worthy of love and happiness is a core belief that drives many SNTs (Black and White thinking in particular). This leads to distorted thought patterns and a negative self-image and inner dialogue that uses criticism and judgment to try to push you to be better. These damaging thoughts can easily convince you that you're *never* deserving of compassion, from yourself or anyone else. Clearly, if you believe that anything short of perfection is intolerable, you'll struggle to exercise kindness and understanding when you inevitably fall short of your own rigid standards.

Perfectionist beliefs fall into one of two categories: perfectionistic *striving*, and perfectionistic *concerns*. Both can be detrimental, though perfectionistic striving, which is more about maxing out your human potential rather than avoiding mistakes and failure, isn't nearly as damaging as perfectionistic concerns are.

Psychologists have found that perfectionist striving involves setting high expectations and goals for oneself, largely from a place of hope and desire for success. Perfectionistic concern, on the other hand, is characterized by a focus on personal mistakes and shortcomings, excessive concern about other people's expectations and judgments, and a fear of failure. Those who engage in perfectionistic striving tend to be motivated to be the best that they *themselves* can be (and when extreme, the pursuit may become unhealthy), while those high in perfectionistic concern are often more motivated by comparisons to *others* and being seen as successful in the eyes of others. As you might imagine, perfectionistic concerns often spur negative emotions and SNTs, which can be crippling. This is because those with perfectionist concerns believe they need to be perfect but won't achieve that standard, often resulting in avoidant behaviors, procrastination, and extreme self-criticism.

We tend to develop perfectionist beliefs as a survival tactic during childhood, often as a way to try and compensate for feelings of inadequacy. Usually, they help us suppress uncomfortable emotions when we feel out of control. We start to figure out as young children that if we can't control our environment, then at least we can control *ourselves*. In fact, that's the most common driver of perfectionist beliefs: a need for control in a world where so many things are completely out of our control.

Perfectionism can help us *feel* like we have things under control, even when we don't. Essentially, if you're supposed to be perfect, you can tell yourself you *are* in control, and therefore you aren't helpless. Of course, this also means you believe you're fully responsible for your *failures* as much as your successes, ramping up your already sky-high personal pressure, and providing ample fodder for your inner critic.

For instance, a student who believes they must maintain a perfect GPA or otherwise be considered an abject failure may struggle with this type of perfectionist thinking. If this type of person has even one slipup and isn't able to study enough or get perfect grades on a paper, it can lead to a slippery slope of internal criticism and judgment. This often triggers a lifelong pattern of SNTs hijacking your happiness when you fail to meet your own personal standards.

When perfectionism becomes the basis of our relationship with ourselves, it can cause a great deal of harm over time, not only to our emotional well-being and peace of mind, but also to our mental and physical health. Some common problems associated with perfectionism include:

- **Increased risk of depression and anxiety** - Research shows that perfectionists are much more likely to develop mental illnesses including depression and anxiety.
- **Difficulty falling or staying asleep** - If you can't stop thinking about the ways you've failed, and a need to be in control, it will be more difficult to get your nervous system in the relaxed state it needs to be in to facilitate sleep. (And losing a Priming pillar is certain to make you feel worse!)
- **Increased irritability** - If you expect to be perfect, your emotional state will suffer during those inevitable times you fall short of the impossible standard.
- **A harsh inner critic and inner voice** - Perfectionist tendencies are rooted in childhood core beliefs and can generate a cruel inner critic who can seem impossible to quiet or ignore.
- **Rumination** - Perfectionists are prone to rumination, which is a key cause of anxiety and depression. When you can't stop pushing yourself to be better and berating yourself for your mistakes, it can easily lead to overthinking and SNTs.
- **Relationship Difficulties** - Perfectionism isn't just an impossible standard you hold yourself to, it's often something you hold *everyone else* to, as well. If you expect perfection from other people, you'll likely be critical of others when they fall short, making it harder to maintain healthy, strong connections.

While you won't always succeed or get what you want in life, you can come to an understanding and acceptance of this reality—that you are *not* perfect, and neither is anyone else in the world—without being detoured on your journey. Self-compassion is THE antidote for perfectionism, and it's your greatest ally in letting go of those impossible expectations.

Research shows that perfection-driven individuals who take up self-compassion experienced an improved mood and reduced feelings of depression—it works! If you can find a way to accept that you aren't perfect, you can find a way to forgive yourself and still feel good, even when life isn't all peaches and cream.

Here are a few proven ways to help rewire your brain away from perfectionist thought patterns, and rewire your brain towards acceptance, understanding and kindness:

- **Do It Badly:** One of the best defenses to overcoming perfectionist behaviors is *doing it badly*. This is exactly what it sounds like. Rather than avoid taking action because you're afraid to fall short, give yourself permission to do a bad, or at least mediocre, job. Don't worry about being perfect; just act, and act *badly,* in order to reduce fear and boost resilience. This technique "How to Cope With Anxiety," works similarly to a technique from Dialectical Behavioral Therapy (DBT) called *Opposite Action,* which essentially asks you to act differently than what your emotions are telling you to do. Over time, 'doing it badly' will lessen the preemptive fear of messing up and activate neuroplasticity to rewire your brain, leading to reduced anxiety and a silencing of perfectionist thoughts.
- **Notice the Damage Done:** Perform a cost/benefit analysis of your perfectionist behaviors. Is the damage to yourself and your life worth the price of maintaining your perfectionist tendencies? Consider what you've gained versus what you've lost, and ask yourself these questions:
    - "What do I get from this?"
    - "What am I getting from being 5% better, at best?"
    - "What is the reward relative to the pain?"
    - "How has this hurt me?"

Recognize What Perfectionism Is

Remember that perfectionism is a core belief, and our core beliefs are often biased and untrustworthy. Keep reminding yourself that while your perfectionist behaviors began with good intentions, and they helped you to protect yourself and feel in control as a child, they're now just an outdated defense mechanism that probably isn't serving you anymore. Apply Socratic questions to outmoded perfectionistic beliefs when they arise.

Change the Standard of Judgment

Does everything *really* have to live up to the standard of 'perfection or bust'? Challenge yourself to change the bar for what's successful and what's not in your life. If you're able to shift your own beliefs about what success looks like, you can rewire your neural networks away from perfectionistic thoughts and actions.

Reframe Black and White SNTs

Go back and revisit the techniques we discussed for shifting your mental activity away from SNTs and negative thought patterns. If you can engage neuroplasticity by repeatedly reframing the belief that you're either perfect or a failure, you can begin to liberate yourself from the shackles of perfectionist core beliefs.

Letting go of perfectionism doesn't mean you give up on setting goals for yourself or striving for success. It simply means unshackling your mind from the chains of impossible standards and accepting yourself for who you are—warts and all, successes and failures, good days, and bad days. If you can accept that you're not perfect, you'll soon realize that you're worthy of self-compassion, too.

Steps and Strategies to Incorporate Self-Compassion into Your Life

While you've now got a firm grasp on what self-compassion is, you may still be wondering: how can I use self-compassion in my daily life?

Well, let's talk about that right now! As we've discussed, compassion towards oneself has been proven to be much more effective and uplifting than self-criticism but doing so when it goes against the negative thoughts and unpleasant emotions swirling around in our heads is easier said than done. Since we know our thoughts aren't 100% within our conscious control, we can work to combat that harsh inner critic by actively practicing self-compassion. So instead of trying to get *rid* of the inner critic, you can replace it (or talk back to it) with the voice of an "inner friend" instead.

Remember, again, that thanks to neuroplasticity, our brains are equipped with an enormous flexibility and capacity for change. While you can't rewire your brain to completely switch off your negativity bias, you can gradually reroute negative, critical thoughts and impulses by consciously choosing to be compassionate with yourself.

The most important thing to remember when practicing self-compassion is to be patient and understanding with yourself. At the beginning, it may feel forced and unnatural, but this is a good time to implement a "fake it till you make it" approach (it works, I promise!). It can take time to develop true feelings of compassion towards yourself, particularly if you've spent your life haunted by an aggressively demeaning inner critic. But just like priming or challenging SNTS, it's worth the time you invest in practicing self-compassion.

If you find that being compassionate towards yourself seems to initially embolden your inner critic, don't freak out—this is a common roadblock. Try to remember that this sort of emotional reverberation is expected as you get used to treating yourself in a completely different way. And of course, remember that the feelings, while unpleasant, can't physically harm you.

Here are some strategies to successfully incorporate self-compassion into your life, and help you enjoy life to the fullest.

- **You're Awesome! Be Nicer to Yourself with The GOLDEN RULE**

    The single most effective way to successfully utilize self-compassion is to commit to the Golden Rule: Treat *yourself* as you'd treat a loved one, a small child, or a close friend.

    While we should strive to treat every single person we encounter with equal amounts of respect, dignity, and compassion, the reality of life is that some people inspire more of our love and care than others. If you are speaking to a stranger, as opposed to your newborn daughter or nephew, for example, which of the two are you likelier to be kinder, gentler, and more affectionate towards?

To get past the initial awkwardness of adopting self-compassion, modeling your self-compassion after the compassion you'd give a loved one is a good way to get started.

Ex. Try imagining a *loved one* dealing with your personal problem at that moment. How would you treat that person you love in their time of need? What would you say to them to make them feel better? How would you *want* them to be treated? I'd bet dollars to donuts you're picturing yourself being gentle, kind, and validating of their feelings. And the way you're envisioning your loved one being treated is *exactly* what you need to be willing to do for yourself.

With the Golden Rule as your constant guide, try adopting these other strategies for cultivating self-compassion and becoming a better friend to yourself:

- **Shift Your Self-Talk**

    How do you talk to yourself inside your own head? Your inner monologue—whether it's positive or negative—can be difficult to control, but you *do* have the ability to choose specific thoughts. If you choose to use your *self-talk* to speak positively and compassionately to yourself, you'll find that those uncontrolled negative thoughts become less distressing.

    Positive and motivational self-talk has been shown to improve professional performance in numerous fields and is commonly practiced by the elite-level athletes. Research has also indicated that actively using positive self-talk can reduce amygdala activation and the fear response that comes with it, reducing our chances of panicking in stressful situations. The important idea here is that what you think influences how you act. How amazing is it that you can *improve* your performance with motivational self-talk?

- **Visualize Yourself Being Compassionate**

  Visualizing yourself in a positive, successful light can also challenge the dominance of a harsh inner critic. Many uber-successful and accomplished professionals are devotees of this self-compassionate technique, known as *mental imagery*. Research has shown conclusively that picturing yourself succeeding before an important task (rather than imaging the worst outcome) results in higher rates of accomplishment. imagine yourself completing the marathon and feeling immense satisfaction. Visualize yourself making those strides every day—pushing through the training, ignoring your inner critic, preparing yourself little by little—and see yourself doing well rather than failing. This exact exercise was shown to increase the chances of Navy SEAL program completion by nearly 33%.

  You can also increase your capacity for self-compassion by visualizing someone else, someone you love, motivating you by saying what you struggle to believe from yourself. Imagine them saying "You got this," or "You're doing an amazing job, I'm so proud of you." Another visualization approach, when anxious or self-critical thoughts arise, is to mentally picture yourself in a safe, comforting place in your mind—a kind of inner sanctuary.

- **Build Yourself a (Modified) NEST**

  Remember the NEST technique for accepting and allowing your negative thoughts and emotions?

  If you recall, one of the best ways to accept uncomfortable emotions is to build a NEST. When it comes to building self-compassion, you can apply this technique to help you accept yourself and your present circumstances, using a slightly different formula:

  - **N**otice yourself being self-critical or judgmental. The first step to solving a problem is recognizing it exists, so be aware and notice when self-criticism arises.

  - **E**xpose yourself to your own imperfection and acknowledge when you make a mistake. Acknowledging the truth—that you may have failed or made a mistake, which is OK, since mistakes can teach us important lessons—can help loosen up any judgments.

- **S**eek support from your loved ones, be it family or friends. When you're working on being kinder to yourself, being with others who offer unconditional compassion can be a big help.
- **T**ake action. In this case, when you notice yourself being critical or judgmental towards yourself, actively shift your self-talk from negative to positive. Acknowledge if you made a mistake or failed, and then *forgive* yourself. Do something nice for yourself to show your love and affection.

- **Goals in Baby Steps**

Goal setting is another strong strategy that helps foster self-compassion, if done in small, achievable steps. Keeping yourself focused on the next task at hand can help you avoid getting overwhelmed by how far you must go on your journey and can prevent you from beating yourself up for not being further along than you think you should be. By narrowing your focus, you're more likely to complete that goal and feel a sense of accomplishment.

As you increase the number of successful goal completions in your life, you naturally feel more positive about yourself and your abilities. After all, those smaller tasks add up, creating a mountain of positive evidence that will make it harder for your negative inner thoughts to pull you down.

- **Tap Your External Compassion Centers**

For most of us, being kind and compassionate towards others is a simple, natural process. If you see someone in pain, whether it's physical or emotional, you may be drawn to comfort and support that person in need. This innate desire to be caring and understanding towards others' misfortunes, however, doesn't always extend to ourselves, and studies have shown that there is little-to-no correlation between compassion towards others and self-compassion.

In other words, if you're generally nice to other people, you're no more likely to be nice to yourself—although, interestingly, the opposite is true. If you're generally nicer to *yourself*, you'll be nicer to *other people*, as well. By consciously practicing self-compassion, then, you can tap into the warm caring we usually reserve for others, wrapping it around yourself, and others, in the process.

- **Incorporate Self-compassion Mindfulness**

    Mindfulness is the foundation of self-compassion: To be kinder to ourselves, we must first be present with ourselves in the moment, without judgment.

    Mindfulness downshifts negative thoughts and emotions by creating space and acceptance around them and can help you remember that you're an imperfect human being, just like everyone else.

Conscious Commitments

Baby Step:

- Every morning when you look in the mirror to wash your face or brush your teeth, take an extra 30 seconds to look at yourself with kindness and give yourself a genuine compliment. It doesn't matter what it is, or how big or small, just find one kind, complementary thing to say to yourself each day.

Bigger Step:

- For one week, commit to practice building a NEST whenever you notice judgmental or self-critical thoughts arising. Keep a journal with you and make notes of what triggers your inner critic, and what works best in quieting it down.

Self-Compassion: Sharing the Love with Yourself

You don't need to judge yourself or melt yourself into a puddle of shame and regret when you struggle in life. Welcome to being human! I'm glad you decided to join the rest of us in our imperfections and difficulties. Being compassionate with yourself is no different from reacting with caring and kindness when someone else is in pain. You're simply turning the tables and treating yourself as you'd treat another.

Even if it's difficult to overcome the brain's negativity bias, practicing self-compassion can rewire your thoughts and emotions in a positive direction over time. Sailing along on your lifelong journey will only become smoother when your kind and compassionate towards yourself.

With an attitude of compassion, you become a lifelong friend to yourself—and this strong and healthy connection with yourself then becomes the basis of your connections with others. From an inner place of connectedness, you build stronger and more fulfilling relationships in your life.

These connections, as we'll see, are one of the most important foundations for a happy life.

CHAPTER 12
Building Better Relationships

When I heard the doctor's diagnosis, my heart stopped. My stomach plunged into the depths of my body. Everything in the room (and, it felt, the entire world) seemed to stop along with my heartbeat, as I struggled to comprehend the words I was hearing. My father—my lifelong rock and refuge—had been diagnosed with Alzheimer's. Sooner rather than later, he would lose most or all his cognitive capabilities. "Eventually, he won't remember who you are at all", said the doctor.

The news hit each of my family members like a ton of bricks, and we huddled together, leaning on each other as we took in this Earth-shattering information. In Persian culture, family is *everything*. My relationship with my father had always been my greatest source of comfort and support.

Our bond, and his love, were crucial to my successful transition from Iran to my new life in the United States. Beyond that, it has been an invaluable resource for my entire life. Although he was living across the country at the time of his diagnosis, we never drifted apart, and if I ever needed him (for any reason whatsoever), I knew he was just a phone call away. When I imagined a future without his paternal presence in my life, I was devastated beyond words. The loss left me with a deep sense of loneliness.

He was a man who dedicated everything, and focused all his energy, into providing for his family. That unwavering, unconditional support had been the wind beneath my wings for decades—literally up until that very moment—and the thought of existing without it left me crestfallen. Without the support of the rest of my family and friends, I could have easily withdrawn into loneliness and depression. They kept me afloat through the darkest days of his illness.

The connections that make up our lives—from close, intimate relationships to casual, friendly acquaintances—aren't just meaningless interactions. They are the literal keys to a long, healthy, and happy life. Surrounding yourself with supportive people, with whom you can be mutually open, honest, and vulnerable, is the foundation for health, happiness, and longevity.

Home is Wherever I'm with You: Our Connections are Our Happiness

Human beings are social creatures. More than anything else, it is our *connections* in life that determine our happiness. This is simply the way we're wired.

What happens when you lack a strong network of social connections? Both your short-term happiness and your long-term mental and physical health decline, while your potential lifespan decreases sharply. Unbeknownst to most people, quality relationships, and close personal connections, aren't just a source of enjoyment; they are as crucial to your physical health and longevity as food or water.

In fact, more than any other factor in a person's life (including diet, genetics, family history and socioeconomic status), having a number of quality relationships is the greatest determining factor in mental and physical health and longevity. The presence of quality social relationships has been shown to reduce one's chances of premature death by a whopping 50%, while the lack of those same relationships is as physically detrimental to one's health as smoking 15 cigarettes per day.

While this somewhat surprising reality has been corroborated through countless studies, it's most prominently demonstrated by the 75-year year Harvard-Grant study, which started in 1938 with a group of undergraduates from various socioeconomic backgrounds—including a young John Fitzgerald Kennedy. The study followed 268 male Harvard undergraduates for three-quarters of a century, collecting data on various aspects of their lives at regular intervals.

From all the data they collected, the researchers came to some strikingly universal conclusions: most notably, the fact that love and connection are our greatest sources of happiness in life.

In fact, the presence of positive, intimate relationships at age 50 (ranging from romantic partners to close friends) was more impactful on one's physical health *at age 80* than a person's cholesterol level at the same age—which is pretty remarkable! The study's lead researcher, George Vaillant, went so far as to say that the study's most important finding is that *the only thing that matters in life is relationships* . A person could have a successful career, wealth, and good health, but without supportive, loving relationships, that person wouldn't be happy, period.

Clearly, if you're hoping to maximize your chances of living a long, healthy life, filled with joy and purpose, then cultivating and maintaining a number of positive, beneficial connections is worth prioritizing. Let's dig in further on why, exactly, close connections are so crucial to thriving.

Together We Stand, Divided We Fall: Why Close Relationships Matter

No man is an island, and our happiness is not something that happens in isolation. Our connections to other people are elemental to our happiness.

Connections with other people nurture feelings of closeness and a sense of belonging. From this, we also derive a sense of security and safety in the world. When we don't feel connection and belonging, we're more likely to be operating in survival mode—with a nervous system on high alert and a negatively-biased brain running amok. As many studies have shown, social support also has a strong protective effect against stress, helping us to become more resilient and adaptive in the face of adversity.

This makes a lot of sense from an evolutionary perspective, where survival is always the top priority. After all, when we trace back thousands of years into the past, living within a group or community—as opposed to being alone and isolated—would drastically increase one's chances of surviving and thriving in the face of many environmental threats.

This has wired our brains to chemically promote connections with other people, particularly through the release of oxytocin, aka 'the love hormone.' Oxytocin is often released through affectionate touching or hugging and works to strengthen positive relationships while steering us away from unhealthy ones. Oxytocin has been shown to enhance a range of social activities, from bonding among couples to parenting behaviors. It's also instrumental in the earliest moments of our lives, in mother-child bonding.

We're wired to take pleasure and find nourishment not only in connection, but also in helping and supporting others. Research has shown that helping other people reduces activity in the stress and threat detections centers and stimulates the reward centers in caregiving areas of the brain.

Alongside the brain's negativity bias, our biological urge to nurture social connections is driven by the Darwinian impulse to survive at all costs. This evolutionary drive can sometimes push us towards unhealthy relationships to avoid being alone. Not all connections are created equal, after all, and just like the way you would set yourself up for success in any endeavor, who you surround yourself with matters.

We all *need* to connect with other people to ensure our health, happiness, and survival, whether you're a buoyant person with a big circle of "best friends," or a quiet individual whose spouse is their *only* "best friend." For instance, I'm an extreme extrovert who absolutely adores social interaction with as many people as possible. I may feel lonely if I'm only connected with, say, two people on a consistent, intimate basis, but that same number of relationships may be perfect for an introverted person, who has less of a need for constant person-to-person contact.

What matters is the quality of your relationships, not the quantity. It's the depth of care, authenticity and support in our relationships that leads to happiness and positive health outcomes.

But the bottom line is that every single person needs some strong and lasting connections in their life. Having lots of people around you doesn't necessarily translate to feeling *supported* and feeling lonely doesn't even mean you're alone—you can feel alone in a room full of people, as the old adage goes.

Let's discuss how close relationships and connections provide social support, and the main ways we both give and receive it.

Lean on Me: Mutuality and Types of Social Support

For a relationship to provide the benefits we've just discussed, there needs to be something mutually offered (without expectation, of course, as close relationships aren't transactional in nature) between both parties. Most importantly, there must be some form of support, by both parties, provided when needed.

The existence of mutuality between parties is at the heart of any healthy relationship. Mutuality is the flow of reciprocity and the sharing of empathy, acceptance, and comfort between two people. This means that a healthy, supportive relationship is a two-way street. Mutuality is perhaps the most important factor in determining the quality of your relationships because it means that *both* people are giving and receiving in relatively equal measure.

Of course, as we've discussed, if the giving and support is transactional or has any sort of "tit for tat" quality, the connection won't become an intimate one. If financial or material support is the driving force of the connection, there won't be the kind of true mutuality that's required for a strong and genuine connection.

Ideally, at least one of five types of support will be found in a close and meaningful connection:

- **Emotional Support:** Provided from a loving source, this type of support is motivated solely by the desire to nurture and care for the other person. Emotional support offers compassion and reassurance when a person is struggling, and encouragement and cheering on when they're doing well. It typically comes from a parent, spouse, close family member, or a close friend.

- **Tangible Support:** This type of support involves financial support, or any kind of assistance where a good or service is provided, as a form of assistance, from a familiar source. This can be a close, intimate connection, a hired professional like a therapist or coach, or an informal acquaintance.
- **Informational Support:** Provides any sort of information (advice, guidance, directions) that can help you diagnose or overcome a problem. This can come from a professional source or a personal relationship.
- **Companionship Support:** The type of support we give and receive when we interact casually with other people in one-on-one or group settings. This may involve teammates on an intramural basketball team, classmates in an academic setting, or fellow patrons at a party, and includes close or casual connections. These connections offer a sense of camaraderie and togetherness.
- **Appraisal Support:** Like emotional support, this type of support will likely come from a close, trusted companion. It gives honest feedback when needed, oftentimes in the form of "tough love." We all make mistakes and sometimes need a dose of cold, hard reality from someone who can help us to see beyond our own distorted perceptions. This type of support offers that in a caring rather than critical manner.

Ask yourself: Are you getting these types of support in your life? If at least one of these forms of social support is being provided when you need it, you'll experience greater fulfillment, ease and a sense of satisfaction in your daily experience. The important thing to acknowledge here is that we all have needs that must be met, and we can't meet them all on our own. Social support helps us to get our own basic needs met so that we can not only survive but thrive in our lives.

As these many types of support suggest, our lives are made up of a vast number of relationships, ranging from the closest, most intimate connections to those unknown people we interact with through chance or circumstance.

Relationship Levels: Inner, Middle, Outer

All the relationships that make up our lives can be categorized into three separate levels, as based on a theory outlined by evolutionary psychologist Dr. Robin Dunbar. Each level correlates with one of the three dimensions of loneliness (which we'll discuss in more detail momentarily). Think of all the relationships in your life as a set of concentric circles that widen as they move outwards. The time that you devote to a particular relationship tends to dictate which level it's situated in. As a rule, our inner-circle relationships require over 60% of our focus.

Naturally, we focus the most energy on those closest to us: our spouses, immediate family members, and closest friends. That being said, the other two levels are just as important, even if they're not as intimate and focal in our lives. More importantly than time, connections can be categorized by the degree of intimacy involved:

- **Inner Level:** Considering the significant time and energy commitment given to those on this level, we tend to have a smaller number of inner level connections. For some (such as an extrovert like myself), there may be up to 15 people in your inner level, but even within *those*, we tend to have no more than five people we'd consider the closest individuals in our lives. There's a deep intimacy and understanding (and mutuality) that exists within these connections, which are often built over many years.

  Those on the inner level may be the only people you ever truly feel comfortable around—maybe the only ones who know the real, unfettered you. This may include your spouse or romantic partner, your parents, children, siblings, or best friends, among others. When there is a lack of relationships on your inner level, you are likely to experience intimate loneliness, which is a longing for close, cherished connections.

- **Middle Level:** This level contains our more generalized companions and acquaintances, those social relationships built on mutual interests, shared history, or any other common interest. While these relationships lack a certain intimacy, they are just as crucial to our capacity for joy. It has been estimated that this level can contain up to 150 people, who share any number of mutual interests that naturally bond one another. This level might include your closer neighbors, coworkers, teachers, casual friendships, and members of any groups that you're a part of.

   Being part of a group with shared desires or interests can bring happiness and a deep sense of belonging. (Just ask any sports fan what it's like watching a game *with* fellow fans, rather than on their own!). When this level of relationships is lacking, one can develop a sense of relational loneliness, which is characterized by feelings of a lack of social engagement in one's life.

- **Outer Level:** The third and final level of connection involves the largest number of people—up to 500 for some—and involves the least amount of intimacy possible while still maintaining a clearly established connection. This level helps foster a sense of community and belonging to a larger collective and can spark a sense of being a part of something greater than yourself. These casual connections—maintained through a friendly hello each morning to your coworker, or perhaps flashing a smile at the other regulars on your bus route—support our overall health and well-being. A lack on this level can lead to feelings of collective loneliness, in which one feels a lack of belonging to a community.

I hope you're beginning to get a clear picture of how your relationships, from your closest connections all the way to your casual acquaintances, are monumentally important to your physical, mental, and emotional health. So, what do you do if your connections are lacking or insufficient? Let's look at an enormous, and often misunderstood, epidemic of modern life: loneliness.

Don't Leave Me All Alone: The Real Risks of Loneliness and Isolation

Loneliness has been on the rise for decades, but one of the most damaging impacts of the global pandemic has been the skyrocketing rates of loneliness and isolation. A 2021 Harvard University report found that 36% of Americans feel "serious loneliness," and that the rates are even higher among young adults and new mothers. Loneliness has reached epidemic levels in our culture—a public health crisis with detrimental effects on our collective health and happiness.

What factors make someone more vulnerable to loneliness? Things like your family and cultural upbringing can play a role. *Interdependent cultures*, like Japan, which are more focused on family and community, have lower reported rates of loneliness, while *independent cultures* like the United States, which are more individualistic, have higher rates of loneliness. Gender can also play a role. Men, in general, have a greater difficulty with overcoming feelings of loneliness, likely stemming from the fact that it is considered taboo in most cultures for men to express any emotional need or vulnerability. Men are expected to be stoic and inflexible, hiding their true feelings from the world rather than seeking help. Women, in general, are more conditioned to express their emotions and seek social support.

Of course, there are many other individual factors as well. This isn't to say that women, or individuals raised within interdependent cultures, are immune to loneliness. We all experience lonely feelings from time to time, and our personal life circumstances and personalities ultimately are the greatest determinants.

Whatever the contributing factors, the negative health impacts of loneliness are universal. Among other discoveries, the Harvard-Grant Study reinforced existing research findings on the negative health impacts of loneliness. Everyone experiences loneliness at some point in their life, so there's no shame if this is something you've struggled with. Have compassion for yourself and remember that loneliness is a universal human experience.

Research has implicated loneliness in a smorgasbord of health problems, including:

- High blood pressure
- Lower lifespan
- Increased depression and anxiety
- Reduce impulse control
- Worsen immune system
- Higher stress levels and feelings of aggression
- Accelerated cognitive decline with aging
- Poor sleep hygiene

Loneliness has been shown to be just as damaging to one's physical health as smoking or obesity. Social psychologist John Cacioppo hypothesizes that the feeling of loneliness triggers a mental alarm like hunger or thirst. When we need to eat, we feel hungry, and when we need to drink, we feel thirsty; ergo, when we need social interaction with another human, we feel lonely. It's an indicator of a basic survival need that is asking to be met.

Those lonely feelings activate the sympathetic nervous system, releasing stress hormones like epinephrine and adrenaline, and triggering the body's fight-flight-freeze response. As you may recall, our brains cannot decipher the difference between physical and emotional pain (and between a real or imagined threat). So, when we feel lonely, our brain and body experiences it as a real survival threat and can remain in a heightened state of stress and hypervigilance over long periods of time. This, in turn, can lead to inflammation and stress-related health problems over time.

This physical danger of loneliness may be best exemplified by an ailment called Takotsubo Syndrome. Colloquially known as 'broken heart syndrome,' it's a rare, occasionally fatal condition where a sudden, extremely stressful event, like the loss of a loved one, severely weakens the heart. Symptoms can mimic those of congestive heart failure, appearing as though the heart literally *breaks* when a vital relationship is lost.

To be clear, my intention in providing this information is to empower you, rather than to add fear or shame on top of the already painful experience of loneliness. I know that being lonely is hard enough already, without adding a worry about all the harmful physical and mental health impacts. But I promise, we'll get into some easy and accessible ways to cultivate strong and meaningful relationships in your life—and to feel a greater sense of connection, even if you find it difficult to meet new people.

A challenge of loneliness is that it often begets more loneliness in a vicious cycle. When you feel isolated is when you need connection the most, but also when it tends to feel the hardest to reach out. Loneliness often exacerbates negative thoughts and emotions, which in turn makes it more difficult to engage in the kind of behaviors and actions that can reduce lonely feelings (like reaching out to a friend or striking up a conversation with a coworker or acquaintance). Breaking the cycle of loneliness isn't always easy, but I assure you, it can be done.

When you feel lonely—which could involve being physically alone or feeling emotionally detached from others—it can be hard to maintain enough self-compassion to overcome the negative thoughts swirling around your mind. But in times of loneliness, self-compassion is the single most valuable tool in your toolkit. Revisit the previous chapter as many times as you need to and draw on the provided practices liberally. Keep reminding yourself that loneliness is a universal human experience. We all feel alone sometimes, and we're all equally deserving of compassion when experiencing the pain of isolation.

Alone But Not Lonely

It's important to note that *alone* does not equal *lonely*. Not all forms of isolation lead to lonely feelings. We've all experienced joyful times when it was just us, doing what we love and feeling full of life, and other times when we've been surrounded by other people and have felt complete disconnection. The term solitude describes the positive state of being alone, when a person actively chooses to disengage from other people for a set period in order to nourish and reconnect with themselves. Solitude can give us a chance to recharge our mental batteries and reflect on who we truly are and wish to be, independent of outside influences. The key factor here is *connection*. If you feel connected to yourself or others, you're unlikely to feel lonely. If you feel disconnected, then you may experience loneliness even if you're in a committed partnership or a strong community.

A healthy practice of solitude can be in small doses, with a conscious intention to connect with oneself. Living in solitude forever is a recipe for misery— just ask any prisoner who's been locked in solitary confinement for an extended period. As this extreme example shows, extended solitude can literally be a form of torture.

Modern technology adds another layer here, as it can simultaneously keep us more connected to others while making us feel more disconnected. Social media can be both a blessing and a curse in our efforts to thwart loneliness, particularly if we don't use our online interactions to blossom real life, face-to-face encounters. It bears repeating it's the *feelings of connection* that matter, not how often we're in contact with others.

When we can't be physically near our closest, inner level companions, online interaction can be a helpful substitute. During the pandemic, for instance, many of my patients experienced immense gratitude for virtual tools like Zoom, FaceTime, and social media, which allowed them to stay connected to their loved ones. But if communicating through social media *replaces* real, person-to-person interactions, the positive impacts will be limited, and the interaction will do little to mitigate feelings of loneliness.

Come A Little Closer: How to Cultivate and Maintain Close Connections

How can you foster new connections, and find greater intimacy and support in the relationships that already exist in your life?

While there's no magic bullet to building strong relationships, there are many strategies that you can draw on to increase the quality and quantity of connections in your life. As long as you stay patient, and commit to putting in the effort over time, you *will* be able to create new relationships and improve your existing ones. And with a stable of strong, positive relationships, you can boost your own capacity for joy and set yourself up for a long life of happiness and fulfillment.

- **Make the Time**

    You're busy—I get it. We all have a lot going on and many demands on our time, but if you truly want to maintain a connection with someone, or start a new relationship, you have to be willing to put in the effort. Active and fulfilling social lives are characterized by people who value their relationships and are prepared to reach out. Make yourself available to people and activities, rather than avoiding socializing. Make that phone call just to check in, invite your friend to go on a walk with you, or strike up a conversation with your co-worker instead of remaining silent.

    These little actions will go a long way in boosting your happiness (trust me!).

- **Be Brave**

    It can be scary to put yourself out there and risk being rejected by another person. Be willing to be courageous! Recognize that you are braver, and stronger, than you may believe during a negative moment. Draw inspiration from Jia Jiang, who sought out rejection every day for 100 days (by doing things like asking a stranger for $100), as a way to desensitize himself to rejection. The outcome? He found that asking for what you want can open up surprising possibilities where there previously were none. I recommend watching Jiang's TED Talk, "What I Learned From 100 Days Of Rejection," if you struggle with a fear of rejection.

- **Use Past Connections**

    We all have relationships that may have become dormant or faded away over the years. Reaching out to people you know and like, who have already demonstrated that they can bring happiness to your life, is a great place to start, particularly if the prospect of meeting new people feels daunting for you. Work your way up by starting with lapsed relationships first.

- **Withhold Judgment**

    Just like you shouldn't judge yourself or be self-critical of your own faults, make sure to do others the same courtesy. Be kind, compassionate and understanding in your interactions. Remember the Golden Rule, and you'll find that developing connections with other people is much easier when you do unto others as you would wish to have done unto you.

- **Share Your Authentic Self**

    If you want to develop a real, genuine connection with another person, you have to be willing to be vulnerable with other people. Tell others your story, share your unfiltered self, and you'll foster close connections with people who accept the real you. False connections won't do much for you, anyway, so just ditch the pseudo-relationships and focus on cultivating the real thing.

- **Share An Experience**

    A great way to cement a relationship is to have shared experiences. Instead of always just meeting for coffee or talking on the phone, try something new with the people you spend time with—like going on a hike, trying a new activity, or volunteering together. Shared experiences create a context for shared memories and a strong connection based on shared values.

When They Long to Be Close to You: 36 Questions to Increase Intimacy

While all relationships are important to living a rich and fulfilling life, our most intimate and lasting relationships are the most consequential for our happiness. The ability to be vulnerable with another human—to bare your soul to another person without fear or judgment or backlash—is a beautiful thing. When you're able to maintain that level of closeness with someone you love, happiness is the natural result.

There's a wonderful researched-backed tool for building intimacy that I love, from husband-and-wife psychology research duo Arthur and Elaine Aron. The Aron's developed a handy questionnaire designed to expedite the often-lengthy process of growing closer as couple.

Popularly known as "The 36 Questions that Lead to Love," these questions have been widely culturally adopted, including in a memorable interaction between Sheldon and Penny on an episode of *The Big Bang Theory* (spoiler alert: the two did not fall in love). The popularity of these questions reflects their value as a tool for improving one's level of intimacy with another person—not only a romantic partner, but also a platonic friend.

When asking these questions with another person—whether it be a romantic partner, a close friend, a family member, or anyone else—it's recommended you take 15 minutes for each set of questions, alternating between who asks and who answers first with each question. Then Aron's advice is to move onto the next set of questions after 15 minutes, whether you've finished or not. However, if you feel so inclined, feel free to take your time and answer every question thoroughly.

Set I

1. Given the choice of anyone in the world, whom would you want as a dinner guest?
2. Would you like to be famous? In what way?

3. Before making a telephone call, do you ever rehearse what you are going to say? Why?
4. What would constitute a "perfect" day for you?
5. When did you last sing to yourself? To someone else?
6. If you were able to live to the age of 90 and retain either the mind or body of a 30-year-old for the last 60 years of your life, which would you want?
7. Do you have a secret hunch about how you will die?
8. Name three things you and your partner appear to have in common.
9. For what in your life do you feel most grateful?
10. If you could change anything about the way you were raised, what would it be?
11. Take four minutes and tell your partner your life story in as much detail as possible.
12. If you could wake up tomorrow having gained any one quality or ability, what would it be?

Set II

13. If a crystal ball could tell you the truth about yourself, your life, the future, or anything else, what would you want to know?
14. Is there something that you've dreamed of doing for a long time? Why haven't you done it?
15. What is the greatest accomplishment of your life?
16. What do you value most in a friendship?
17. What is your most treasured memory?
18. What is your most terrible memory?
19. If you knew that in one year you would die suddenly, would you change anything about the way you are now living? Why?
20. What does friendship mean to you?
21. What roles do love, and affection play in your life?
22. Alternate sharing something you consider a positive characteristic of your partner. Share a total of five items.
23. How close and warm is your family? Do you feel your childhood was happier than most other people's?

24. How do you feel about your relationship with your mother?

Set III

25. Make three true "we" statements each. For instance, "We are both in this room feeling…"
26. Complete this sentence: "I wish I had someone with whom I could share…"
27. If you were going to become a close friend with your partner, please share what would be important for them to know.
28. Tell your partner what you like about them; be very honest this time, saying things that you might not say to someone you've just met.
29. Share with your partner an embarrassing moment in your life.
30. When did you last cry in front of another person? By yourself? 31. Tell your partner something that you like about them [already].
31. What, if anything, is too serious to be joked about?
32. If you were to die this evening with no opportunity to communicate with anyone, what would you most regret not having told someone? Why haven't you told them yet?
33. Your house, containing everything you own, catches fire. After saving your loved ones and pets, you have time to safely make a final dash to save any one item. What would it be? Why?
34. Of all the people in your family, whose death would you find most disturbing?
35. Why?
36. Share a personal problem and ask your partner's advice on how they might handle it. Also, ask your partner to reflect back to you how you seem to be feeling about the problem you have chosen.

> **CONSCIOUS COMMITMENTS**
>
> **Baby Step:**
> - Pick up the phone! Commit once a week to making one extra phone call to check in with a friend or family member and just say hello.
>
> **Bigger Step:**
> - Get involved! Join a book club, intramural sport, community group or volunteer organization—anything that involves doing something that you care about and meeting new people at the same time.

Never Thought I'd Need So Many People: Connections Make Happiness

Soon after my father's diagnosis, he moved back to L.A. to live with me, my husband, and our five-year-old son. We were unsure what to expect, and I was terrified of what the future had in store. I wondered *who* exactly was coming to live with us—which version of the man I'd known and loved my whole life. As I confided in my husband and several dear, close friends, it was horrifying to imagine my strong and vibrant father as a shell of his former self.

Even with those fears, which weren't exactly quelled by his continual confusion as to why he was staying with us, it was never a question, between my husband and I, whether we'd welcome my father into our home. This was my father, after all, and he had given *so much* to me throughout my lifetime. Now that the time had come to return the favor, I knew in my heart that I needed to step up to the plate.

As time went on, with my father slowly losing his grip on his day-to-day reality, it became more and more necessary to lean on those closest to me, drawing strength from their compassion, love and understanding. The ability to text a close friend, or get together with a beloved companion, was a lifesaver during those rough days.

Those relationships meant the world to me. My friends knew how grateful I was for them, and they knew that they could, in turn, reach out to me for care and comfort whenever they needed it. I'd always be there for them like they were there for me.

Even as his condition slowly deteriorated, having my father with me at his most vulnerable time was undoubtedly one of the best decisions I've ever made. Beyond the ability to remain recognizable to him as his disease progressed, it was a deeply rewarding experience to pay forward the same kind of compassion and comfort that he had always offered me. Helping the person who'd helped me the most in my life fostered feelings of personal satisfaction, and boosted my personal self-worth, giving me the strength to meet the challenges inherent to caretaking a person with Alzheimer's.

While my father remains alive—in theory, at least, since his presence does little more than serve as a living reminder of the man who no longer exists—I miss him every day. As heartbreaking as this reality is, I have no choice but to accept the hand we've been dealt and find comfort and support in the presence of the people I love.

My relationship with my father has provided countless joyful moments, while also helping me through life's inevitable setbacks and obstacles. As he faded from a coherent state of mind over the years, I depended on my closest friends and family. I've been able to continue onward—finding moments of happiness in my life every single day—because of those connections.

While my father may not be able to hear me tell him how grateful I am for all he's done for me, *I* can still express my gratitude, and use his example to be sure I savor every single second of my life's happiest moment. Let's complete our exploration of connection by looking at the single most important determinant of happiness: The ability to connect with the beauty and joy of life as a whole through gratitude and savoring the good.

CHAPTER 13

Happiness From the Inside Out: Finding Gratitude & Savoring the Good

Cindy, a 42-year-old married physician with two teen boys, started therapy because she was concerned about her inability to enjoy her life.

"Work sucks, my kids don't listen to me, and I can't see my friends or travel because of the pandemic," she complained. "Why would I want to be present, if being present means being more engaged in moments that suck?"

Cindy knew that mindfulness was a good thing, but she couldn't summon the energy or drive to practice it because she felt that the experiences of her life weren't worth being present for. She even started asking herself: "What's the point of my life?" It wasn't that her life was so awful, she admitted, but somehow, she still didn't feel like engaging in it! Cindy suddenly understood why people had midlife crises and bought ridiculous sports cars. Joy was nowhere to be found in their lives, and they just needed to shake things up.

Listening to Cindy, I knew that she wasn't ready to start with priming. Before she could begin taking small actions towards happiness, we had to go straight to the source: to the feeling and experience of happiness itself. Cindy needed to see what she was missing and to connect with the feelings that she knew she could *choose* to bring into her life. So, I went straight to the most powerful tool in the happiness arsenal: *gratitude*.

Teaching her how to practice gratitude was my way of giving her a jump start, helping her to generate the motivation and will she needed to start taking daily actions towards building a happier life.

The Hidden Power of Gratitude

While there's no one simple method for finding happiness, one practice stands above the rest, and that's *gratitude*. Look around at how lucky you are to be alive...right now!

Have you ever heard the expression "happiness is wanting what you have"? *That's* the power of gratitude. It takes us out of lack, judgment, jealousy, worry and negativity, and trains our focus on the many blessings available to us, right here and right now. The concept of gratitude is quite simple: Gratitude is an active appreciation for what you have in your life. Gratitude is about expressing, either to yourself or to others, your thankfulness for the people you care about; for yourself; for the natural wonders of the world; for *simply being alive*. That begins with noticing and focusing on the positive aspects of yourself and your life. And it's one of the greatest tools in your neuroplasticity arsenal to make your brain work for you in your pursuit of happiness. There is a huge amount of research on the many benefits of gratitude, which we'll get into shortly. But it wasn't just the wealth of data that convinced me of the direct correlation between gratitude and happiness. More than anything else, it was my firsthand experience of my patients' transformations over the years through the practice of gratitude. Witnessing the power of gratitude transform people's lives was the reason I felt compelled to share this information with you.

As I suspected, gratitude was just what Cindy needed. After a few weeks of various gratitude practices, including writing a letter of appreciation to her older sister, who had been instrumental in raising Cindy and helping her through medical school, she walked into my office one afternoon and said, "Fatemeh, I can't believe it. I am looking at all my relationships in a whole new light. I feel closer than I have ever felt to my family and friends. I feel truly blessed for all the love and support that I have in my life."

Nothing had changed in Cindy's life—but she was finally opening her eyes to what had been there all along. Gratitude opened her up to a greater level of connection. That's why we're discussing gratitude as part of Step 3: *Connect*. When we live with an attitude of gratitude, we cultivate a deeper connection with ourselves, the people we care about, and life.

No matter what is going on in our lives, we can find countless things to be grateful for. In today's world, alongside the many difficulties, uncertainties and injustices, there is also plenty to be grateful for. When you consider the breadth of information available to us, or the unfathomably advanced technology that we are able to access, to say nothing of the majestic beauty of the natural world we're blessed to live within, it truly is a wonderful time to be alive. Life is a miracle!

Stop worrying about what you *don't* have in your life and start finding and expressing gratitude for what you *do* have.

You'll always catch more flies with honey than with vinegar, as the old saying goes. Be actively grateful towards who or whatever brings you happiness when it occurs, and you'll keep finding more and more things to be happy about in the future.

Why is it often so hard, then, to tap into gratitude? Even when we have so many things to be thankful for, we can't seem to get our focus off everything that's going wrong. As good as gratitude feels, most of us don't wake up in the morning feeling a rush of thankfulness for everything we're fortunate to have in our lives. Instead, we tend to focus on what we *don't* have, and how we can try to get whatever we perceive to be missing.

It should come as no surprise that when it comes to gratitude, our brain can work against us. Because of the way the brain is wired, we rarely focus on the positive things that we're grateful for. Instead, our brains try to protect us by focusing on the negative so that we can find ways to "fix" the problem or avoid it in the future.

As you recall, our brains are wired to remember and learn from negative things—as a way of trying to protect us from having them happen again. We become hypersensitive to anything negative that comes our way. As neuroscientist Rick Hanson puts it in his book *Hardwiring Happiness*, "The mind is like Velcro for negative experiences and Teflon for positive ones."

By practicing gratitude, we can consciously and actively rewire our brain's negativity bias, so that negative experiences stick less, and positive ones begin to take hold. Gratitude creates a total figure-ground perspective shift, bringing the good things in our lives to the forefront of our attention, and letting those things that are negative or lacking fade into the background.

Benefits of Gratitude

The benefits of expressing gratitude are practically endless. This list is by no means exhaustive, but it will give you a taste of how gratitude improves your health, well-being, happiness, and relationships. While there are many physical health benefits of gratitude (including improved sleep and a lowered risk for many diseases), I've focused on the ways that gratitude can improve your mental outlook and your life as a whole:

- **Improved Ability to Interpret Events Positively:** Gratitude helps you to see the good in all things. The conscious, consistent expression of gratefulness pushes you towards a positive interpretation of stimuli and events over a negative one. This means that gratitude helps activate and prioritize positive pathways in your brain, allowing you to find the silver lining in every situation in your life (like remembering that your family will continue loving you unconditionally even if you don't get the job you interviewed for).
- **Kick Jealousy to the Curb:** When you're grateful for what you have, and feel positively about yourself, you're much less likely to feel envious of other people, studies show. In fact, it's almost impossible to be grateful and jealous at the same time. After all, if you're truly grateful for your job, family, and home, then you won't be focused on someone else's job, family, or home. Gratitude makes your brain work for you by appreciating yourself, rather than lamenting what others have that you don't.
- **Boost Positive Feelings and Lower Depressive Ones:** People who feel and express gratitude for the good things in their

lives are much more likely to feel positive about themselves overall and experience positive emotions. Another study shows that those who express gratitude have a higher propensity for positive thoughts and emotions about themselves, leading to a more positive outlook on life, while reducing depressive feelings over time. And the more you think and feel positively, the more neuroplasticity shifts your neural pathways towards the positive.

- **Reduced Negative Thoughts and Emotions:** Those SNTs won't stand a chance when you're anchored in an attitude of gratitude! Expressing gratitude leads to increased positive thoughts and emotions. By triggering neuroplasticity, it creates and reinforces positive neural pathways in your brain, leading to fewer negative thoughts and emotions. In fact, research shows that practicing gratitude leads to a lower percentage of negative thoughts within just three weeks!
- **Improve Relationships and Feel More Connected to Others:** Expressing gratitude for the people we care about can boost our feelings of closeness to others, whether it's a platonic or romantic relationship. Considering how vital the presence of strong interpersonal relationships are to our happiness, anything that can boost the intimacy and genuineness of those connections should be welcomed with open arms. Go ahead, be thankful!

In one study, students who were asked to both express and think grateful things about a friend demonstrated a stronger connection with that friend, as well as feelings of greater personal investment in their friend's life. Another study showed that high school students who expressed gratitude towards their parents or other close adults increased their connection to that person.

In essence, feeling gratitude for the people in your life causes you to feel more positively towards them and treat them better, which in turn improves their feelings and behaviors towards you.

- **Positive Self-Image & Self-Compassion:** Self-compassion researcher Dr. Kristen Neff describes self-appreciation as the "flip side" of self-compassion. People who express gratitude are more able to find the good in themselves, and to see themselves and their personal traits from a glass-half-full perspective. Expressing gratitude can also make overcoming setbacks easier, by helping you to identify and utilize your personal strengths, and to feel capable and worthy of achieving your goals.
- **Foster Growth and Self-Improvement:** When you truly appreciate yourself and your life, you're more likely to place a high value on your own well-being, and to feel that you're worthy of the effort for self-growth. Gratitude can support you in believing in your ability to move towards the person you want to be and kick you into action. Gratitude for yourself also means you'll be motivated to take care of yourself, particularly through increased exercise, which will both PRIME your brain to work for you and improve your overall health.

Gratitude = Connection

Gratitude is not only the quickest route to achieving happiness but is also the best way to build and improve our connections with the people in our lives. Underpinning the many interpersonal benefits of gratitude is its ability to make us more trustworthy and appreciative in the eyes of others. If you're in a relationship and want to make your partner, feel good, research suggests that you should start by showing some gratitude for them. Day-to-day words of appreciation and small acts of kindness can go a long way, but if you're looking for a more unique way to express your love and gratitude, try putting thank-you notes in your partner's pocket, their drawer or any place where they may unexpectedly find it.

It's not only romantic relationships that benefit from expressions of gratitude, but also friendships. If you're looking to strengthen your friendships, gratitude is the answer. When you appreciate others and feel appreciated in return, you'll be more open to working through any problems, conflicts or concerns that may arise.

One of the greatest blessings in my life is the quality friendships that I have fostered over the years. All my friendships are extremely special to me, but my love and appreciation for my best friend of 40-plus years is the one that fills my heart with the most gratitude. Aside from regular texts expressing my feelings of gratitude for her, I decided recently to do something a little different to put a smile on her face. I gave her a framed picture of us when we were teenagers on vacation together—awkward hairdos and all—knowing that it would bring back for her the same fond memories of our time together.

Practicing gratitude *with* the people you love is also a great way to build intimacy and nurture strong relationships. Wanting my family to reap the benefits of gratitude, I introduced a dinner ritual of going around the table and sharing what we were grateful for that day. I was worried my pre-teen son might accuse me of "doing therapy on him," and, to be sure, he was a little resistant at first. But after a week or so, before I even had a chance to bring it up, my son would say, "What are you guys grateful for?" (Remember, gratitude feels good, so once we get started, it's very easy to want to continue!)

This practice has been amazing for my family. It really is a wonderful way for me to hear about what is going on in my fifth grader's life, beyond the usual "How was your day?" I recently learned that he had a classmate who lost his dog. For a few weeks after that, he would say from time to time, "I am so happy that Freddie is healthy," expressing heartfelt gratitude for our beloved family dog.

These statements of gratitude have really connected us as a family and allowed my husband and I to be more aware of where our son is emotionally in his life.

Tips For Practicing Gratitude In Your Community

Practicing gratitude within your wider community can also boost feelings of happiness, connection and belonging. Here are a few opportunities to integrate expressions of gratitude into your daily interactions:

- **Eating out:** Whenever you eat out at a restaurant, compliment the server on their positive attitude or their smile, and make sure to tip them, which lets them know you are thankful for their service.
- **Common courtesy:** Use basic words of appreciation like "thank you" and "please" at the bank or with the cashier at the grocery store, or simply hold open the door for someone else. Our actions impact others.
- **Random kindness:** An act of kindness can be as simple as helping someone with directions or lending a hand to someone carrying a heavy load.

Gratitude Journaling: Making Thankfulness a Daily Habit

To reap the many rewards of being grateful, we need to generate new habits and routines to create new neural pathways of gratitude in the brain. My personal favorite technique—and one that is backed by science and utilized by many psychologists, therapists, and coaches—is gratitude journaling.

Almost every single one of my clients also wants to know if there is a shortcut or a quicker road to being happy. Surprisingly, the answer is YES—and that shortcut is gratitude journaling.

There is a great deal of research that supports the power of this practice. You might think it sounds silly, but before you give up on the idea, let me explain *how* it is that gratitude journaling can work wonders in your life.

When you write down a list of what you're grateful for, you immediately and automatically shift your focus from the negative to the positive. This shift allows you to move away from obsessing about all the things that are wrong in your life to focusing on all the blessings that are present in your day-to-day life.

This shift in focus triggers a release of feel-good chemicals in your brain that promote happiness and well-being.

When you experience any type of gratitude, whether it's writing down what you're appreciating in the moment, noticing what's good in your life or expressing thanks to others for loving and supporting you, you're helping your brain to release dopamine (and we all know that dopamine makes us feel good!). Because it feels so good, you're naturally going to want more, which will trigger thoughts and actions that lead to more positive emotions and feelings of optimism.

But wait—there's more. When you put pen to paper and actually write down the blessings in your life, your brain also releases serotonin, that all-powerful, mood-enhancing chemical that has been called the "happy molecule." This means that you are actively building the gratitude circuits which will create new neural pathways to release even more feel-good chemicals on a regular and automatic basis—wiring your brain for happiness. Remember, "neurons that fire together wire together, "so get those positive neurons wiring with daily gratitude journaling!

The easiest way to get started with gratitude journaling is simply to list 5-10 things that you're grateful for, big or small, either in the morning or at the end of the day.

If you need a little help getting inspired, I put together some simple prompts that you can use at any time to get the words flowing. But before you put pen to paper and experiment with the prompts, keep in mind that it's ideal to do your journaling first thing in the morning, every day, to establish it as a ritual that ultimately becomes a strong habit. (Bonus points for "habit stacking": pair your journaling with five minutes of meditation to turbo charge your morning with positivity!

To get started, take in a few deep breaths, and consider what you're grateful for in the moment.

(Hint: it could be something as small as your delicious cup of coffee).

Gratitude Journal Prompts:

- ➤ What's a recent experience with a loved one that makes you feel grateful?
- ➤ What's a small thing that happened today that you're grateful for?
- ➤ What comforts in your life are you grateful for?
- ➤ What fond memories are you grateful for? Why are you grateful for those experiences?
- ➤ What do you appreciate about having the people in your life?

Incorporating Gratitude Into Your Life

Like many ancient proverbs, the saying "you reap what you sow"—or you get what you give in life—is rooted in actual truth. As a general rule, the more you express gratitude and kindness towards others, the more likely you are to receive gratitude in return.

Here are several proven ways to evoke feelings of gratitude, and reap the benefits of its awesome power:

- **Mental Subtraction:** Imagine your life *without* an important positive experience you've had, or without an immensely important person. What would your life be like if you had never met your spouse, or if you grew up without your mother or father? Perhaps you're a marine biologist, who fell in love with ocean life after a trip to the Great Barrier Reef in Australia. How would your life be different if you'd never taken that trip, and never discovered the aquatic amazement you so deeply love? Research shows that taking the time to appreciate the things or people you have in your life by imagining a world *without* them, can boost your ability to be grateful.

- **Gratitude Letters and Visits:** Devised by renowned psychologist Martin Seligman, founding father of the field of positive psychology, this technique involves writing out a letter of thanks towards someone you care about, then taking the time to read the letter to the person. In fact, one study showed that people who wrote gratitude letters once a week for 10 minutes, for a total of six weeks, experienced a stark increase in life satisfaction as compared to a control group.

  Making gratitude visits with people you feel you've taken for granted is another way to not only increase your joyfulness, but also ameliorate feelings of guilt or shame if you suspect that you've neglected people you care about.

- **Remember What You've Overcome:** You've been through hell before—as we all have in one way or another. How did it feel when you emerged? Reflect on the challenges you've overcome in your life and appreciate how lucky you are to still be living and breathing—and perhaps even thriving.

- **"Three Good Things" Nightly Journal:** Each night before bed, take a few minutes to write down three good things that happened during your day. When you make yourself search for positive moments on a consistent, nightly basis, you'll be much more likely to notice and appreciate those positive, happy events when they happen. Keeping a "three good things" nightly journal will help you overcome your negativity bias, rewiring your brain away from quick-trigger negative thoughts, not unlike the process of 'mental dumping' that you learned in the sleep chapter.

> ## Conscious Commitments
>
> **Baby Step:**
> - Keep a "three good things" nightly journal every night for one week. Notice at the end of the week if you're noticing more positive and pleasurable things in your daily life.
>
> **Bigger Step:**
> - Write a gratitude letter once a week for one month, and make sure to read the letter to the person you wrote it for. At the end of the month, write a reflection in your journal about the experience. Notice any shifts that may have occurred in your feelings of appreciation for your relationships.

Savoring Life's Great Wonders and Delights

Have you ever experienced an almost perfect moment in your life? A moment in time so spectacular that you wished it would last forever. We've all been there, whether it was eating an exquisitely delicious meal, enjoying a warm gathering with loved ones, or a tranquil stroll through a beautiful forest. There's nothing better than that glow of joy radiating from within. In those rare instances when you find yourself feeling immeasurably content, the natural response is to want to *fully savor them.*

What does it mean to savor the good? Right at the intersection of gratitude and mindfulness is the act of *savoring. Savoring* positive experiences in your life means allowing your focus to linger on a pleasant or joyful experience in order to really soak up and extend those joyous feelings. When you savor, you're taking the time to actively engross yourself in a wonderful moment—both during and after it occurs—to ensure that you make the most of it. Savoring is one of the greatest secrets to happiness because of its power to exponentially increase your levels of gratitude, which is why we're going to focus on it now.

By lingering and focusing on positive experiences, savoring literally rewires your brain towards the positive, allowing you to better absorb those moments and recognize them with greater frequency. Life may not be a constant stream of sunshine and lollipops, but it's not an endless stream of hellfire and brimstone, either. Savoring can increase your ability to *see* those pleasurable aspects of life that you may have been ignoring or overlooking when you were distracted by your internal dialogue or focused on the negative.

Simply put, savoring entails lingering in a positive moment, with mindful presence, for as long as possible. While it shares many benefits with mindfulness, savoring differs in that it involves assigning a positive label to your experience, rather than just neutrally observing it. Additionally, savoring utilizes neuroplasticity to overcome the brain's negativity bias over time, training your focus on positive experiences so that you can let in more of the good.

Proactively savoring those moments of sheer joy, rapture and even simple contentment literally rewires your brain to put more attention on positive experiences over negative ones. Research on people who practice savoring shows unanimous and staggering increases in happiness, self-satisfaction, and mental resilience.

The next time you find yourself flooded with delight, take notice, and let yourself really *feel* the positive feelings by bringing your full attention to them. It doesn't necessarily have to be an extraordinary event that is the trigger for savoring—often, it's those every day, simple pleasures that fill our hearts with good feelings. Maybe you're lounging on the beach on a sunny day without a care in the world or sitting on the couch with your husband binging Marvelous Mrs. Maisel, feeling full of warmth and comfort. Or you might be witnessing the majestic beauty of the stars on a clear evening. Whatever the experience, recognize that feeling and harness it, with focused attention, in the present moment.

Even if positivity isn't our default state of mind, we're all still capable of experiencing great pleasure and fulfillment in the positive moments of our lives as they occur. Stop and smell the roses, as they say, and *really* do it with your whole being: witness the vibrant color, admire the floral, earthy aroma, and how the scent tickles your nose as it dances its way in. Being mindful of life's small pleasures can help your brain gradually reroute its default neural state from negative to positive. This also means that you'll be more likely to remember positive events, creating a storehouse of happy memories to support you on your path to a happy life.

Benefits of Savoring

Savoring those positive, joyful experiences can help negate some of the negativity that we naturally may feel in response to life's challenges, frustrations, and setbacks, while also supporting feelings of gratitude. Some of the other noteworthy benefits of savoring include:

- **Less Negative Emotions:** Savoring has been shown to decrease your negative feelings, while lowering your stress and depression levels. Additionally, the chances of dealing with anhedonia (the inability to feel any pleasure) drastically drop when you practice savoring.
- **Improved Relationships (Romantic and Platonic):** When you savor the joyful moments within your romantic relationships, particularly in the company of your significant other, the bonds deepen between you. In fact, research shows that both male and female partners who had savored and felt savored by their partner, too-were more likely to be happier and more secure in their relationship seven years later.

When you take the time to savor those wonderful moments, big and small, you'll find that these seemingly rare moments of unabated happiness likely occur more often than you realized. You'll quickly learn that life is full of beauty, wonder and joy for anyone whose eyes are open enough to see it.

Savoring In Daily Life

Here are some easy and enjoyable ways to incorporate savoring in your daily life.

- **Consider Yourself Lucky**

We all know how hard life can be. When things are going well, count your blessings and enjoy the good times—instead of just waiting for the other shoe to drop. Remind yourself of how lucky you are to be where you are, doing what you're doing, instead of being stuck somewhere you don't like doing something you don't want to do.

- **Celebrate YOU**

 When good things happen to you, *enjoy them*! Luxuriating in your joys and successes helps maximize your ability to feel pleasure and letting yourself get lost in your own enjoyment increases the likelihood of that positive moment being stored in your memory, allowing you to continually draw on it as a source of joy. Give yourself permission to celebrate *you*.

- **Save a Keepsake**

 If it's possible, try retaining some sort of souvenir from a notably pleasurable experience (say, the ticket stub from a fun concert or a pressed flower from a beautiful wedding). Having a keepsake will improve your ability to recall that memory and its associated feelings using the physical reminder.

- **Utilize Memory Building**

 We've talked about how mentally visualizing yourself completing a task can help you to complete the task successfully. Similarly, taking the time to cement a mental picture of a savored experience can enhance your ability to recall the memory in the future.

- **Remember: All Things Must End**

 Impermanence can be a beautiful reminder of the preciousness of life. Keep in mind the fleeting nature of life—and the fact that all good things must come to an end—as a way to remember to appreciate and enjoy every experience in the moment.

- **Share the Moment**

    Considering the importance of connection, it should come as no surprise that sharing joyful moments with others is the best way to enrich the experience. Research has shown that people who share exciting news or positive moments with their friends, family, or anyone else in their lives, experience greater happiness than those who simply celebrate in the dark. In fact, simply *thinking* about sharing good news with another person can boost your bliss.

- **Improve Romantic Relationships with Anticipation**

    Savoring your experiences in relationships can also include anticipating a positive experience with that person, which has been shown to strengthen the connection. This anticipatory thinking has the power to accurately predict future happiness within a relationship, according to research.

- **Reminisce on Happy Times**

    Research has shown that actively taking the time to reminisce and reflect on past positive experiences can increase your feelings of happiness, in as little as one week. Taking a positive trip down memory lane can also reduce depressive feelings as you get older and has the potential to improve cognitive functionality as you age.

Bringing It All Together: Taking Your Next Steps Towards a Happier Life

So, what's next? Clearly, as much as we wish it were different, human beings aren't neurologically wired to simply *be* or *feel happy*. Happiness is about what we *do*. It requires a series of conscientious and repetitive actions—daily, over the long term—to ensure we find genuine, sustainable contentment throughout our lives. Throughout this book, I've shared a number of individual life choices proven to stimulate positivity while also breaking down some of the innate brain barriers we all face as human beings in maximizing our own happiness.

We've established that fostering joyful feelings is dependent on both internal and external factors. Anyone can be happy, despite their genetics and life circumstances, by making the *choice* to be happy and by *acting* on that choice. Choosing happiness, as you've learned, involves both internal shifts in our mindset and emotional regulation as well as external changes in the way we act and live our lives. Remember the 75-year-long Harvard study, which concluded that relationships are the greatest determinant of long-term health and happiness. But while the power and importance of strong connections and social support can't be overstated, it doesn't change the fact that cultivating sustainable happiness is an inside-out affair.

The three-step **Prime, Shift, Connect** system is designed to help you address both the inner and the outer factors of happiness in the easiest, most efficient way possible, starting with the foundation. Operating at your peak personal potential—guided by what *you* value and desire in *your* life—is a step-by-step process of gradually changing your behavior and rewiring your brain over time. To recap, the basic steps are:

PRIME:
1. *Prime* your brain through *Exercise, Sleep, & Meditation/Mindfulness*

SHIFT:
2. *Shift* your *Routines & Habits*, replacing bad ones with healthy and positive ones
3. *Reset your mindset by learning* to *understand* and *cope* with your Emotions and Thoughts
4. Discover *Values* and reorient your life around them

CONNECT:
5. Practice *Self-Compassion* to build a more loving and supportive relationship with yourself
6. Connect with other people, and maintain strong, healthy *Relationships*

7. Deepen your connection and appreciation with all of life through *Gratitude and Savoring*

Thanks to neuroplasticity, if you're able to integrate and practice the steps listed above, I guarantee that you will have taken monumental strides towards rewiring your brain for greater happiness and fulfillment.

I've already laid out several evidence-based techniques and strategies, backed by research, along with some thorough explanations on the natural difficulties found in finding happiness. Frankly, at this point, you already know the majority of available tools in your arsenal with everything we've discussed thus far. Now, the idea is to take everything you've learned, and make sure you're squeezing every last beneficial drop from the research presented.

The Journey Ahead

Here we are at the end of *Wired For Happiness,* and I would like to leave you with a few final thoughts to help you continue your journey to a happier, more fulfilling life. Here are some of the most important things that I hope you will take away from this book:

We will all experience obstacles, losses, pain, and disappointments in our lives, but no matter how far off track you may feel, remember that you always have the choice to turn things around with tiny steps and repeated actions.

Rewiring your brain for happiness takes time, so celebrate the successes along the way, savoring even the tiny ones. I know how difficult it can be to develop positive new habits and to commit to shifting negative patterns of thought and emotion, but I am hoping that with the tools you've gained, you will be able to move forward and build those new, positive neural pathways

You don't need to change the circumstances of your life or get anything that you don't already have to find happiness. You have the power to improve what's already here. Remember to be thankful for the positives in your life and to cherish and nurture supportive connections as if your life depends on it—because, in fact, it does.

Don't underestimate the priming step. Our happiness is cultivated from within, and the starting point is how you take care of yourself and prioritize your wellbeing. Give yourself breaks along the way, knowing that you may veer off the path at times. Catch yourself having those black and white thoughts and the need for perfectionism, for instance, and instead focus on being grateful for all that you have in the present moment.

Over the years in my work with thousands of patients who had anxiety and depression, or were simply feeling disconnected and dissatisfied, I heard one thing repeatedly, and that is their wish to live a more fulfilling and happier life. It is my hope that by using the strategies in *Wired For Happiness*, you will be able to experience more joy and connection in your life, experience more gratitude for the blessings that are present day-to-day, and flourish in your connections with yourself and others.

After using the three-step strategy of **Prime-Shift-Connect**, one of my patients said to me, "I feel a deeper level of satisfaction in my life that I didn't think was possible." What could be better than that?

We all long for sustainable happiness, for the rich connections with our loved ones and a sense of wellbeing. We are all capable of achieving this through the magical abilities of our brain and our own committed actions.

I have also created the Wired For Happiness Planner for those of you who want an actionable daily blueprint to using the strategies in this book and living your best life.

In closing, there are many free resources for you to continue your journey of happiness on my website at **www.farahanterhapy.com** . I wish you all the best in your new journey.

Acknowledgments

Gratefulness is a big part of my life, as well as my book. So, I would like to take this opportunity to express how thankful I am to all the people who have helped to make my book possible and to all those who have contributed to making my life happier and more joyous.

First, I am grateful to my son who is my greatest source of happiness and greatest achievement. Thank you to my family, of course being Persian, which includes not only my parents who laid the foundation for my happiness but in particular my mom, aunt, brother, cousins and my husband whose regular practical and emotional support made it possible for me to complete this book.

I couldn't have written this book without Adam Swierk who helped develop the writing, and the tone of this book contributing countless hours of revisions and invaluable feedback.

Dr. Richard Nongard. Thank you for your wisdom, and patience.

Deep thanks to my wonderful research assistant Katherine Iwasiutyn for her endless persistence. Much gratitude to Carolyn Gregorie for her editing and thoughtful suggestions. My thanks also go to my dear friend and amazing writer Stacey Rukeyser for providing her expert recommendations on the structure of the book.

It's impossible to think of what my life would be like without my clients and all that they add to my life daily. Thank you.

I am blessed to have so many people in my life that support my son, husband, and I. Our friends, neighbors, and school community, thank you for helping us and bringing so much joy into our lives.

REFERENCES

Chapter 1

Brickman, P., Coates, D., & Janoff-Bulman, R. (1978). Lottery winners and accident victims: is happiness relative?. *Journal of personality and social psychology*, *36* (8), 917–927.

Dunn, E. W., Gilbert, D. T., & Wilson, T. D. (2011). If money doesn't make you happy, then you probably aren't spending it right. *Journal of Consumer Psychology*, *21* (2), 115-125.

Danner, Deborah D.,Snowdon, David A.,Friesen, Wallace V.(2001) Positive Emotions in Early Life and Longevity: Findings From the Nun Study, Journal of Personality and Social Psychology 80(5), 804-813

Tierney, J and Baumeister, R (2021) The Power of Bad

Herculano-Houzel, S. (2012). The remarkable, yet not extraordinary, human brain as a scaled-up primate brain and its associated cost. *Proceedings of the National Academy of Sciences*, *109* (Supplement 1), 10661-10668.

Ware, D. Neurons that Fire Together Wire Together. *Psychologists Guide to Emotional Wellbeing*.

Vaish, A., Grossmann, T., & Woodward, A. (2008). Not all emotions are created equal: the negativity bias in social-emotional development. *Psychological bulletin*, *134* (3), 383–403.

Ilona Papousek, Karin Nauschnegg, Manuela Paechter, Helmut K. Lackner, Nandu Goswami, Günter Schulter,(2010) Trait and state positive affect and cardiovascular recovery from experimental academic stress,Biological Psychology, 83(2) 108-115,

Chapter 3

Norris, C. J. (2021). The negativity bias, revisited: Evidence from neuroscience measures and an individual differences approach. *Social neuroscience*, *16* (1), 68-82.

Demarin, V., & MOROVIĆ, S. (2014). Neuroplasticity. *Periodicum biologorum, 116* (2), 209-211.

Chapter 4

Lardone, A., Liparoti, M., Sorrentino, P., Rucco, R., Jacini, F., Polverino, A., Minino, R., Pesoli,

M., Baselice, F., Sorriso, A., Ferraioli, G., Sorrentino, G., & Mandolesi, L. (2018). Mindfulness

Meditation Is Related to Long-Lasting Changes in Hippocampal Functional Topology during Resting State: A Magnetoencephalography Study. *Neural plasticity*, *2018*, 1-9.

Lazar, S. W., Kerr, C. E., Wasserman, R. H., Gray, J. R., Greve, D. N., Treadway, M. T.,

McGarvey, M., Quinn, B. T., Dusek, J. A., Benson, H., Rauch, S. L., Moore, C. I., & Fischl, B. (2005). Meditation experience is associated with increased cortical thickness. *Neuroreport*, *16* (17), 1893–1897.

Jha, A.P., Krompinger, J. & Baime, M.J. (2007). Mindfulness training modifies subsystems of attention. *Cognitive, Affective, & Behavioral Neuroscience, 7*, 109–119.

Taren, A. A., Creswell, J. D., & Gianaros, P. J. (2013). Dispositional mindfulness co-varies with smaller amygdala and caudate volumes in community adults. *PloS one*, *8* (5), e64574.

Kral, T., Schuyler, B. S., Mumford, J. A., Rosenkranz, M. A., Lutz, A., & Davidson, R. J. (2018). Impact of short- and long-term mindfulness meditation training on amygdala reactivity to emotional stimuli. *NeuroImage* , *181* , 301–313.

Hölzel, B. K., Carmody, J., Vangel, M., Congleton, C., Yerramsetti, S. M., Gard, T., & Lazar, S. W. (2011). Mindfulness practice leads to increases in regional brain gray matter density. *Psychiatry research* , *191* (1), 36–43.

Luders, E., Cherbuin, N., & Kurth, F. (2015). Forever Young(er): potential age-defying effects of long-term meditation on gray matter atrophy. *Frontiers in psychology*, *5* , 1551.

Lutz, A., Greischar, L. L., Rawlings, N. B., Ricard, M. Davidson, R. J. (2004). Long-term meditators self-induce high-amplitude gamma synchrony during mental practice. *PNAS, 101* (46), 16369-16373.

Gamboa, P. M., Jáuregui, I., Gonzalez, G., Fernandez, J. C., & Antépara, I. (1991). Allergic contact dermatitis from tali (missanda) wood (Erythrophleum guianense). *Contact dermatitis* , *24* (4), 309.

Turakitwanakan, W., Mekseepralard, C., & Busarakumtragul, P. (2013). Effects of mindfulness meditation on serum cortisol of medical students. *Journal of the Medical Association of Thailand, 96 Suppl 1* , S90–S95.

Davidson, R. J., Kabat-Zinn, J., Schumacher, J., Rosenkranz, M., Muller, D., Santorelli, S. F., Urbanowski, F., Harrington, A., Bonus, K., & Sheridan, J. F. (2003). Alterations in brain and immune function produced by mindfulness meditation. *Psychosomatic medicine* , *65* (4), 564–570.

Epel, E., Daubenmier, J., Moskowitz, J. T., Folkman, S., & Blackburn, E. (2009). Can meditation slow rate of cellular aging? Cognitive stress, mindfulness, and telomeres. *Annals of the New York Academy of Sciences* , *1172* , 34–53.

Mehta, R., Sharma, K., Potters, L., Wernicke, A. G., & Parashar, B. (2019). Evidence for the Role of Mindfulness in Cancer: Benefits and Techniques. *Cureus*, *11* (5), e4629.

Lam, A. G., Sterling, S., Margines, E. (2015). Effects of Five-Minute Mindfulness Meditation on Mental Health Care Professionals. *J Psychol Clin Psychiatry*, *2* (3), 00076.

He, X., Shi, W., Han, X., Wang, N., Zhang, N., & Wang, X. (2015). The interventional effects of loving-kindness meditation on positive emotions and interpersonal interactions. *Neuropsychiatric disease and treatment*, *11*, 1273–1277.

Levine, G. N., Lange, R. A., Bairey-Merz, C. N., Davidson, R. J., Jamerson, K., Mehta, P. K., Michos, E. D., Norris, K., Ray, I. B., Saban, K. L., Shah, T., Stein, R., & Smith, S. C. (2017). Meditation and cardiovascular risk reduction. *J ournal of the American Heart Association, 6* (10), 1-57.

Chapter 5

Xie, L., Kang, H., Xu, Q., Chen, M. J., Liao, Y., Thiyagarajan, M., O'Donnell, J., Christensen, D. J., Nicholson, C., Iliff, J. J., Takano, T., Deane, R., & Nedergaard, M. (2013). Sleep drives metabolite clearance from the adult brain. *Science (New York, N.Y.)*, *342* (6156), 373–377.

Gorgoni, M., D'Atri, A., Lauri, G., Rossini, P. M., Ferlazzo, F., & De Gennaro, L. (2013). Is sleep essential for neural plasticity in humans, and how does it affect motor and cognitive recovery?. *Neural plasticity*, *2013*, 103949.

Fultz, N. E., Bonmassar, G., Setsompop, K., Stickgold, R. A., Rosen, B. R., Polimeni, J. R., & Lewis, L. D. (2019). Coupled electrophysiological, hemodynamic, and cerebrospinal fluid oscillations in human sleep. *Science (New York, N.Y.)*, *366* (6465), 628–631.

Joo, E. Y., Kim, H., Suh, S., & Hong, S. B. (2014). Hippocampal substructural vulnerability to sleep disturbance and cognitive impairment in patients with chronic primary insomnia: magnetic resonance imaging morphometry. *Sleep*, *37* (7), 1189–1198.

Tempesta, D., Salfi, F., De Gennaro, L., & Ferrara, M. (2020). The impact of five nights of sleep restriction on emotional reactivity. *Journal of sleep research*, *29* (5), e13022.

Bourdillon, N., Jeanneret, F., Nilchian, M., Albertoni, P., Ha, P., & Millet, G. P. (2021). Sleep Deprivation Deteriorates Heart Rate Variability and Photoplethysmography. *Frontiers in neuroscience*, *15*, 642548.

Pesoli, M., Rucco, R., Liparoti, M., Lardone, A., D'Aurizio, G., Minino, R., Troisi Lopez, E., Paccone, A., Granata, C., Curcio, G., Sorrentino, G., Mandolesi, L., & Sorrentino, P. (2022). A night of sleep deprivation alters brain connectivity and affects specific executive functions. *Neurological sciences : official journal of the Italian Neurological Society and of the Italian Society of Clinical Neurophysiology*, *43* (2), 1025–1034.

Morselli, L., Leproult, R., Balbo, M., & Spiegel, K. (2010). Role of sleep duration in the regulation of glucose metabolism and appetite. *Best practice & research. Clinical endocrinology & metabolism*, *24* (5), 687–702.

Copinschi G. (2005). Metabolic and endocrine effects of sleep deprivation. *Essential Psychopharmacology, 6* (6), 341-347.

Irwin M. R. (2019). Sleep and inflammation: partners in sickness and in health. *Nature reviews. Immunology*, *19* (11), 702–715.

Bishir, M., Bhat, A., Essa, M. M., Ekpo, O., Ihunwo, A. O., Veeraraghavan, V. P., Mohan, S. K.,

Mahalakshmi, A. M., Ray, B., Tuladhar, S., Chang, S., Chidambaram, S. B., Sakharkar, M. K., Guillemin, G. J., Qoronfleh, M. W., & Ojcius, D. M.

(2020). Sleep Deprivation and Neurological Disorders. *BioMed research international*, *2020*, 5764017.

Van Someren, E. J., Cirelli, C., Dijk, D. J., Van Cauter, E., Schwartz, S., & Chee, M. W. (2015). Disrupted Sleep: From Molecules to Cognition. *The Journal of neuroscience : the official journal of the Society for Neuroscience*, *35* (41), 13889–13895.

Scharf, M. T., Naidoo, N., Zimmerman, J. E., & Pack, A. I. (2008). The energy hypothesis of sleep revisited. Progress in neurobiology, 86(3), 264–280.

Arble, D. M., Bass, J., Behn, C. D., Butler, M. P., Challet, E., Czeisler, C., Depner, C. M.,

Elmquist, J., Franken, P., Grandner, M. A., Hanlon, E. C., Keene, A. C., Joyner, M. J.,

Karatsoreos, I., Kern, P. A., Klein, S., Morris, C. J., Pack, A. I., Panda, S., Ptacek, L. J., ... Wright, K. P. (2015). Impact of sleep and circadian disruption on energy balance and diabetes: A summary of workshop discussions. Sleep, 38(12), 1849–1860.

Herring, M. P., Monroe, D. C., Kline, C. E., O'Connor, P. J., & MacDonncha, C. (2018). Sleep quality moderates the association between physical activity frequency and feelings of energy and fatigue in adolescents. European child & adolescent psychiatry, 27(11), 1425–1432.

Rasch, B., & Born, J. (2013). About sleep's role in memory. *Physiological reviews*, *93* (2), 681–766.

P. Schwarz, W. Graham, F. Li, M. Locke, J. Peever (2013) Sleep deprivation impairs functional muscle recovery following injury,Sleep Medicine,14(1),262,

Taheri, S., Lin, L., Austin, D., Young, T., & Mignot, E. (2004). Short sleep duration is associated with reduced leptin, elevated ghrelin, and increased body mass index. *PLoS medicine*, *1* (3), e62.

Yang, D. F., Shen, Y. L., Wu, C., Huang, Y. S., Lee, P. Y., Er, N. X., Huang, W. C., & Tung, Y. T. (2019). Sleep deprivation reduces the recovery of muscle injury induced by high-intensity exercise in a mouse model. *Life sciences*, *235*, 116835.

Ben Simon, E., & Walker, M. P. (2018). Sleep loss causes social withdrawal and loneliness. *Nature communications*, *9* (1), 3146.

Cacioppo, J. T., Hawkley, L. C., Berntson, G. G., Ernst, J. M., Gibbs, A. C., Stickgold, R., & Hobson, J. A. (2002). Do lonely days invade the nights? Potential social modulation of sleep efficiency. *Psychological science*, *13* (4), 384–387.

Gordon, A. M., Mendes, W. B., & Prather, A. A. (2017). The social side of sleep: Elucidating the links between sleep and social processes. *Current directions in psychological science*, *26* (5), 470–475. https://doi.org/10.1177/0963721417712269

Jackson, M. L., Croft, R., Kennedy, G. A., Owens, K., & Howard, M. E. (2012). Cognitive components of simulated driving performance: sleep loss effects and predictors. *Accid Anal Prev, 50*, 438-444.

Brown, R. E., Basheer, R., McKenna, J. T., Strecker, R. E., & McCarley, R. W. (2012). Control of sleep and wakefulness. *Physiol Rev, 92,* 1087-1187

Van Dongen, H. P., Maislin, G., Mullington, J. M., & Dinges, D. F. (2003). The cumulative cost of additional wakefulness: dose-response effects on neurobehavioral functions and sleep physiology from chronic sleep restriction and total sleep deprivation. *Sleep*, *26* (2), 117–126.

Centers for Disease Control and Prevention. (2016, February 16). *1 in 3 adults don't get enough sleep*. Centers for Disease Control and Prevention.

Retrieved April 26, 2022, from
https://www.cdc.gov/media/releases/2016/p0215-enough-sleep.html

Scherer, M. (2009, April 21). *Scientists claim CIA misused work on sleep deprivation* . Time. Retrieved April 26, 2022, from
http://content.time.com/time/nation/article/0,8599,1892897,00.html

Leproult, R., Copinschi, G., Buxton, O., & Van Cauter, E. (1997). Sleep loss results in an elevation of cortisol levels the next evening. *Sleep* , *20* (10), 865–870.

Lateef, O. M., & Akintubosun, M. O. (2020). Sleep and Reproductive Health. *Journal of circadian rhythms* , *18* , 1.

Nagai, M., Hoshide, S., & Kario, K. (2010). Sleep duration as a risk factor for cardiovascular disease- a review of the recent literature. *Current cardiology reviews* , *6* (1), 54–61.

Knutson, K. L., & Van Cauter, E. (2008). Associations between sleep loss and increased risk of obesity and diabetes. *Annals of the New York Academy of Sciences, 1129* , 287–304.

Davis, S., & Mirick, D. K. (2006). Circadian disruption, shift work and the risk of cancer: a summary of the evidence and studies in Seattle. *Cancer Causes and Control* , 17(4), 539–545.

Bryant, P. A., Trinder, J. & Curtis, N. (2004). Sick and tired: Does sleep have a vital role in the immune system? *Nat Rev Immunol* , *4* , 457–467

Poe, G. R., Walsh, C. M., & Bjorness, T. E. (2010). Cognitive neuroscience of sleep. Progress in Brain Research, 185, 1–19.

Nagai, M., Hoshide, S., & Kario, K. (2010). Sleep duration as a risk factor for cardiovascular disease- a review of the recent literature. *Current cardiology reviews, 6* (1), 54–61.

Anderson, C., Platten, C. R. (2011). Sleep deprivation lowers inhibition and enhances impulsivity to negative stimuli. *Behav Brain Res*., *217*, 463–466.

University Of Pennsylvania Medical Center. (2003, March 14). 'Sleep Debts' Accrue When Nightly Sleep Totals Six Hours Or Fewer; Penn Study Find People Respond Poorly, While Feeling Only 'Slightly' Tired.

Works, H. I., Treat, C. W., & Schweig, S. Improving Your Life With Better Sleep.

Okamoto-Mizuno, K., & Mizuno, K. (2012). Effects of thermal environment on sleep and circadian rhythm. *Journal of physiological anthropology*, *31* (1), 14.

Gooley, J. J., Chamberlain, K., Smith, K. A., Khalsa, S. B., Rajaratnam, S. M., Van Reen, E., Zeitzer, J. M., Czeisler, C. A., & Lockley, S. W. (2011). Exposure to room light before bedtime suppresses melatonin onset and shortens melatonin duration in humans. *The Journal of clinical endocrinology and metabolism*, *96* (3), E463–E472.

Noyed, D. (2022, March 11). *How to choose a Mattress*. Sleep Foundation. Retrieved April 26, 2022, from https://www.sleepfoundation.org/mattress-information/how-to-choose-a-mattress Epstein, L. J., & Mardon, S. (2007). *The Harvard Medical School Guide to a good night's sleep*. McGraw-Hill.

Pietilä, J., Helander, E., Korhonen, I., Myllymäki, T., Kujala, U. M., & Lindholm, H. (2018). Acute Effect of Alcohol Intake on Cardiovascular Autonomic Regulation During the First Hours of Sleep in a Large Real-World Sample of Finnish Employees: Observational Study. *JMIR mental health*, *5* (1), e23.

Hammond, C. (n.d.). *6 yoga nidra scripts for sleep, Deep Relaxation & More*. World of Lucid Dreaming. Retrieved April 26, 2022, from https://www.world-of-lucid-dreaming.com/yoga-nidra-scripts.html

Black, D. S., O'Reilly, G. A., Olmstead, R., Breen, E. C., & Irwin, M. R. (2015). Mindfulness meditation and improvement in sleep quality and daytime impairment among older adults with sleep disturbances: a randomized clinical trial. *JAMA internal medicine*, *175* (4), 494–501.

Johns Hopkins Medicine. (2021, August 8). *Exercising for better sleep* . Johns Hopkins Medicine. Retrieved April 26, 2022, from https://www.hopkinsmedicine.org/health/wellness-and-prevention/exercising-for-better-sleep#:~:text=Based%20on%20available%20studies%2C%20%E2%80%9CWe,at%20Howard%20Count y%20General%20Hospital.

Dubocovich, M. L. (2007). Melatonin receptors: role on sleep and circadian rhythm regulation. *Sleep medicine, 8* , 34-42.

Yang, G., Lai, C. S., Cichon, J., Ma, L., Li, W., & Gan, W. B. (2014). Sleep promotes branch-specific formation of dendritic spines after learning. *Science (New York, N.Y.)* , *344* (6188), 1173–1178.

Walker, M. (2018). *Why We Sleep* . Penguin Books.

Chapter 6

Tarr, B., Launay, J., Benson, C., & Dunbar, R. I. M. (2017). Naltrexone Blocks Endorphins

Released when Dancing in Synchrony. *Adaptive Human Behavior and Physiology, 3,* 241–254.

Yorgason, J. B., Johnson, L. N., Hill, M. S., & Selland, B. (2018). Marital Benefits of Daily Individual and Conjoint Exercise Among Older Couples. *Fam Relat* ., *67* (2), 227–39.

Bjørnebekk, A., Mathé, A. A., & Brené, S. (2005). The antidepressant effect of running is associated with increased hippocampal cell proliferation . *The international journal of neuropsychopharmacology*, *8* (3), 357–368.

Dietrich, A., & McDaniel, W. F. (2004). Endocannabinoids and exercise. *British Journal of Sports Medicine*, *38*, 536-541.

Dang, L. C., Castrellon, J. J., Perkins, S. F., Le, N. T., Cowan, R. L., Zald, D. H., & Samanez-Larkin, G. R. (2017). Reduced effects of age on dopamine D2 receptor levels in physically active adults. *NeuroImage*, *148*, 123–129.

Karnib, N., El-Ghandour, R., El Hayek, L., Nasrallah, P., Khalifeh, M., Barmo, N., Jabre, V., Ibrahim, P., Bilen, M., Stephan, J. S., Holson, E. B., Ratan, R. R., & Sleiman, S. F. (2019). Lactate is an antidepressant that mediates resilience to stress by modulating the hippocampal levels and activity of histone deacetylases. *Neuropsychopharmacology : official publication of the American College of Neuropsychopharmacology*, *44* (6), 1152–1162.

Fleshner, M., Maier, S. F., Lyons, D. M., & Raskind, M. A. (2011). The neurobiology of the stress-resistant brain. *Stress*, *14* (5), 498-502.

Zamani Sani, S. H., Fathirezaie, Z., Brand, S., Pühse, U., Holsboer-Trachsler, E., Gerber, M., & Talepasand, S. (2016). Physical activity and self-esteem: testing direct and indirect relationships associated with psychological and physical mechanisms. *Neuropsychiatric disease and treatment*, *12*, 2617–2625.

Egan, E., & Zierath, J. R. (2013). Exercise metabolism and the molecular regulation of skeletal muscle adaptation. *Cell Metabolism*, *17* (2), 162–184.

Scott, S. J. (2014). *Habit stacking: 97 small life changes that take five minutes or less*. Archangel Ink.

Milkman, K. L., Minson, J. A., & Volpp, K. G. (2014). Holding the Hunger Games Hostage at the Gym: An Evaluation of Temptation Bundling. *Management science*, *60* (2), 283–299.

McGonigal, K. (2019). *The joy of movement* . Avery, an imprint of Penguin Random House LLC.

Durkheim, Émile. (1965). *The Elementary Forms of the Religious Life* . (J. W. Swain, Trans.). The Free Press. (Original work published 1912)
Howell, N. A., Tu, J. V., Moineddin, R., Chu, A., & Booth, G. L. (2019). Association Between

Neighborhood Walkability and Predicted 10-Year Cardiovascular Disease Risk: The CANHEART (Cardiovascular Health in Ambulatory Care Research Team) Cohort. *Journal of the American Heart Association* , *8* (21), e013146.

Chapter 7

Society for Personality and Social Psychology. (2014, August 8). How we form habits, change existing ones. *ScienceDaily*

Neal, D. T., Wood, W., Wu, M., & Kurlander, D. (2011). The Pull of the Past: When Do Habits Persist Despite Conflict With Motives? *Personality and Social Psychology Bulletin* , *37* (11), 1428-1437.

Lally, P., Jaarsveld, C.H., Potts, H.W., & Wardle, J. (2010). How are habits formed: Modelling habit formation in the real world. *European Journal of Social Psychology, 40* , 998-1009.

Huberman, A. (Host). (2022, January, 3). The science of making and breaking habits. (No. 65) [Audio Podcast Episode]. In *Huberman Lab*. Scicomm Media. https://hubermanlab.com/the-science-of-making-and-breaking-habits/

Buijze, G. A., Sierevelt, I. N., van der Heijden, B. C., Dijkgraaf, M. G., & Frings-Dresen, M. H. (2016). The Effect of Cold Showering on Health and Work: A Randomized Controlled Trial. *PloS one* , *11* (9), e0161749.

Bernard W. Balleine, Mauricio R. Delgado and Okihide Hikosaka (2007) The Role of the Dorsal

Striatum in Reward and Decision-Making. Journal of Neuroscience 1, 27 (31) 8161-8165

Wood, W., & Rünger, D. (2016). Psychology of Habit. *Annual review of psychology*, *67*, 289–314.

Yin, H., & Knowlton, B. (2006). The role of the basal ganglia in habit formation. *Nat Rev Neurosci* , *7* , 464–476.

Eilam, D., Izhar, R., & Mort, J. (2011). Threat detection: Behavioral practices in animals and humans. *Neuroscience & Biobehavioral Reviews*, *35* (4), 999-1006.

Korb, A. (2015). *The upward spiral: Using neuroscience to reverse the course of depression, one small change at a time.*

Fogg, B. J. (2020). *Tiny habits: the small changes that change everything.* Boston: Houghton Mifflin Harcourt.

Duhigg, C. (2014). *The power of habit: why we do what we do in life and business.* New York: Random House Trade Paperbacks.

Clear, J. (2018). *Atomic habits: tiny changes, remarkable results : an easy & proven way to build good habits & break bad ones.* New York: Avery, an imprint of Penguin Random House.

Zumrut, G. (2019). Self-compassion and health-promoting lifestyle behaviors in college students. *Psychology, Health & Medicine* , 24(*1*), 108-114.

Neff, K. D. & Germer, C. (2017). *Self-Compassion and Psychological Wellbeing* . In J. Doty (Ed.) Oxford Handbook of Compassion Science, Chap. 27. Oxford University Press.

Halvorson, H. G. (2012). *Nine Things Successful People Do Differently* . Harvard Business Review Press.

Ariely, D. (2016). *Payoff: The Hidden Logic That Shapes Our Motivations* . Simon Schuster/ TED.

Rachlin, H. (2004). *The Science of Self-Control* . Harvard University Press.

Chapter 8

Ekman, P. (1992). An argument for basic emotions. *Cogn. Emot.* 6, 169–200

Beck, A. T. (1967). *Depression: Causes and treatment* . Philadelphia: University of Pennsylvania Press.

Beck, A. T., Epstein, N., & Harrison, R. (1983). Cognitions, attitudes and personality dimensions in depression. British Journal of Cognitive Psychotherapy.

Ellis, A. (1957). Rational Psychotherapy and Individual Psychology. Journal of Individual Psychology, 13: 38-44.

Ellis, A. (1962). Reason and Emotion in Psychotherapy. New York: Stuart.

Linehan, M. M. (1993). *Cognitive-behavioral treatment of borderline personality disorder.* Guilford Press.

Vanderhasselt, M. A., Baeken, C., Van Schuerbeek, P., Luypaert, R., and De Raedt, R. (2013). Inter-individual differences in the habitual use of cognitive reappraisal and expressive suppression are associated with variations in prefrontal cognitive control for emotional information: an event related fMRI study. *Biol. Psychol. 92* , 433–439

Mehrabian, A. (1972). *Nonverbal Communication* . New Brunswick: Aldine Transaction.

Carlson, M., & Miller, N. (1987). Explanation of the relation between negative mood and helping. Psychological Bulletin, 102(1), 91-108.

Williams, L. E., Bargh, J. A., Nocera, C. C., & Gray, J. R. (2009). The unconscious regulation of emotion: Nonconscious reappraisal goals modulate emotional reactivity. *Emotion, 9* (6), 847–854.

Taylor, J. B. (2009). *My stroke of insight* . New American Library.

Neacsiu, A. D., Bohus, M., & Linehan, M. M. (2014). Dialectical behavior therapy: An intervention for emotion dysregulation. In J. J. Gross (Ed.), *Handbook of emotion regulation* (pp. 491–507). The Guilford Press.

Lieberman, M. D., Eisenberger, N. I., Crockett, M. J., Tom, S. M., Pfeifer, J. H., & Way, B. M. (2007). Putting feelings into words: affect labeling disrupts amygdala activity in response to affective stimuli. *Psychological science, 18* (5), 421–428.

Chapter 9

Beck, A. T. (1963). Thinking and depression: I. Idiosyncratic content and cognitive distortions.

Archives of General Psychiatry, 9(4), 324-333.

Vaish, A., Grossmann, T., & Woodward, A. (2008). Not all emotions are created equal: the negativity bias in social-emotional development. *Psychological bulletin , 134* (3), 383–403.

Beck, J. S. (2011). *Cognitive behavior therapy: Basics and beyond* (2nd ed.). New York, NY: Guilford Press.

Belloch, A., Morillo, C., Lucero, M., Cabedo, E., Carrió, C. (2004). Intrusive thoughts in non-clinical subjects: The role of frequency and unpleasantness on appraisal ratings and control strategies. Clinical Psychology & Psychotherapy, 11, 100-110.

Ciarrochi, J., Robb, H., Godsell, C. (2005). Letting a little nonverbal air into the room: Insights from Acceptance and Commitment Therapy Part 1: Philosophical and theoretical underpinnings.

Journal of Rational-Emotive & Cognitive-Behavior Therapy, 23, 79-106

Clark, D. A., Beck, A. T. (2011). Cognitive Therapy of Anxiety Disorders. New York, NY: Guilford Press.

Belloch, A., Morillo, C., Lucero, M., Cabedo, E., Carrió, C. (2004). Intrusive thoughts in non-clinical subjects: The role of frequency and unpleasantness on appraisal ratings and control strategies. Clinical Psychology & Psychotherapy, 11, 100-110.

Deacon, B. J., Fawzy, T. I., Lickel, J. J., Wolitzky-Taylor, K. B. (2011). Cognitive defusion versus cognitive restructuring in the treatment of negative self-referential thoughts: An investigation of process and outcome. Journal of Cognitive Psychotherapy: An International Quarterly, 25, 218-228.

Hayes, S. C. (2015). Foreword. In Hooper, N., Larsson, A. (Eds.), The research journey of Acceptance and Commitment Therapy (ACT) (pp. x-xvii). London, England: Palgrave Macmillan.

Hayes, S. C., Strosahl, K. D., Wilson, K. G. (1999). Acceptance and Commitment Therapy: An y, 6, 164-185.

Hooper, N., McHugh, L. (2013). Cognitive defusion versus thought distraction in the mitigation of learned helplessness. The Psychological Record, 63, 209-218.

Hooper, N., Saunders, J., McHugh, L. (2010). The derived generalization of thought suppression. Learning & Behavior, 38, 160-168.

Larsson, A., Hooper, N., Osborne, L. A., Bennett, P., & McHugh, L. (2016). Using Brief Cognitive Restructuring and Cognitive Defusion Techniques to Cope With Negative Thoughts. *Behavior Modification*, *40* (3), 452–482.

Ellis, A (1980). Rational-emotive therapy and cognitive behavior therapy: Similarities and differences. *Cogn Ther Res* 4, 325–340

Chapter 10

Ryan, R. M., & Deci, E. L. (2000). Intrinsic and extrinsic motivations: Classic definitions and new directions. *Contemporary Educational Psychology* , *25* , 54–67.

Dahl, J., Plumb, J. C., Stewart, I., & Lundgren, T. (2009). T *he Art and Science of Valuing in Psychotherapy: Helping Clients Discover, Explore, and Commit to Valued Action Using Acceptance and Commitment Therapy* (1st ed.). New Harbinger Publications.

Chase, J. A., Houmanfar, R., Hayes, S. C., Ward, T. A., Vilardaga, J. P., & Follette, V. (2013).

Values are not just goals: Online ACT-based values training adds to goal setting in improving undergraduate college student performance. *Journal of Contextual Behavioral Science* , *2* (3-4), 79-84.

Chapter 11

Neff, K. D. (2004). Self-compassion and psychological well-being. *Constructivism in the Human Sciences, 9* , 27-37.

Marsh, J., & Neff, K. (2012, March 14). *The Power of Self-Compassion* . Greater Good. https://greatergood.berkeley.edu/article/item/the_power_of_self_compassion

Neff, K. (2010). Review of The mindful path to self-compassion: Freeing yourself from destructive thoughts and emotions. *British Journal of Psychology, 101* , 179-181.

Homan, K. J., & Sirois, F. M. (2017). Self-compassion and physical health: Exploring the roles of perceived stress and health-promoting behaviors. *Health psychology open, 4* (2), 1-9.

Zabelina, D. L., & Robinson, M. D.(2010). Don't be so hard on yourself: Self-compassion facilitates creative originality among self-judgmental individuals. *Creativity Research Journal*, *22* (3), 288-293.

Breines, J. G., & Chen, S. (2012). Self-Compassion Increases Self-Improvement Motivation. *Personality and Social Psychology Bulletin*, *38* (9), 1133–1143.

Breines, J. G., & Chen, S. (2012). Self-compassion increases self-improvement motivation. Personality & social psychology bulletin, 38(9), 1133–1143.

Sirois, F. M. (2014). Procrastination and stress: Exploring the role of self-compassion. *Self and Identity*, *13* (2), 128 - 145.

Neff, K. D. & McGeehee, P. (2010). Self-compassion and psychological resilience among adolescents and young adults. *Self and Identity*, *9*, 225-240.

Mongrain, M., Chin, J. M., & Shapira, L. B. (2011). Practicing compassion increases happiness and self-esteem. J *ournal of Happiness Studies: An Interdisciplinary Forum on Subjective Well-Being, 12* (6), 963–981.

Neff, K. D & Beretvas, N.S. (2011) The Role of Self-compassion in Romantic Relationships. Self and Identity, 12 (1), 78-98

Kirschner, H., Kuyken, W., Wright, K., Roberts, H., Brejcha, C., & Karl, A. (2019). Soothing Your Heart and Feeling Connected: A New Experimental Paradigm to Study the Benefits of Self-Compassion. *Clinical Psychological Science*, *7* (3), 545–565.

Slade, P. D., & Owens, R. G. (1998). A dual process model of perfectionism based on reinforcement theory. *Behavior modification*, *22* (3), 372–390.

Smith, M. M., Saklofske, D. H., Yan, G., & Sherry, S. B. (2015). Perfectionistic strivings and perfectionistic concerns interact to predict negative emotionality: Support for the tripartite model of perfectionism in Canadian and Chinese university students. *Personality and Individual Differences*, *81*, 141–147.

Woodfin, V., Hjeltnes, A., & Binder, P. E. (2021). Perfectionistic individuals' understanding of how painful experiences have shaped their relationship to others. *Frontiers in psychology*, *12*, 619018.

Ferrari, M., Yap, K., Scott, N., Einstein, D. A., & Ciarrochi, J. (2018). Self-compassion moderates the perfectionism and depression link in both adolescence and adulthood. *PloS one, 13* (2), e0192022.

Schmidt, R. E., Courvoisier, D. S., Cullati, S., Kraehenmann, R., & der Linden, M. V. (2018). Too Imperfect to Fall Asleep: Perfectionism, Pre-sleep Counterfactual Processing, and Insomnia. F *rontiers in psychology, 9*, 1288.

Lozano, L. M., Valor-Segura, I., García-Cueto, E., Pedrosa, I., Llanos, A., & Lozano, L. (2019). Relationship Between Child Perfectionism and Psychological Disorders. *Frontiers in psychology*, *10*, 1855.

Lin, R. M., Xie, S. S., Yan, Y. W., Chen, Y. H., & Yan, W. J. (2019). Perfectionism and adolescent sleep quality: The mediating role of repetitive negative thinking. *Journal of health psychology, 24* (12), 1626–1636.

Slaney, R. B., Pincus, A. L., Uliaszek, A. A., & Wang, K. T. (2006). Conceptions of perfectionism and interpersonal problems: evaluating groups using the structural summary method for circumplex data. *Assessment*, *13(*2), 138–153.

Abdollahi, A., Allen, K. A., & Taheri, A. (2020). Moderating the Role of Self-Compassion in the Relationship Between Perfectionism and Depression. *J Rat-Emo Cognitive-Behav Ther, 38*, 459–471.

Remes, O. (2019, March 13). *How to cope with anxiety* [Video]. TED Talks.

https://www.ted.com/talks/olivia_remes_how_to_cope_with_anxiety?language=en Hatzigeorgiadis, A., Zourbanos, N., Galanis, E., & Theodorakis, Y. (2011). Self-Talk and Sports Performance: A Meta-Analysis. *Perspectives on psychological science: a journal of the Association for Psychological Science* , *6* (4), 348–356.

Blankert, T., & Hamstra, M. R. (2017). Imagining Success: Multiple Achievement Goals and the Effectiveness of Imagery. *Basic and applied social psychology* , 39(1), 60–67.

Vasquez N. A., & Buehler R. (2007). Seeing future success: Does imagery perspective influence achievement motivation? *Personality and Social Psychology Bulletin* , *33* (10), 1392–1405.

López, A., Sanderman, R., Ranchor, A. V., & Schroevers, M. J. (2018). Compassion for Others and Self-Compassion: Levels, Correlates, and Relationship with Psychological Well-being. *Mindfulness* , *9* (1), 325–331.

Chapter 12

Holt-Lunstad, J., Smith, T. B., Baker, M., Harris, T., & Stephenson, D. (2015). Loneliness and social isolation as risk factors for mortality: a meta-analytic review. *Perspectives on psychological science: a journal of the Association for Psychological Science, 10* (2), 227–237.

Vaillant, G. E. (2015). *Triumphs of Experience: The Men of the Harvard Grant Study* (Reprint ed.). Belknap Press: An Imprint of Harvard University Press.

Ozbay, F., Johnson, D. C., Dimoulas, E., Morgan, C. A., Charney, D., & Southwick, S. (2007). Social support and resilience to stress: from neurobiology to clinical practice. Psychiatry (Edgmont (Pa. : Township)), 4(5), 35–40.

Love T. M. (2014). Oxytocin, motivation and the role of dopamine. *Pharmacology, biochemistry, and behavior* , *119* , 49–60

Inagaki, T. K., Bryne Haltom, K. E., Suzuki, S., Jevtic, I., Hornstein, E., Bower, J. E., & Eisenberger, N. I. (2016). The Neurobiology of Giving Versus Receiving Support: The Role of Stress-Related and Social Reward-Related Neural Activity. *Psychosomatic medicine*, *78* (4), 443–453.

Sarason, B. R., Sarason, I. G., & Pierce, G. R. (1990). *Traditional views of social support and their impact on assessment.* In B. R. Sarason, I. G. Sarason, & G. R. Pierce (Eds.), *Social support: An interactional view* (pp. 9–25). John Wiley & Sons.

Dunbar, R. I. M. (1992). Neocortex size as a constraint on group size in primates. *J. Hum. Evol.*, *20*, 469–493.

Chapter 13

Hanson, Rick (2016) Hardwiring Happiness

Lambert, N. M, Graham, S. M, Fincham, F. D, & Stillman, T. F, (2009) A Changed Perspective: How Gratitude Can Affect Sense of Coherence Through Positive Reframing. Journal of Positive Psychology 4(6), 461-470

Xiang, Y., Chao, X., & Ye, Y. (2018). Effect of Gratitude on Benign and Malicious Envy: The Mediating Role of Social Support. *Frontiers in psychiatry*, *9*, 139.

Koo, M., Algoe, S. B., Wilson, T. D., & Gilbert, D. T. (2008). It's a wonderful life: mentally subtracting positive events improves people's affective states, contrary to their affective forecasts. *Journal of personality and social psychology*, *95* (5), 1217.

Lyubomirsky, S. (2008). The how of happiness: A scientific approach to getting the life you want.

Seligman, Martin (2002) Authentic Happiness: Using the New Positive Psychology to Realize Your Potential.

Kashdan, T. B, Unswatte, G., Julian, T. (2006). Gratitude and hedonic and eudaimonic well-being in Vietnam war veterans. Behaviour Research and Therapy, 44(2) 177-199

Froh, J. J, Sefick W. J, & Emmons, R. A. (2008) Counting blessings in early adolescents: An experimental study of gratitude and subjective well-being. Journal of School Psychology, 46(2) 213-233

Layous, K., Sweeny, K., Armenta, C., Na, S., Choi, I., & Lyubomirsky, S. (2016). The proximal experience of gratitude.

Seligman, M. E., Steen, T. A., Park, N., & Peterson, C. (2005). Positive psychology progress: empirical validation of interventions. *The American psychologist* , *60* (5), 410–421.

Algoe, S. B., Gable, S. L., & Maisel, N. C. (2010). It's the little things: Everyday gratitude as a booster shot for romantic relationships. *Personal relationships*, *17* (2), 217-233.

Lambert, N. M., Clark, M. S., Durtschi, J., Fincham, F. D., & Graham, S. M. (2010). Benefits of expressing gratitude: Expressing gratitude to a partner changes one's view of the relationship. *Psychological Science*, *21* (4), 574-580.

Emmons, R. A. (2007). *Thanks!: How the new science of gratitude can make you happier* . Houghton Mifflin Harcourt.

McCullough, M. E., Kilpatrick, S. D., Emmons, R. A., & Larson, D. B. (2001). Is gratitude a moral affect?. *Psychological bulletin* , *127* (2), 249.

Emmons, R. A., & McCullough, M. E. (Eds.). (2004). *The psychology of gratitude* . Oxford University Press.

Emmons, R. A., & Mishra, A. (2011). Why gratitude enhances well-being: What we know, what we need to know. *Designing positive psychology: Taking stock and moving forward* , 248-262.

Emmons, R. A., McCullough, M. E., & Tsang, J. A. (2003). The assessment of gratitude.

Amin, A. (2014). The 31 benefits of gratitude you didn't know about: How gratitude can change your life. *Happier Human*.

Algoe, S. B., Fredrickson, B. L., & Gable, S. L. (2013). The social functions of the emotion of gratitude via expression. *Emotion*, *13* (4), 605.

Lambert, N. M., & Fincham, F. D. (2011). Expressing gratitude to a partner leads to more relationship maintenance behavior. *Emotion*, *11* (1), 52.

Boehm, J. K., Lyubomirsky, S., & Sheldon, K. M. (2011). A longitudinal experimental study comparing the effectiveness of happiness-enhancing strategies in Anglo Americans and Asian Americans. *Cognition & Emotion*, *25* (7), 1263-1272.

Lyubomirsky, S., Dickerhoof, R., Boehm, J. K., & Sheldon, K. M. (2011). Becoming happier takes both a will and a proper way: an experimental longitudinal intervention to boost well-being. *Emotion*, *11* (2), 391.

Jose, P. E., Lim, B. T., & Bryant, F. B. (2012). Does savoring increase happiness? A daily diary study. *The Journal of Positive Psychology*, *7* (3), 176-187.

Smith, J. L., & Hollinger-Smith, L. (2015). Savoring, resilience, and psychological well-being in older adults. *Aging & mental health*, *19* (3), 192-200.

McCullough, M. E. (2002). Savoring life, past and present: Explaining what hope and gratitude share in common. *Psychological Inquiry*, *13* (4), 302-304.

Irvin, K. M., Bell, D. J., Steinley, D., & Bartholow, B. D. (2020). The thrill of victory: Savoring positive affect, psychophysiological reward processing, and symptoms of depression. *Emotion*.

Lenger, K. A., & Gordon, C. L. (2019). To have and to savor: Examining the associations between savoring and relationship satisfaction. *Couple and Family Psychology: Research and Practice, 8* (1), 1.

Bryant, F. B., & Veroff, J. (2017). *Savoring: A new model of positive experience*. Psychology Press.

Lenger, K. A., & Gordon, C. L. (2019). To have and to savor: Examining the associations between savoring and relationship satisfaction. *Couple and Family Psychology: Research and*

Practice, 8 (1), 1.

Bryant, F. B., Smart, C. M., & King, S. P. (2005). Using the past to enhance the present: Boosting happiness through positive reminiscence. *Journal of Happiness Studies, 6* (3), 227-260.

ABOUT THE AUTHOR

FATEMEH FARAHAN, LMFT, is a licensed marriage and family therapist who runs a thriving group psychotherapy practice in Southern California. She is a nationally recognized speaker and a leading expert on happiness and relationships. With over 25 years of experience, Fatemeh has helped thousands of individuals and families to build happier lives and more authentic and fulfilling connections. She also works with Fortune 500 companies (including Hulu), to improve wellbeing, productivity, and satisfaction in the workplace. Through working with Farahan, patients and clients can learn the tools to rewire their brain, by utilizing cutting-edge insights from neuroscience and psychology. In her therapy sessions, teaching, and writing, Fatemeh seeks to increase understanding of how the brain can thwart our efforts towards true happiness. She provides an easy-to-follow system to maximize joy and connectedness with self and others.

You can learn more about her work at farahantherapy.com

Fatemeh Farahan
Fatemeh Farahan, Marriage Family Therapist, PC
10350 Santa Monica Blvd., Suite 310
Los Angeles, CA 90025
(310) 962-5935
www.farahantherapy.com
Fatemeh Farahan, LMFT is available to speak at your business or conference event on a variety of topics. Email us at info@farahantherapy.com for booking information.

Made in United States
Orlando, FL
03 April 2025